Careers in Communications & Media

Careers in Communications & Media

Editor
Michael Shally-Jensen, Ph.D.

SALEM PRESS
A Division of EBSCO Information Services, Inc.
Ipswich, Massachusetts

GREY HOUSE PUBLISHING

∞ The paper used in these volumes conforms to the American National Standard for Permanence of Paper for Printed Library Materials, Z39.48-1992 (R1997).

Library of Congress Cataloging-in-Publication Data

Careers in communications & media / editor, Michael Shally-Jensen. --
[1st ed.].
p. : ill. ; cm. -- (Careers in--)
Includes bibliographical references and index.
ISBN: 978-1-61925-230-1
1. Mass media--Vocational guidance. 2. Communication--Vocational guidance. I. Shally-Jensen, Michael. II. Title: Careers in communications and media

P91.6 .C37 2013
302.23/023

First Printing

PRINTED IN THE UNITED STATES OF AMERICA

CONTENTS

PUBLISHER'S NOTE

Careers in Communications & Media contains twenty-five alphabetically arranged chapters describing specific fields of interest in communications and media. These chapters provide a current overview and a future outlook of specific occupations in communications and media industries. Merging scholarship with occupational development, this single comprehensive guidebook provides communications and media students and readers alike with the necessary insight into potential careers, and provides instruction on what job seekers can expect in terms of training, advancement, earnings, job prospects, working conditions, relevant associations, and more. *Careers in Communications & Media* is specifically designed for a high school and undergraduate audience and is edited to align with secondary or high school curriculum standards.

Scope of Coverage

Understanding the interconnected nature of the different and varied branches of communications and media is important for anyone preparing for a career in these fields. *Careers in Communications & Media* comprises twenty-five lengthy chapters on a broad range of branches and divisions within these industry segments, including tradition¬al and long-established fields such as Advertising Director and Journalist, as well as in-demand and cutting-edge fields such as Software Developer, Web Developer, and Animator. This excellent reference also presents possible career paths and occupations within high-growth and emerging fields in these industries.

Careers in Communications & Media is enhanced with numerous charts and tables, including projections from the US Bureau of Labor Statistics, and median annual salaries or wages for those occupations profiled. Each chapter also notes those skills that can be applied across broad occupation categories. Interesting enhancements, like **Fun Facts, Famous Firsts**, and dozens of photos, add depth to the discussion. A highlight of each chapter is **Conversation With** – a two-page interview with a professional working in a related job. The respondents share their personal career paths, detail potential for career advancement, offer advice for students, and include a "try this" for those interested in embarking on a career in their profession.

Essay Length and Format

Each chapter ranges in length from 3,500 to 4,500 words and begins with a Snapshot of the occupation that includes career clusters, interests, earnings and employment outlook. This is followed by these major categories:

- **Overview** includes detailed discussions on: Sphere of Work; Work Environment; Occupation Interest; A Day in the Life. Also included here is a Profile and outlines working conditions, educational needs, and physical abilities. You will also find the occupation's Holland Interest Score, which matches up character and personality traits with specific jobs.

- **Occupational Specialties** lists specific jobs that are related in some way, like Advertising Managers, Marketing Managers, and Promotions Managers, with detailed comparisons. This section also includes a list of Duties and Responsibilities.
- **Work Environment** details the physical, human, and technological environment of the occupation profiled.
- **Education, Training, and Advancement** outlines how to prepare for this occupation while in high school, and what college courses to take, including licenses and certifications needed. A section is devoted to the Adult Job Seeker, and there is a list of skills and abilities needed to succeed in the job profiled.
- **Earnings and Advancements** offers specific salary ranges, and includes a chart of metropolitan areas that have the highest concentration of the profession.
- **Employment and Outlook** discusses employment trends, and projects growth to 2020. This section also lists related occupations.
- **Selected Schools** list those prominent learning institutions that offer specific courses in the profiles occupations.
- **More Information** includes associations that the reader can contact for more information.

Special Features

Several features continue to distinguish this reference series from other career-oriented reference works. The back matter includes:

- Appendix A: Guide to Holland Code. This discusses John Holland's theory that people and work environments can be classified into six different groups: Realistic; Investigative; Artistic; Social; Enterprising; and Conventional. See if the job you want is right for you!
- Appendix B: General Bibliography. This is a collated collection of annotated suggested readings.
- Subject Index: Includes people, concepts, technologies, terms, principles, and all specific occupations discussed in the occupational profile chapters.

Acknowledgments

Special mention is made of editor Michael Shally-Jensen, who played a principal role in shaping this work with current, comprehensive, and valuable material. Thanks are due to the many academicians and professionals who worked to communicate their expert understanding of communications and media to the general reader. Finally, thanks are also due to the professionals who communicated their work experience through our interview questionnaires. Their frank and honest responses provide immeasurable value to *Careers in Communications and Media*. The contributions of all are gratefully acknowledged.

EDITOR'S INTRODUCTION

An Industry Overview

Media and communications is a segment of industry encompassing a wide variety of activities and businesses. Media and communications companies are involved in television and radio broadcasting, motion picture/video production, publishing, advertising, and telecommunications (including the Internet and social media). The media and communications industry is an exciting one to be part of because it is the work of its professionals to inform, entertain, and connect people across the nation and around the world.

Industry Makeup

The two main areas of the media and communications field overlap but display some differences, as well. The media segment traditionally focuses on content, and includes 1) motion picture/video producers who create movies, television shows, and other videos to sell to broadcasters; 2) publishers who produce and distribute material such as books, newspapers, magazines, and recorded music; and 3) television and radio broadcasters who acquire or generate media content (including news programs) and channel it to consumers.

The communications segment traditionally focuses on information and providing access to information. It includes the telecommunications field—that which makes voice, data, and video communication possible—as well as the Internet and new media, which make online social networking, shopping, video viewing, research, and electronic gaming possible.

Positioned in between these two broad areas, at once drawing on and contributing to them, are the large and important fields of advertising and public relations. Advertising professionals use media and communications technologies to create and distribute ads for targeted audiences, while public relations professionals make use of information and media to organize and manage the "public face" of their clients.

At the core of each of these industry segments are the people who do the work. These include the director and the producer, the camera operator and the sound technician, the journalist and the radio announcer, the writer and the editor, the graphic artist and the web developer, the photographer and the production coordinator, the copywriter and the advertising manager, the translator and the public relations specialist, the newscaster and the broadcast technician. These and a number of other communications and media occupations are the subject of this book, although the size of the industry precludes complete coverage.

Industry Concentration

The media and communications industry is fairly heavily concentrated, both in terms of the companies that make it up and in terms of the locations where its businesses operate. This means that production in this industry tends to be dominated by a relatively small number of large firms that shape the industry's direction and price levels, and, many of these companies tend to be located in major cities such as New York, Los Angeles, Chicago, and Boston. This is not to suggest that career opportunities do not exist for those not living in or around these cities, only that the highest concentration of businesses occurs in these cities and similar large metropolises.

The media and entertainment segment is comprised of many companies, from multi-billion dollar corporate conglomerates to small, independent movie studios and production facilities. Similarly, the Internet/new media segment may be dominated by a small number of large, influential firms, but thousands of smaller firms either work as independent contracting units for these larger firms or are involved in the development and marketing of their own products. As these fields continue to thrive, so too will the allied fields of marketing, advertising, and public relations thrive. In fact, these are some of the strongest components of the industry.

History

For centuries, print (pamphlets, newspapers, books, etc.), was the only effective means of mass communication. In 1876, Alexander Graham Bell invented the electric speaking machine, the original telecommunications device. The telephone immediately became the Internet of its age, spawning massive amounts of investment and numerous types of new businesses. The recording industry took off, on a smaller scale, at about the same time, following Thomas Edison's invention of the phonograph in 1877. Cinema and radio both arrived at the dawn of the 20th century and quickly became extremely popular. As viewing and listening audiences grew, so too did the film and broadcasting industries that served them. Televisions first became available in the 1930s, but, due to cost and technical difficulties, it wasn't until the late 1940s and early 1950s, that more and more households began to own one.

In the next forty years, each of these industries continued to grow and consolidate, leading to the establishment of several mega media empires and a variety of smaller companies. Aiding them every step of the way, of course, and experiencing significant growth in their own right, were the many advertising and marketing firms that often "pushed the envelope" in terms of creative use of media resources.

The 1990s saw a major revolution in the industry as the Internet and World Wide Web entered the mainstream. These new forms of media afforded individuals the ability to reach millions of people for a fraction of the cost of traditional media. The video game industry emerged experienced marked growth, and social networking exploded in its first decade. Now, many of the world's largest corporations work in and around what is commonly called "new" media.

Trends

Perhaps the most important trend affecting the media and communications industry today is the convergence of technology. Communications equipment is being combined with computer technologies and other consumer electronics applications to create multifunctional devices. A popular example is the cell phone, or smart phone. There are more sales of smart phones with MP3 digital audio capability than sales of stand-alone MP3 players, and more sales of smart phones with cameras than sales of cameras as such. Additionally, with the convergence of smart phone technology with other wireless technologies, phones are increasingly being used for conducting financial transactions, from depositing checks to making online purchases to swiping credit cards.

A major trends today is a push toward making media of all kinds available on communications devices of all kinds. People want to see and share, to show and tell. It is a trend toward social media. Increasingly, we have access to books, magazines, newspapers, movies, television shows, news, music, talk shows, videos, art, and games on a single mobile platform. And, increasingly, users can interact with other users. This is best exemplified, perhaps, by one of the fastest growing markets, social gaming. Not only are there such minor diversions as "Candy Crush Saga," "Angry Birds," and "Farmville," but more and more people are playing so-called massively multiplayer online role-playing games (MMORGs), in which users create an environment for themselves and others to interact in and help or hinder one another's progress through the game.

All of which is to say that the communications and media industry is likely to continue to grow in this direction. New equipment, new services, and new applications should create ongoing demand in the consumer market. And such demand, in turn, should fuel a continued or expanded need in the labor market for qualified employees. The innovation and invention characteristic of the communications and media industry should keep consumer interest high and employment opportunities strong for the foreseeable future.

Future Outlook

According to one recent poll of industry executives, that conducted by KPMG (2013), more than 70 percent of American top executives report that their company's revenues increased from the previous year, and as much as 75 percent expect their company's revenues to increase over the coming years. Almost half of those polled expected revenues to increase by 6 percent or more, a percentage that is significantly higher than that for the economy as a whole.

About 80 percent of the executives polled believe that revenues from the distribution of digital content (media) should continue to increase. Half expected "moderate" growth in distribution through mobile devices, specifically, while nearly 20 percent expected "significant" growth in mobile distribution.

Of the two broad fields, media and communication, executives on the media side were more optimistic about their companies' projected overall revenues: 83 percent expected an increase. On the communications side, 68 percent expected an increase. In either case, these are very strong numbers.

When asked to identify the most critical elements in their businesses for continued growth, 80 percent of the executives pointed to the ability to evaluate information regarding customer purchases, sentiments, and preferences—a clear indication of the importance of market research and advertising. Nearly 70 percent stated that equally important was the maximizing of digital revenues through expanding markets (the convergence theme again).

The most significant challenges facing the executives were 1) staying on top of emerging technologies, ensuring that their products were up to the task; and 2) addressing pressures on pricing, ensuring that their products meet consumer expectations regarding price while also returning a profit to the business.

Although the KPMG survey did not address hiring specifically, it did report that a sizeable majority (almost 60 percent) of the executives said that their companies planned to increase capital spending in the immediate future, compared to a somewhat lower percentage (about 50 percent) for the previous year. Specifically, they expected to increase spending on 1) new products and services; 2) geographic expansion; and 3) information technology.

All of this is good news for job seekers interested in the communications and media field. Indeed, using the U.S. Bureau of Labor Statistics' (BLS) employment projections for the occupations included in the present book, one can note that an increase of nearly 20 percent is expected in the number of communications and media jobs over the next several years (to 2020). Given that the BLS estimate for all jobs (in all industries) is for 14 percent growth, people seeking to find employment in the communications and media industry should have a better chance than most. It seems a good time to get in.

Career Options

Depending on your skills, interests, and educational background, working in the communications and media industry can translate into a wide assortment of career-paths, all dealing with the creation and dissemination of information in one form or another. Working in the industry could mean one-on-one exchanges regarding a particular project, or it could mean trying to reach as many people as possible through a mass mailing or advertising campaign. It could mean sharing factual information on a news broadcast, or it could mean presenting an artful or humorous brand of entertainment. It could mean disseminating information through the written medium, or it could mean developing a multimedia product. Depending on who you are and what you enjoy, working in communications and media could find you performing any one of these functions.

As noted, the communications industry includes a variety of fields such as advertising and marketing, journalism, public relations, entertainment, new media, and publishing. Within each field, a variety of career paths exist. For example, entertainment could mean working in film, television, radio, or a variety of other careers. Journalism could mean working for a newspaper, a website, or a television news station. Each of these subfields is divided into further subfields and specialized career areas. The opportunities are quite literally endless.

Although it can seem overwhelming at first to get started in the industry, the multiplicity of options may work to your advantage. Whether you are currently in the process of looking for a job or expect to be someday, it is never too early to begin exploring your options and begin shaping yourself for a career in this exciting and rewarding industry.

—M. Shally-Jensen, Ph.D.

Sources

Bureau of Labor Statistics. 2013. Occupational Outlook Handbook. http://www.bls.gov/ooh/

KPMG. 2013. "Media and Telecom Execs Optimistic on Revenue Growth." http://www.kpmg.com/US/en/IssuesAndInsights/ArticlesPublications/Press-Releases/Pages/Media-And-Telecom-Execs-Optimistic-On-Revenue-Growth-Worry-About-Keeping-Pace.aspx

Advertising & Marketing Manager

Snapshot

Career Cluster: Business, Management & Administration, Marketing, Sales & Service, Media & Communications, Public Relations
Interests: Advertising, Business, Media & Communications, Products, Project Management
Earnings (Yearly Average): $104,246
Employment & Outlook: Average Growth Expected

OVERVIEW

Sphere of Work

Advertising and marketing managers work as staff members in corporate marketing and advertising departments. They can also work in specialized ad agencies or marketing firms. Their work falls within the communication, information, and business sectors. They serve as one of the main links or points of contact between the marketplace and the company or agency for which they work. Advertising and marketing managers coordinate print, television, radio, and

digital media advertising campaigns and projects; in some cases, they may also be responsible for sales and developing new business opportunities.

While advertising and marketing managers contribute to campaign development, they are not technically part of an agency's creative (or design) team. Their primary role is to ensure that campaigns are priced, administered, and executed smoothly and efficiently, and with the company's (or client's) interests in mind. They ensure that campaign milestones are met and elements of the campaign are delivered on time and within budget. Aside from working closely with the director of advertising and marketing, they coordinate the work activities of personnel such as copywriters, graphic designers, production assistants, public relations personnel, and market researchers. They may interact with sales representatives and have additional project managers responsibilities, as well. Advertising and marketing managers are generally supervised by a departmental director or client services supervisor.

Work Environment

Advertising and marketing managers work in an office environment within small to large companies or agencies. Air and car travel may be occasionally required to attend trade conferences or meet with clients. Evening and weekend work is also often required. Advertising and marketing managers frequently work under pressure and adhere to strict budgets and tight deadlines.

Profile

Working Conditions: Office Environment
Physical Strength: Light Work
Education Needs: Bachelor's Degree
Licensure/Certification: Usually Not Required
Physical Abilities Not Required: No Heavy Lifting, Climbing, Kneeling
Opportunities For Experience: Internship, Apprenticeship, Volunteer Work
Holland Interest Score*: AES

* See Appendix A

Occupation Interest

Graduates and professionals with a strong interest in advertising and marketing, mass media and communications, and project management are often attracted to the advertising industry. In particular, the role suits people who have an interest in coordinating multiple activities in a fast-paced environment and who are comfortable working closely with others.

Aside from excellent collaborative, communication, and organizational skills, advertising and marketing managers must also possess strong research and analytical skills and solid business acumen. They may be expected to formulate and execute budgets, monitor expenses, and assist with financial reporting. In some instances, they will be expected to make sales calls or develop and present new business proposals.

Successful advertising and marketing managers must be able to speak and write fluently, work with a diverse range of people, adapt to new industries, clients, products and services, and deliver consistent results under pressure. The role also requires considerable tact and diplomacy.

A Day in the Life—Duties and Responsibilities

The typical work day of an advertising and marketing manager includes frequent meetings with staff, supervisors, department heads, and, in the case of independent agencies, clients. The campaign deliverables, which advertising and marketing managers coordinate, are usually subject to tight timeframes and strict deadlines. Therefore, on a daily basis, the role demands excellent organizational and time management skills. Advertising and marketing managers must be adept at multi-tasking, adapting to change, and problem solving.

Advertising and marketing managers generally gain a high level of exposure to different customer types, industries, products, and services (although some may specialize in specific industries). The role demands high business (and possibly sales) acumen and the ability to analyze new information quickly and effectively. An advertising and marketing manager is expected to thoroughly research and understand the industry in which their company operates, as well as their competitors and any competing products and marketing campaigns. This includes developing a deep understanding of the company's (or client's) customer base, methods and processes, challenges and opportunities, and target markets.

Advertising and marketing managers are expected to have competent computing skills to help them prepare campaign-related and organizational materials, such as financial and marketing reports, budget proposals, "pitches" (presentations) to acquire new business, and other work-related documents. They may also be expected to develop and manage spreadsheets and databases for project management and accounting purposes.

OCCUPATION SPECIALTIES

Advertising Managers

Advertising managers seek to generate interest in a product or service by means of ads placed in various media. They work with sales staff and others to create ideas for an advertising campaign. Some advertising managers specialize in a particular field or type of advertising. For example, media directors determine the way in which an advertising campaign reaches customers; they can use any or all of various media, including radio, television, newspapers, magazines, the Internet, and outdoor signs. Advertising managers known as account executives manage clients' accounts, but they do not necessarily develop or supervise the creation or presentation of the advertising. That is the work of the creative services department.

Marketing Managers

Marketing managers gather and use data to estimate the demand for products and services that an organization and its competitors offer. They identify potential markets, develop pricing strategies to help maximize profits, and ensure that customers are satisfied (by using surveys, etc.). They work with sales, advertising, and product development staffs to identify and target customers and keep the firm's products or services competitive in the marketplace. In smaller firms individuals may function as both marketing and advertising managers as well as promotions managers.

Promotions Managers

Promotions managers oversee programs that combine advertising with purchasing incentives to increase sales. Often, the programs use

Duties and Responsibilities

- **Preparing advertising and marketing campaigns, schedules, and budgets**
- **Consulting with people in sales, market research, and creative departments**
- **Overseeing staff in layout, copy, and production**

direct mail, inserts in newspapers, Internet advertisements, in-store displays, product endorsements, or special events to target customers. Purchasing incentives may include discounts, samples, gifts, rebates, coupons, sweepstakes, and contests.

WORK ENVIRONMENT

Physical Environment

Office settings predominate. Advertising and marketing managers work for small to large advertising and marketing departments or agencies, usually in urban or semi-urban locations. Some travel may be required.

Job security is sometimes tenuous in the advertising industry. Economic or sector downturns, changes to a firm's customer base, or reduced customer spending can lead to layoffs. This tends to create an atmosphere of intense competition.

Human Environment

Advertising and marketing manager roles demand strong collaborative and team skills. Advertising and marketing managers interact with sales, advertising, business, and creative specialists, such as brand and product managers, marketing managers, brand strategists, public relations executives, graphic designers, art directors, multimedia technicians, copywriters, production assistants, and editors. They are likely to work with multiple departmental or client contacts, as well as outside service providers or freelancers. They usually report to an agency/department director or owner, or to an area supervisor.

Technological Environment

Advertising and marketing managers use standard business technologies, including computer systems and networks, telecommunications tools, Internet and social media tools, presentation tools and software, and financial and database software.

In smaller firms, where greater overlap between marketing and design functions often exists, managers sometimes need to be familiar with graphic design software and basic production technologies (such as desktop publishing).

EDUCATION, TRAINING, AND ADVANCEMENT

High School/Secondary

High school students can best prepare for a career as an advertising and marketing manager by taking courses in business, math (with an accounting focus), computer literacy, and communications (for example, journalism or business communications). Courses such as social studies, history, and economics will also prepare the student for synthesizing research into written materials. The creative aspects of the advertising industry may be explored through art and graphic design. However, it is important to note that advertising and marketing managers work in an administrative, rather than a creative, capacity. In addition, psychology and cultural studies may provide an understanding of group and individual responses to advertising and other forms of communication.

Students should also become involved in extracurricular school activities and projects that develop business and communication skills to gain hands-on experience prior to graduation. Additionally, serving as a club secretary,

Skills and Abilities

Analytical Skills
- Critical thinking and reasoning
- Information processing

Communication Skills
- Listening to others
- Persuading others
- Speaking and writing effectively

Interpersonal/Social Skills
- Being able to work with others
- Cooperating with others
- Having good judgment
- Motivating others

Organization & Management Skills
- Making sound decisions
- Managing time and budget
- Meeting goals and deadlines
- Paying attention to and handling details
- Solving problems
- Supervising others as necessary

Other Skills
- Appreciating both the business and the creative sides

treasurer, or other office holder will help to develop organizational skills. Participation in student newsletters and similar publications will help to build an understanding of print and multimedia communications.

Suggested High School Subjects

- Business Data Processing
- Business Math
- Communications
- Composition
- Computer Science
- Economics
- English
- Graphic Arts
- Journalism
- Psychology
- Statistics

Famous First

The first use of coupons in a promotional campaign was in 1865, when soap maker B. T. Babbitt of New York City began selling soap bars in wrappers. At first people resisted buying the product because they worried they were being charged extra for the wrapper. Babbitt then printed the word "coupon" on the wrapper and offered to give away a lithographic print for every 10 coupons returned. The strategy was so successful that Babbitt soon had to create a "premium department" to manage this and other such giveaways.

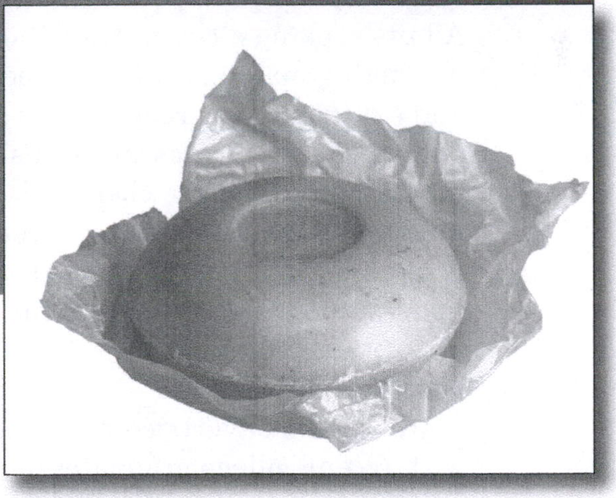

College/Postsecondary

At the college level, students interested in becoming an advertising and marketing manager should work toward earning an undergraduate degree in communications, advertising, marketing, or business administration.

Alternatively, they should build a strong liberal arts background. Owing to strong competition among professional business candidates, a master's degree is sometimes expected, although practical experience is often more highly regarded than formal qualifications.

A large number of colleges and universities offer advertising, marketing, communications, and business degree programs. Some programs offer internships or work experience with advertising departments or agencies. These experiences may lead to entry-level opportunities. Aspiring advertising and marketing managers can also gain entry into the advertising industry via other roles, such as market research, administration, or sales.

Related College Majors

- Advertising
- Business Administration
- Communications
- Journalism
- Management/Management Science
- Marketing & Merchandising
- Psychology
- Public Relations
- Statistics

Adult Job Seekers

Adults seeking a career transition into or return to an advertising and marketing manager role will need to highlight qualifications, skills, and experience in areas such as business administration, advertising, and marketing. Necessary skills for a successful transition include account coordination, client liaison, and project management. Marketing and advertising experience with a non-agency corporation is often highly regarded because agency firms value employees who understand the client side of the relationship.

Networking is critical—candidates should not rely solely on online job searches and advertised positions to explore work opportunities. As with recent college graduates, adult job seekers may wish to consider entry to the advertising industry via an alternative route, such as market research, administration, or sales.

Professional Certification and Licensure

There are no formal professional certifications or licensing requirements for advertising and marketing managers.

Additional Requirements

The most important attributes for advertising and marketing managers are a passion for advertising and marketing communications, coupled with excellent business, organizational, and people skills. Advertising and marketing managers must be skilled and diplomatic coordinators, negotiators, and problem solvers. They should be willing to persist under often heavy workloads and with demanding stakeholders.

Fun Fact

Ninety three percent of marketers use social media for business.
Source: the Website Marketing Group, 2013.

EARNINGS AND ADVANCEMENT

Earning potential increases as advancement occurs. Advancement may be quick in corporate ranks, partly because turnover can be high as a result of account success or failure. Many firms provide their employees with continuing education opportunities, either in-house or at local colleges and universities, and encourage employee participation in seminars and conferences.

According to a salary survey by the National Association of Colleges and Employers, graduates with a bachelor's degree in advertising had starting salaries of $47,343 in 2012. Advertising and marketing managers had median annual earnings of $104,246 in 2012. The lowest ten percent earned less than $52,592, and the highest ten percent earned more than $176,384. Performance incentives and bonuses are granted according to the employee's record of performance.

Advertising and marketing managers may receive paid vacations, holidays, and sick days; life and health insurance; and retirement benefits. These are usually paid by the employer. Top executives in the field may receive additional benefits (such as stock options).

Metropolitan Areas with the Highest Concentration of Jobs in this Occupation

Metropolitan area	Employment(1)	Employment per thousand jobs	Hourly mean wage
New York-White Plains-Wayne, NY-NJ	14,930	2.89	$76.50
Chicago-Joliet-Naperville, IL	9,170	2.52	$54.10
Los Angeles-Long Beach-Glendale, CA	9,100	2.35	$65.45
Minneapolis-St. Paul-Bloomington, MN-WI	7,320	4.18	$56.99
Boston-Cambridge-Quincy, MA	5,710	3.34	$64.11
Seattle-Bellevue-Everett, WA	5,410	3.84	$59.63
Washington-Arlington-Alexandria, DC-VA-MD-WV	5,120	2.19	$61.81
San Francisco-San Mateo-Redwood City, CA	4,530	4.53	$70.42

(1) Does not include self-employed. Source: Bureau of Labor Statistics, 2012

Conversation With . . .
JESSICA MOODY

Vice President of Marketing, 10 years

1. What was your individual career path in terms of education, entry-level job, or other significant opportunity?

I have a bachelors degree from Colgate University. I majored in English with a double minor in Education and Natural Sciences. Shortly after graduating college, I set out to find a position in publishing. I joined Grey House Publishing as an editorial assistant in 1997, but moved into their marketing department soon after I was hired. My responsibilities within the marketing department grew as our product line expanded. Sixteen years later, now as Vice President of Marketing for Grey House, I manage our direct mail, advertising and email marketing campaigns; trade show exhibits and our presence on the web, including social media outlets; assist with new product creation and market research; and support our sales team with campaign creation and lead generation to identify potential markets or sales opportunities.

2. Are there many job opportunities in your profession? In what specific areas?

Given companies' need to promote what they're doing – a product, a service – sales and marketing positions will always be around. The nitty gritty of what those tasks are may shift, but they will never go away. Because marketing, as a profession, spans all industries, take a step back and say, "What industries do I like?" I liked English, so that's why I went into publishing. From the entertainment to the automotive industries, electronics and technology, consumer goods, or anything in between, companies need to sell their product or service to expand and grow. Delivering a message to your target audience – a message to take action and buy a product, or make use of a service – is what marketing is all about. Marketing and advertising are everywhere, on television and radio, in newspapers and magazines, on the web, in your email inbox, bundled with apps and on social media. The challenge that marketers face is to make their message stand out from the crowd and be heard.

3. What do you wish you had known going into this profession?

Marketing is all about testing and trying new strategies. Some work and some don't, but you don't know until you test. I wish I had known to be even more fearless – to try new methods and to test different strategies, no matter how off-the-wall. I've found that creativity, flexibility and a willingness to collaborate are critical to success in this field.

4. How do you see your profession changing in the next five years?

The landscape of online marketing has been changing and growing by leaps and bounds and I expect that technology will continue to advance and create new ways to reach an audience with even more targeted, personalized messages. A marketer's ability to take advantage of those new technologies will contribute to his or her success.

5. What role will technology play in those changes, and what skills will be required?

The advancements in the ways in which marketing messages will be delivered, and the technology behind those advancements, will expand the basic skills necessary for marketers in the future. Candidates wishing to join the marketing field will benefit from courses or experience in art and web design, computer programming, social media and new technologies – all this combined with the more basic tools needed in creative writing, communications and presentation skills.

6. Do you have any general advice or additional professional insights to share with someone interested in your profession?

A career in marketing can be incredibly rewarding and creatively satisfying. For someone who enjoys working on new projects, creating new ideas or putting a new spin on an existing idea, this profession can provide lasting appeal.

7. Can you suggest a valuable "try this" for students considering a career in your profession?

If you reach into your mailbox or inbox, chances are good that you will find a number of examples of types of marketing. Examine each piece, and make note of the various messages they contain, what they look like, how they were delivered, and how they call the recipient to action. How could they say things differently? How could the piece say the same message using different graphics or delivery vehicles? For those who enjoy taking a creative "whack" at these types of questions, marketing can be an excellent career path. Marketing internships are also a great place to gain experience and learn more about the field.

EMPLOYMENT AND OUTLOOK

There were approximately 200,000 advertising and marketing managers employed nationally in 2012. Positions exist not only in advertising agencies, but also with public relations firms, printing and publishing firms, computer services firms, and many others. There is also a strong demand for advertising and marketing managers in the non-profit sector, including colleges/universities and philanthropic organizations. Employment is expected to grow about as fast as the average for all occupations through the year 2020, which means employment is projected to increase approximately 14 percent. Increasingly intense domestic and global competition in products and services offered to consumers should require greater need for this occupation as companies want to maintain and expand their share of the market.

Employment Trend, Projected 2010–20

Total, All Occupations: 14%

Marketing Managers: 14%

Advertising, Promotions, and Marketing Managers: 14%

Advertising and Promotions Managers: 13%

Note: "All Occupations" includes all occupations in the U.S. Economy. Source: U.S. Bureau of Labor Statistics, Employment Projections Program

Related Occupations

- Advertising Director
- Advertising Sales Agent
- Copywriter
- Electronic Commerce Specialist
- Market Research Analyst
- Public Relations Specialist
- Sales Manager

SELECTED SCHOOLS

Many large universities, especially those with business schools, offer programs in marketing and advertising. The student can also gain initial training through enrollment at a liberal arts college or community college. Below are listed some of the more prominent institutions in this field.

Indiana University–Bloomington
107 S. Indiana Avenue
Bloomington, IN 47405
812.855.4848
www.indiana.edu

New York University
70 Washington Square
New York, NY 10012
212.998.1212
www.nyu.edu

University of California–Berkeley
110 Sproul Hall
Berkeley, CA 94720
510.642.6000
www.berkeley.edu

University of Michigan–Ann Arbor
Ann Arbor, MI 48109
734.764.1817
www.umich.edu

University of North Carolina–Chapel Hill
South Building, CB 9100
Chapel Hill, NC 27599
919.962.2211
unc.edu

University of Pennsylvania
3541 Walnut Street
Philadelphia, PA 19104
215.898.5000
www.upenn.edu

University of Southern California
University Park
Los Angeles, CA 90089
213.740.2311
www.usc.edu

University of Texas–Austin
Austin, TX 78712
512.471.3434
www.utexas.edu

University of Virginia
Charlottesville, VA 22904
434.924.0311
www.virginia.edu

University of Wisconsin–Madison
500 Lincoln Drive
Madison, WI 53706
608.262.1234
www.wisc.edu

MORE INFORMATION

Advertising Research Foundation
432 Park Avenue South, 6th Floor
New York, NY 10016-8013
212.751.5656
thearf.org

Advertising Women of New York
25 West 45th Street, Suite 403
New York, NY 10036
212.221.7969
www.awny.org

American Advertising Federation
1101 Vermont Avenue, NW
Suite 500
Washington, DC 20005-6306
800.999.2231
www.aaf.org

American Association of Advertising Agencies
405 Lexington Avenue, 18th Floor
New York, NY 10174-1801
212.682.2500
www.aaaa.org

American Marketing Association
311 S. Wacker Drive
Suite 5800
Chicago, IL 60606
312.542.9000
www.marketingpower.com

Association of National Advertisers
708 Third Avenue, 33rd Floor
New York, NY 10017-4270
212.697.5950
www.ana.net

Direct Marketing Association
1120 Avenue of the Americas, 13th Floor
New York, NY 10036-6700
212.768.7277
thedma.org

Kylie Grimshaw Hughes/Editor

Advertising Director

Snapshot

Career Cluster: Business, Management & Administration, Marketing, Sales & Service, Media & Communications, Public Relations
Interests: Entrepreneurship, Marketing, Finances/Budgets, People, Products
Earnings (Yearly Average): $104,246
Employment & Outlook: Average Growth Expected

OVERVIEW

Sphere of Work

Advertising directors lead teams of promotional and marketing professionals in the conception, creation, and implementation of campaigns to generate public interest in goods and services. The position requires a unique combination of skills, including both creative ingenuity and management savvy.

Directors oversee the creative, financial, and clientele aspects of advertising campaigns, ensuring their timely development and quality execution. Directors of advertising work with other executives to identify marketing strategies, form advertising budgets, and contribute to the conceptualization of the public face of corporations and organizations.

Advertising directors are seasoned professionals with tested management skills who possess several years of experience in the lower tiers of the marketing and promotions field or a closely related discipline, such as public relations or communications development.

Work Environment

Advertising directors work predominantly in professional and office settings. The managerial aspects of the position may require their presence in several different offices and similar professional settings on a daily basis, depending on the realm of industry. Advertising directors work with professionals involved in finance, creative design, and product development. Directors who oversee creative firms (ad agencies), as opposed to marketing departments of single companies, are often required to visit clients at their place of business.

Profile

Working Conditions: Office Environment
Physical Strength: Light Work
Education Needs: Bachelor's Degree
Licensure/Certification: Usually Not Required
Physical Abilities Not Required: No Heavy Physical Work
Opportunities For Experience: Prior Employment As Advertising & Marketing Manager
Holland Interest Score*: ESA

* See Appendix A

Occupation Interest

Executive positions in advertising are almost exclusively given to those with at least five to seven years of lower-level experience in marketing and promotions. While specific undergraduate or postgraduate work can prepare students for the position, advertising professionals come from a variety of secondary and postsecondary programs related to marketing and promotions, from communications to graphic design and business management.

A Day in the Life—Duties and Responsibilities

The day-to-day responsibilities of an advertising director consist of monitoring project development, communicating with top executives and external clients to ensure their continued satisfaction, and, in the case of ad agencies, recruiting new clients through demonstrations of the firm's capabilities. Monitoring project development is a supervisory duty that entails ensuring all deadlines and timelines are being adhered to by the marketing staff. The ability to complete advertising campaigns in a timely and financially sound manner is a crucial responsibility of advertising directors.

While client representatives may handle the day-to-day interactions with clients, advertising directors also share the responsibility of representing their firm (or department) and its work, both to their clientele and to other members of the organization. Such interactions can often include soliciting new business with an organization or an advertising firm's sales staff. In such settings, advertising directors must demonstrate how their firm/department has successfully handled major projects in the past both on time and on budget. This is done through effective interpersonal communication, portfolio presentations, and other visual demonstrations. Professionals with an outgoing personality and an interest in working daily with a variety of different people are often best suited for the networking and team-oriented nature of the position. People who prefer to work alone or in small groups may not be well suited for the large amount of collaboration necessary to carry out the role.

Duties and Responsibilities

- **Managing the staff that puts together an advertising package**
- **Making and maintaining many contacts with clients, freelancers and business people**
- **Overseeing the visual communication aspects of advertising, such as illustrations, art and photography**
- **Researching consumer buying trends and the possible market for a specific product**
- **Deciding which media avenue is best to use for the advertising package**
- **Developing catchy phrases or jingles and explaining the product and service verbally and in writing**

WORK ENVIRONMENT

Physical Environment

Advertising directors generally work in professional and office settings. They are also often called to meetings off-site, in locations dictated by particular clients. In addition, the may attend trade conferences and professional development seminars.

Skills and Abilities

Analytical Skills

- Ability to read markets and customer needs

Communication Skills

- "Pitching" or presenting ideas persuasively
- Speaking and writing effectively
- Understanding others

Creative/Artistic Skills

- Recognizing and applying effective audiovisual media

Interpersonal/Social Skills

- Being adept at networking
- Exhibiting confidence and knowledge
- Possessing strong team leadership abilities

Organization & Management Skills

- Handling challenging situations
- Managing time and finances
- Meeting goals and deadlines
- Overseeing staff members
- Solving problems

Human Environment

Strong collaborative and leadership skills are preferable. In addition to positively interacting with clients, advertising directors must also possess the capability to motivate large groups of team members working simultaneously on numerous projects with strict deadlines. Optimum candidates possess the deft public-speaking skills necessary for all positions of leadership.

Technological Environment

Applicable technologies range from networked computer systems and web conferencing tools to software for design, finances, and communications—in short, the full range of contemporary office technologies.

EDUCATION, TRAINING, AND ADVANCEMENT

High School/Secondary

High-school students can best prepare for a career in advertising with courses in business administration, English composition, graphic arts, communications, computers, and economics. Participation in student politics can equip students with basic leadership skills that can be utilized in future management positions. Beneficial skills such as communication, teamwork, and problem solving are often garnered through participation in scholastic sports and clubs such as debate, community service, and theater arts.

Unpaid or volunteer experience at a marketing or advertising firm can help students learn the entry-level responsibilities of the field and can potentially bolster college applications.

Suggested High School Subjects

- Business Math
- Arts
- Audio-Visual
- Business Operations
- Composition
- English
- Foreign Languages
- Geometry
- Graphic Communications
- Humanities
- Journalism
- Literature
- Photography

Famous First

The first advertising show for business professionals was held in Madison Square Garden in New York City in 1906. The slogan for the show was "If your business isn't with advertising, advertise it for sale."

College/Postsecondary

Advertising directors traditionally have an undergraduate education in advertising itself or a related field, such as marketing, public relations, management, or graphic design. Undergraduate advertising majors supplement a traditional liberal-arts curriculum with a basic introduction to advertising, including course work in mass communications research, communication theory, new media design, persuasion, and communication law.

Professionals aspiring to careers in advertisement at the managerial level often seek a graduate degree in the field. Graduate studies in advertising allow students to explore an individual project related to a facet of advertising that interests them, in concert with advanced course work in media research, creative strategy development, and communications management.

Related College Majors

- Advertising
- Business Administration
- Communications
- Management/Management Science
- Marketing & Merchandising
- Psychology
- Public Relations

Adult Job Seekers

Advertising is a considerably competitive field that requires an intense amount of dedication, particularly in the early part of one's career. Those who achieve management-level positions have often worked tirelessly at developing both their frame of reference and their knowledge of contemporary advertising strategies. They have also embraced positions of leadership and project management throughout their career.

Professional Certification and Licensure

No specific certification is required.

Additional Requirements

Advertising professionals who ascend to managerial positions in the field are effective communicators and proactive problem solvers who can motivate large groups to tackle complex creative problems. Organization, professionalism, and amicability are highly sought-after traits for advertising executives, as is the ability to motivate in an encouraging and proactive manner.

Fun Fact

Ninety two percent of Americans think free content (news, weather, blogs) is important to the overall value of the Internet; 75 percent prefer ad-supported content as opposed to paying for ad-free content; 68 percent want some ads directed at their interests; and 16 percent like to see ads for general products and services.

Source: Zogby Analytics poll commissioned by the Digital Advertising Alliance (DAA)

EARNINGS AND ADVANCEMENT

In smaller firms, advancement occurs more slowly than at larger firms. Emphasis is placed on experience, ability, and leadership. Depending on the company, the rank above advertising director may be vice president of the company, executive director over several advertising directors, or president of the company. According to a salary survey by the National Association of Colleges and Employers, graduates with a bachelor's degree in advertising had starting salaries of $47,343 in 2012. Advertising directors had median annual earnings of $104,246 in 2012. The lowest ten percent earned less than $52,592, and the highest ten percent earned more than $176,384.

Advertising directors may receive paid vacations, holidays, and sick days; life and health insurance; and retirement benefits. These are usually paid by the employer.

EMPLOYMENT AND OUTLOOK

Employment in the occupation of advertising director is expected to grow about as fast as the average for all occupations through the year 2020, which means employment is projected to increase about 14 percent. This is due to increasing domestic and global competition in products and services offered to consumers via advertising. Opportunities for employment will be in larger cities such as New York, Chicago, and Los Angeles because the concentration of business is higher. Job competition is extremely tough because top jobs are highly sought.

Related Occupations

- Advertising & Marketing Manager
- Advertising Sales Agent
- Art Director
- Copywriter
- Electronic Commerce Specialist
- Motion Picture/Radio/TV Art Director
- Online Merchant
- Public Relations Specialist

Conversation With . . .
DENELL NUESE

Advertising Director, 25 years in profession

1. What was your individual career path in terms of education, entry-level job, or other significant opportunity?

I received my undergraduate degree in communications and a master's degree in integrated advertising & marketing. During my senior year in college I had an internship as the assistant to a shopping mall marketing manager. She left and I was hired to fill her position prior to my college graduation. This job allowed me to learn about advertising as well as special events and public relations.

2. Are there many job opportunities in your profession? In what specific areas?

Yes, there seem to be a lot of jobs available right now, particularly in e-commerce, mobile, and online advertising including search and social media. When I started working years ago, the world of advertising was basically buying an ad in a newspaper or on television. Now there's mobile advertising, there's search, and there are all these different areas where you can buy or manage advertising that didn't exist years ago. When I first started out it was a much more narrow approach. You could buy an ad on a billboard. Now you can buy an ad on a truck or van. I've had to continually adjust and learn about new industries and products. In my previous job, which I left more than a decade ago, we never even talked about pay-per-click and online digital advertising and bidding on key words. And now that's part of what I do.

3. What do you wish you had known going into this profession?

That advertising is math! You really have to have a command of numbers because it all comes down to formulas. Television is sold as "reach times frequency." That formula tells you how many people your commercial will reach and how often it will air. Media buyers have software systems that allow them to run those formulas in order to determine the best ways to spend their advertising dollars.

The best advice I received when starting out was to be thorough in my communication and never assume that someone knows what you are thinking or talking about. This is true of the people you work with as well as with the consumer. When creating advertising, you have to assume that the consumer doesn't know anything about the product or service, nor do they really care about it. That helps me figure out what the ad has to say or do to get through to them.

4. How do you see your profession changing in the next five years?

It has changed so much over the past 20 years and will continue to change based upon new technology, products and programs. Ten years ago, mobile marketing (advertising via a cell phone) didn't even exist, social media didn't exist, and online advertising was in its infancy. It's constant learning and adapting and I find that I rely more frequently on experts in different areas. I find you almost have to have at least a few people in your department to master all of the different areas where you can advertise.

5. What role will technology play in those changes, and what skills will be required?

New technologies will continue to change the landscape of advertising. The skills necessary to thrive in that environment are strong analytics and the ability to adapt and learn quickly. I find that I do a lot of research on my own. There's always something new to learn or investigate. You also need a willingness to embrace and thrive on change.

6. Do you have any general advice or additional professional insights to share with someone interested in your profession?

Try to obtain internships and work with as many different types of companies as you can to determine what part of the advertising world you want to be in. An advertising director might work for an agency providing services to many different clients. That requires a different type of personality than say, an ad director who works for the company itself and who gets to call the shots. Within those positions, there can be specialties: an ad director might specialize in media buying, project management, tracking the results of advertising. Others are involved heavily in the development of ads, so that might be a good fit for somebody who is creative.

7. Can you suggest a valuable "try this" for students considering a career in your profession?

Go online and look up sample marketing plans. Use those as a guide to write your own for either a real or imaginary product or service. You might also see if there's a professional organization in your area for the advertising industry. Tap into their resources and learn about the profession.

SELECTED SCHOOLS

Many large universities, especially those with business schools, offer programs in marketing and advertising. The student can also gain initial training through enrollment at a liberal arts college or community college. Below are listed some of the more prominent institutions in this field.

Indiana University–Bloomington
107 S. Indiana Avenue
Bloomington, IN 47405
812.855.4848
www.indiana.edu

New York University
70 Washington Square
New York, NY 10012
212.998.1212
www.nyu.edu

University of California–Berkeley
110 Sproul Hall
Berkeley, CA 94720
510.642.6000
www.berkeley.edu

University of Michigan–Ann Arbor
Ann Arbor, MI 48109
734.764.1817
www.umich.edu

University of North Carolina–Chapel Hill
South Building, CB 9100
Chapel Hill, NC 27599
919.962.2211
unc.edu

University of Pennsylvania
3541 Walnut Street
Philadelphia, PA 19104
215.898.5000
www.upenn.edu

University of Southern California
University Park
Los Angeles, CA 90089
213.740.2311
www.usc.edu

University of Texas–Austin
Austin, TX 78712
512.471.3434
www.utexas.edu

University of Virginia
Charlottesville, VA 22904
434.924.0311
www.virginia.edu

University of Wisconsin–Madison
500 Lincoln Drive
Madison, WI 53706
608.262.1234
www.wisc.edu

MORE INFORMATION

The Advertising Club of New York
235 Park Avenue S., 6th Floor
New York, NY 10003-1450
www.theadvertisingclub.org
212-533-8080
Grants & Scholarships:
www.theadvertisingclub.org/winners

Advertising Research Foundation
432 Park Avenue South, 6th Floor
New York, NY 10016-8013
212.751.5656
thearf.org

Advertising Women of New York
25 West 45th Street, Suite 403
New York, NY 10036
212.221.7969
www.awny.org

American Advertising Federation
1101 Vermont Avenue, NW,
Suite 500
Washington, DC 20005-6306
800.999.2231
www.aaf.org

American Association of Advertising Agencies
405 Lexington Avenue, 18th Floor
New York, NY 10174-1801
212.682.2500
www.aaaa.org

American Marketing Association
311 S. Wacker Drive
Suite 5800
Chicago, IL 60606
312.542.9000
www.marketingpower.com

Association of National Advertisers
708 Third Avenue, 33rd Floor
New York, NY 10017-4270
212.697.5950
www.ana.net

Direct Marketing Association
1120 Avenue of the Americas, 13th Floor
New York, NY 10036-6700
212.768.7277
thedma.org

John Pritchard/Editor

Art Director

Snapshot

Career Cluster: Arts, Business, Management & Administration, Media & Communications
Interests: Advertising, Art, Media & Communications
Earnings (Yearly Average): $85,468
Employment & Outlook: Slower Than Average Growth Expected

OVERVIEW

Sphere of Work

Art directors work in a variety of industries, including advertising, theatre, film, video games, and publishing. While these fields involve different media, the essential task of an art director is the same: an art director oversees the aesthetic direction of a project from its conception to completion. The art director typically does not play an active role in the creation of the various elements of a project; rather, he or she works closely with artists and writers to reach a shared goal.

Work Environment

Depending on the industry and the size of the project, an art director can expect to work with varying numbers of artists and writers on a particular project. No matter what the industry, the art director has executive control of the work. All artistic decisions must be made with the art director's consent and approval before being made public. In a large advertising firm, an art director may report to an executive creative director. Art directors usually work during standard business hours. Long hours may be required to meet deadlines.

Profile

Working Conditions: Office Environment/Studio Environment
Physical Strength: Light Work
Education Needs: Bachelor's Degree
Licensure/Certification: Usually Not Required
Physical Abilities Not Required: No Heavy Physical Labor
Opportunities For Experience: Internship Part-Time Work
Holland Interest Score*: AES

* See Appendix A

Occupation Interest

Working as an art director appeals to individuals with creative vision who are able to articulate and carry out that vision in an effective manner. Those drawn to this occupation have a firm grasp of the history of their media, are aware of cultural trends, and have creative minds. They can imagine the final product, whether it's an advertising campaign, a book, a magazine, or a film; and they can coordinate the various tasks and elements involved in the creative process. Art directors have strong people skills and work with a team to realize an idea. Those with an undergraduate degree in advertising, art history, or graphic design, or previous experience as a visual artist, actor, or filmmaker would be suited to the field. Successful art directors should be problem solvers, have strong communication skills, and must be well organized.

A Day in the Life—Duties and Responsibilities

An art director's daily duties vary by industry. Art directors commonly work for film, advertising, and publishing companies.

In large film productions, an art director meets with the prop master and costume and set designers to develop the overall "look" of a movie. He or she reports to the film's production director. The art director is often responsible for scheduling and hiring individuals working in construction, sound, and special effects and ensuring that the set construction and location are ready for filming. The art director also often manages a portion of a film's budget. Art directors for smaller productions may be required to take on more responsibilities and tasks.

In an advertising agency, an art director collaborates with one or more artists, such as graphic designers, illustrators and animators, and copywriters to develop the overall concept for a project. The art director organizes face-to-face or virtual meetings to discuss the relationship between the textual and visual components of an advertisement and any related promotional material. Suggestions may be made from one department to another, with copywriters and artists exchanging ideas about visual and textual aspects of the advertising campaign. During these conversations, the art director acts as facilitator and executive decision maker. Once aesthetic decisions have been made, the art director may supervise the work itself.

An art director working in publishing performs a similar job function to that of an advertising art director. He or she works closely with writers, editors, and designers to establish an aesthetic approach for the layout of a book or magazine. The art director typically has the final say on matters such as the typeface of a book, the visual details of the book interior, and the jacket design that best fits the work.

Duties and Responsibilities

- **Working with and directing copywriters, assistants, artists, illustrators, cartoonists, and designers**
- **Performing duties as graphic designer, illustrator, or artist**
- **Reviewing portfolios of photographers, illustrators, artists, directors, and producers**

WORK ENVIRONMENT

Physical Environment

Art directors working in advertising or publishing usually work in an office setting. A large creative department may have separate studio spaces for the various creative personnel who work there. Artists and directors working in theatre or film work predominately in offices, but also spend time on the set.

Human Environment

While art directors do not usually hold the top position in any industry, they have considerable control over their specific projects, acting in a guiding, executive role with the various artists, assistants, and writers they supervise.

Technological Environment

Art directors interact with clients and colleagues using standard telecommunications tools (email, phone, video conferencing) and in face-to-face meetings. Computers play a large role in their daily activities. Art directors should have familiarity with graphic and photo-imaging software, as they may make adjustments to a project or need to demonstrate a compositional idea. (Art directors in the film industry may be familiar with even more sophisticated graphic technologies depending on their field.) Experience with web design and computer code can also be valuable as more companies expand their efforts in Internet and social media marketing.

Skills and Abilities

Communication Skills
- Translating concepts into concrete ideas

Creative/Artistic Skills
- Being skilled in art, music, or other expressive forms

Interpersonal/Social Skills
- Working with and directing a team of creative individuals

Organization & Management Skills
- Balancing art requirements with business goals
- Identifying and coordinating tasks

EDUCATION, TRAINING, AND ADVANCEMENT

High School/Secondary

Students aspiring to become an art director should pursue a rigorous college preparatory program, with an emphasis on coursework in the arts, such as theatre, media arts, computers, drafting, art history, visual art, and English. Students particularly interested in the financial and administrative aspects of art direction may also find advanced courses in arts management and economics helpful.

Interested students should research and apply to postsecondary schools that offer a relevant major. Some professional organizations provide career workshops for high school students, as well as scholarships for postsecondary studies in art direction.

Suggested High School Subjects

- Arts
- Audio-Visual
- Business
- Drafting
- English
- Geometry
- Graphic Communications
- Humanities
- Journalism
- Literature
- Mechanical Drawing
- Photography
- Psychology
- Speech

Famous First

The first modern photographic print in a publication appeared in the *New York Daily Graphic* in 1880. It showed a shantytown in the city. The print was produced by means of the halftone process, which uses tiny dots of different sizes and gradations to create the optical illusion that the viewer is seeing shades of gray along with black and white.

College/Postsecondary

At the university level, students should consider a major in visual art, film studies, art history, English, theatre, art administration, or advertising, depending on their industry of interest. An aspiring art director should major in art administration or pursue summer internships in an industry relevant to his or her interests.

Related College Majors

- Art Administration
- Art History
- Commercial Art & Illustration
- Graphic Design
- Media Studies
- Theater Arts

Adult Job Seekers

Art direction is a highly competitive field; most employers hire those with experience in the industry. Entry-level positions that may lead to a career in art direction are often unpaid or low paying. Young adults may opt for internships to make connections in a particular industry. Artists may easily enter the field and advance to an art director position.

Professional Certification and Licensure

No certifications or licenses are needed to become an art director. In the film industry, however, some art directors do pursue specialized certificates, particularly if they are serving in the capacity of creative director or a similar role.

Additional Requirements

Owing to the competitive nature of the field, most art directors are extremely motivated, hardworking, efficient, organized, and creative individuals. Successful art directors are excellent communicators and comfortable working collaboratively. Working well under pressure can be a deciding factor for future success, as art directors commonly serve a central role on film productions or advertising campaigns where
Art directors held about 32,000 jobs nationally in 2012. Employment is expected to grow slower than the average for all occupations through the year 2020, which means employment is projected to increase approximately 9 percent. Job growth in traditional print publications will slow but will be replaced with new opportunities in electronic and Internet-based publications.

EARNINGS AND ADVANCEMENT

The path of advancement most often is receiving a similar job in a larger, more prestigious corporation, agency or organization. This usually results in increased responsibilities and earnings.
Median annual earnings of art directors were $85,468 in 2012. The lowest ten percent earned less than $45,410, and the highest ten percent earned more than $173,236.
Art directors may receive paid vacations, holidays, and sick days; life and health insurance; and retirement benefits. These are usually paid by the employer.

Metropolitan Areas with the Highest Concentration of Jobs in This Occupation

Metropolitan area	Employment[1]	Employment per thousand jobs	Hourly mean wage
New York-White Plains-Wayne, NY-NJ	5,940	1.15	$62.83
Los Angeles-Long Beach-Glendale, CA	2,830	0.73	$57.01
Chicago-Joliet-Naperville, IL	1,650	0.45	$38.67
Boston-Cambridge-Quincy, MA	1,010	0.59	$45.34
San Francisco-San Mateo-Redwood City, CA	970	0.96	$59.28
Minneapolis-St. Paul-Bloomington, MN-WI	730	0.42	$39.45
Seattle-Bellevue-Everett, WA	630	0.45	$48.69
Washington-Arlington-Alexandria, DC-VA-MD-WV	590	0.25	$40.97

[1]Does not include self-employed. Source: Bureau of Labor Statistics, 2012

EMPLOYMENT AND OUTLOOK

Art directors held about 32,000 jobs nationally in 2012. Employment is expected to grow slower than the average for all occupations through the year 2020, which means employment is projected to increase approximately 9 percent. Job growth in traditional print publications will slow but will be replaced with new opportunities in electronic and Internet-based publications.

Employment opportunities may be found in areas such as advertising and public relations agencies, specialized design services, direct marketing agencies, motion picture and video industries, and publishers. Art directors should expect strong competition for available openings.

Employment Trend, Projected 2010–20

Total, All Occupations: 14%

Arts, Designing, Entertainment, Sports and Media Occupations: 13%

Art Directors: 9%

Note: "All Occupations" includes all occupations in the U.S. Economy. Source: U.S. Bureau of Labor Statistics, Employment Projections Program

Related Occupations

- Advertising Director
- Graphic Designer
- Medical & Scientific Illustrator
- Motion Picture/Radio/TV Art Director
- Multimedia Artist & Animator
- Photographer

Conversation With . . .
PATRICK CALKINS

Art Director, 30 years in the profession

1. What was your individual career path in terms of education, entry-level job, or other significant opportunity?

At the age of fifteen, I found out what a commercial artist was at 'career day' at my high school. I knew immediately that it was what I wanted to do. I showed my high school portfolio and was accepted at The Burnley School of Design in Seattle and studied figure drawing and illustration, graphic design, lettering and typography, advertising design, industrial and sign design, and printing.

After graduation I got an assistant art director job at a start-up ad agency. It was a beginning, and I created some real-world portfolio pieces. I then took the advice of my art school teachers who said, "If you want a variety of opportunities to work in this field go to Los Angeles or New York." I chose New York. I got a non-art job and went back to art school at the Parson's School of Design, and added to my portfolio. I applied to a magazine company for a beginning job in the art department and was hired. I learned a lot about how magazines were designed and put together. Again, I built up my portfolio and found a better job with more pay and was on my way. At one point I bought a good camera and studied photography so I could illustrate a magazine story or do an ad with my own photos.

2. Are there many job opportunities in your profession? In what specific areas?

Every magazine has an art director, an assistant art director, and sometimes an associate art director and/or a junior designer. Art departments change personnel as experienced artists move up and change jobs. Advertising agencies always have art departments. Freelancing is also a possible way into the industry. Webpage design is a basic design course offered in any modern art school along with graphic design, animation, video game design, film and video plus sound and technical studies. Pretty much all of it is hands-on practical application. When a student graduates, he or she would have a digital media portfolio. It would show a variety of disciplines from print media to animation and video to sample web pages complete with sound and music.

3. What do you wish you had known going into this profession?

When I started out I didn't know anything about photography. That includes composition, artificial versus natural lighting, exposures and flash, color versus black and white, studio and location shooting and other technical subjects. Today, anybody can take a photo with their phone or digital camera but learning the art of photography is very important to an art director.

4. How do you see your profession changing in the next five years?

I think the future of graphic design and related careers will be within the internet where everything will be online. Printed media will become less and less of a factor so learning digital design for the web would be an advantage. At the present time tablet computers are outselling desktops by an increasing margin yearly. Mobility is the key here which means you could also work from home. Another change is that many editors and writers are learning how to design pages which only makes it harder to find art jobs. The smart art director should learn to write.

5. What role will technology play in those changes, and what skills will be required?

Apple Macs are still the industry standard but now the design program is an all Adobe package called the Indesign Suite. It includes the Indesign publishing graphics system in combination with Photoshop and Illustrator. If you want to be in this industry you need to learn these programs inside and out to even compete.

6. Do you have any general advice or additional professional insights to share with someone interested in your profession?

A solid design education is essential to get a foothold in this industry. But that is not the only thing that makes a great art director. Learning is an ongoing endeavor and should be pursued every day. Know what's going on in the world. Learn world and American history, study all the arts and sciences. Get familiar with popular culture and not just American culture. The more you know, the more resources you can draw on to make intelligent design decisions. I learned this definition of design when I was 18 and never forgot it. "Design is the logical selection and arrangement of visual elements for order plus interest."

7. Can you suggest a valuable "try this" for students considering a career in your profession?

Start with a written story or an editorial from a local newspaper or a school newsletter. Read it a couple of times and visualize what the writer is trying to say. Come up with an idea or two and sketch it out or compose a photo and put them together to create one article. You could also pick a product or service and compose an advertisement. Lastly, why not design your own business card and stationery? It can be a good way to show what you can do and you can hand out your work. Working in an art department is a creative and fun way to earn a living. Good luck.

SELECTED SCHOOLS

Many large universities, especially those with schools of art and design, offer programs in the arts. The student can also gain initial training through enrollment at a liberal arts college or community college. Below are listed some of the more prominent institutions in this field.

Art Center College of Design
1700 Lida Street
Pasadena, CA 91103
626.396.2200
www.artcenter.edu

Carnegie-Mellon University
5000 Forbes Avenue
Pittsburgh, PA 15213
412.268.2000
www.cmu.edu

Massachusetts Institute of Technology
77 Massachusetts Avenue
Cambridge, MA 02139
617.253.1000
www.mit.edu

Parsons The New School for Design
66 5th Avenue
New York, NY 10011
212.229.8900
www.newschool.edu/parsons

Pratt Institute
2000 Willoughby Avenue
Brooklyn, NY 11205
718.636.3600
www.pratt.edu

Rhode Island School of Design
2 College Street
Providence, RI 02903
401.454.6100
www.risd.edu

Rochester Institute of Technology
1 Lomb Memorial Drive
Rochester, NY 14623
585.475.2400
www.rit.edu

Savannah College of Art and Design
342 Bull Street
Savannah, GA 31402
912.525.5100
www.scad.edu

Stanford University
450 Serra Mall
Stanford, CA 94305
650.723.2300
www.stanford.edu

University of Cincinnati
2600 Clifton Avenue
Cincinnati, OH 45221
513.556.1100
www.uc.edu

MORE INFORMATION

The Advertising Club of New York
235 Park Avenue S., 6th Floor
New York, NY 10003-1450
212-533-8080
www.theadvertisingclub.org
Grants & Scholarships:
www.theadvertisingclub.org/winners

AIGA (American Institute of Graphic Arts)
164 5th Avenue
New York, NY 10010
www.aiga.org

Art Directors Club, Inc.
106 West 29th Street
New York, NY 10001
212.643.1440
www.adcglobal.org

Art Directors Guild
Headquarters Office
11969 Ventura Boulevard, 2nd Floor
Studio City, CA 91604
818.762.9995
www.adg.org

Association for Women in Communications (AWC)
National Headquarters
3337 Duke Street
Alexandria, VA 22314
703.370.7436
www.womcom.org

Mark Boccard/Editor

Broadcast Technician

Snapshot

Career Cluster: Arts, A/V Technology & Communications, Manufacturing Science, Technology, Engineering & Mathematics
Interests: Broadcast Media & Technology, Audio/Visual Techniques, Film Production
Earnings (Yearly Average): $37,227
Employment & Outlook: Slower Than Average Growth Expected

OVERVIEW

Sphere of Work

Broadcast technicians are responsible for the maintenance and operation of audio or audiovisual equipment that transmits signals to listeners or viewers. They may control radio equipment, regulating the sound quality and volume level, or monitor the fidelity, brightness, and other visual elements of a television broadcast. They also frequently control technical operations within a radio or television station and direct various aspects of transmission, such as

transferring from local to network broadcasts, signaling when video or audio footage is over, and ensuring that the program operates within Federal Communications Commission (FCC) regulations. Broadcast technicians at large stations tend to specialize in specific operations, while technicians at smaller stations oversee a number of responsibilities.

Work Environment

Broadcast technicians generally work in radio and television stations. When shows and programs are broadcast from off-site locations, technicians may travel to these locations. They may be required to climb antennae, power poles, or broadcast towers; perform moderate lifting; or otherwise engage in physical activity during the course of their jobs. Broadcast technicians generally work forty-hour weeks, but since a majority of television and radio stations remain on the air during nights, weekends, and holidays, technicians may work erratic shifts.

Profile

Working Conditions: Office/Production Studio Some Out Side Work
Physical Strength: Light To Moderate Work
Education Needs: Technical/ Community College Bachelor's Degree
Licensure/Certification: Recommended
Physical Abilities Not Required: No Strenuous Work
Opportunities Or Experience: Apprenticeship, Military Service Volunteer Work, Part-Time Work
Holland Interest Score*: RCE

* See Appendix A

Occupation Interest

Broadcast technicians play an integral role in ensuring that broadcasts are transmitted properly, making their work a fulfilling career for individuals who thrive in a complex and fast-paced technological environment. The broad range of equipment used in radio and television, including microphones, sound recorders, lights, cameras, and transmitters, provides technicians with the opportunity to gain hands-on experience in a variety of areas or choose to specialize in one particular field.

A Day in the Life—Duties and Responsibilities

Broadcast technicians coordinate with station managers, producers, and directors to ensure that audiovisual systems operate properly while radio or television programs are running. To this end, they monitor the strength and clarity of outgoing and incoming signals, regulate sound and visual effects using sound boards and video monitors, and report any equipment failures or issues. Broadcast technicians repair or disconnect faulty or outdated hardware and install new equipment as needed. Furthermore, they are frequently responsible for maintaining detailed programming logs in accordance with the established policies of the station and the FCC.

In the case of large stations, the work of broadcast technicians is dependent on the specialized field in which they work. For example, lighting technicians spend most of their time ensuring that lights are positioned properly, while transmitter technicians work primarily at the location of the station's transmitter, often in a different building from the main studio. Audio control technicians (or sound engineering technicians), meanwhile, work in master control booths and specialize in operating the complex computer-based sound systems used in modern radio and television stations.

In contrast, smaller stations frequently have few or no specialized technicians. Consequently, broadcast technicians working in these environments are often generalists, responsible for lights, sound, transmitters, and all other aspects of the station's technical systems.

Duties and Responsibilities

- **Operating equipment that regulates the quality of sound and pictures being recorded or broadcast**
- **Operating controls that switch broadcasts from one camera or studio to another, from film to live programming or from network to local programs**
- **Setting up, testing, and operating broadcasting equipment at different locations**
- **Dismantling and returning equipment to the studio**

OCCUPATION SPECIALTIES

Video Operators

Video Operators control video consoles to regulate the transmission of television screens and control the quality, brightness, and contrast of the video output. Also called Video Technician.

Audio Operators

Audio Operators control audio equipment to regulate volume level and sound quality during television broadcasts. Also called Sound Technician or Sound Engineering Technician.

Field Engineers

Field Engineers install and operate portable field transmission equipment to broadcast programs or events originating outside the studio. Also called Field Technician.

Transmitter Operators

Transmitter Operators are responsible for monitoring and logging outgoing signals and for operating the transmitter. Also called Transmitter Technician.

Plant and Maintenance Technicians

Plant and Maintenance Technicians repair, adjust, set up and service electronic broadcasting equipment. It is their job to determine the cause of signal breakdown and repair it.

Recording Engineers

Recording Engineers operate and maintain video and sound recording equipment. They operate the disk or recording machine to record music, dialogue or sound effects during recording sessions, radio and television broadcasts or conferences.

WORK ENVIRONMENT

Physical Environment

Broadcast technicians primarily work in television and radio stations. However, they often work outdoors, either with on-site shooting crews or on outdoor equipment, such as transmitters, located away from the station. Broadcast technicians may face some danger of electrocution or other injury when working with high voltages and equipment that is difficult to access.

Human Environment

Depending on their area of work, broadcast technicians may interact with directors, producers, camera and microphone operators, set construction crews, electricians, or on-air personalities. In addition, they may work closely with broadcast technicians specializing in particular tasks.

Skills and Abilities

Communication Skills

- Listening to and understanding others
- Speaking/communicating with others

Interpersonal/Social Skills

- Working as a member of a team

Organization & Management Skills

- Following instructions
- Paying attention to and handling details

Technical Skills

- Applying technology to a task
- Performing mechanical and technical work
- Working with machines, tools, or other objects

Technological Environment

The equipment used by broadcast technicians varies based on their responsibilities or specialty and may include sound mixers, cameras, lighting systems and towers, boom microphones, transmitter equipment, master control switchers, oscilloscopes, satellite receivers, and video editors. Technicians may also use video creation, graphic and photo imaging, and office suite computer software.

EDUCATION, TRAINING, AND ADVANCEMENT

High School/Secondary

High school students interested in becoming broadcast technicians should take industrial arts courses related to radio and television operation/repair and electronics. Courses in geometry, trigonometry, and algebra are also highly useful for aspiring technicians. Participation in the school's audiovisual department, as well as theater and other extracurricular activities focused on lighting or sound, is strongly encouraged.

Suggested High School Subjects

- Algebra
- Applied Communication
- Applied Math
- Applied Physics
- College Preparatory
- Electricity & Electronics
- English
- Geometry
- Media Arts
- Physics
- Radio & TV Repair
- Theatre & Drama
- Trigonometry

Famous First

The first telecast of a moving object took place in 1925 from a radio station in Washington, DC. It showed a windmill turning. The technology used was called "vision-by-radio." Two years later the first telecast of an image accompanied by sound occurred. It showed Herbert Hoover, then Secretary of Commerce, reading a speech. The picture screen at the receiving end was 2 by 3 inches, a little smaller than those on today's smart phones.

Postsecondary

Following high school, aspiring broadcast technicians frequently complete a technical training program at a vocational school or similar institution. A growing number of broadcast technicians hold associate's or bachelor's degrees, which give those candidates an edge in this highly competitive field and opens up possibilities for career advancement. Some senior-level technicians even hold advanced degrees in engineering.

Related College Majors

- Broadcast Journalism
- Radio & Television Broadcasting
- Radio & Television Broadcasting Technology

Adult Job Seekers

Experienced broadcast technicians are encouraged to apply directly to open positions, while candidates who are new to the field can gain hands-on experience in a variety of areas through internships or entry-level jobs at smaller stations. Unions and trade associations, such as the National Association of Broadcast Employees and Technicians (NABET) and the National Association of Broadcasters (NAB), offer training, resources, and valuable networking opportunities.

Professional Certification and Licensure

No certification is required in order to become a broadcast technician. However, technicians may choose to become certified by the Society of Broadcast Engineers (SBE). As with any voluntary certification process, it is beneficial to consult credible professional associations within the field and follow professional debate as to the relevancy and value of any certification program.

Additional Requirements

Broadcast technicians must have strong mechanical skills, with an ability to quickly analyze often-complex electronic systems and equipment. They must demonstrate both dexterity and monitoring skills, which help identify and correct mechanical issues while under strict time constraints. Some broadcast technicians may be required to lift equipment or climb high structures when necessary, so a degree of physical fitness is helpful.

EARNINGS AND ADVANCEMENT

Earnings of broadcast technicians can vary greatly depending on the size and geographic location of the city or town. Television stations usually pay better than radio stations; commercial broadcasting usually pays more than educational broadcasting; and stations in large markets pay more than those in small ones.

Median annual earnings of broadcast technicians were $37,227 in 2012.

Broadcast technicians may receive paid vacations, holidays, and sick days; life and health insurance; and retirement benefits. These are usually paid by the employer.

Metropolitan Areas with the Highest Employment Level in This Occupation

Metropolitan area	Employment[1]	Employment per thousand jobs	Hourly mean wage
Los Angeles-Long Beach-Glendale, CA	4,160	1.07	$23.78
New York-White Plains-Wayne, NY-NJ	3,360	0.65	$26.03
Chicago-Joliet-Naperville, IL	820	0.23	$23.69
Washington-Arlington-Alexandria, DC-VA-MD-WV	750	0.32	$29.42
Boston-Cambridge-Quincy, MA	610	0.35	$26.46
Virginia Beach-Norfolk-Newport News, VA-NC	580	0.81	n/a
Nassau-Suffolk, NY	580	0.47	$24.38
Miami-Miami Beach-Kendall, FL	510	0.51	$16.55

[1] Does not include self-employed. Source: Bureau of Labor Statistics, 2012

EMPLOYMENT AND OUTLOOK

There were approximately 32,000 broadcast technicians employed nationally in 2012. About one-fourth worked in radio and television broadcasting, and about 15 percent worked in the motion picture, video and sound recording industries. Broadcast technician jobs in television are located in virtually all cities, whereas jobs in radio also are found in many small towns. The highest paying and most specialized jobs are concentrated in New York City, Los Angeles, Chicago, and Washington, DC - the originating centers for most network or news programs. Motion picture production jobs are concentrated in Los Angeles and New York City.

Employment is expected to grow slower than the average for all occupations through the year 2020, which means employment is projected to increase 3 percent to 9 percent. Job prospects are expected to remain competitive because of the large number of people attracted to this relatively small field. Most of these openings will be the result of the need to replace experienced broadcast technicians who leave the occupation.

Employment Trend, Projected 2010–20

Total, All Occupations: 14%

Audio and Video Equipment Technicians: 13%

Broadcast and Sound Engineering Technicians: 10%

Broadcast Technicians: 9%

Sound Engineering Technicians: 1%

Note: "All Occupations" includes all occupations in the U.S. Economy. Source: U.S. Bureau of Labor Statistics, Employment Projections Program

Related Occupations

- Camera Operator/Videographer
- Computer Network Architect
- Computer Support Specialist
- Electrical & Electronics Engineer
- Electronic Engineering Technician
- Motion Picture Projectionist
- Radio Operator
- Sound Engineering Technician

Conversation With . . .
ANTRON L. ROSE
Broadcast Technician, 5 years

1. What was your individual career path in terms of education, entry-level job, or other significant opportunity?

I was working as a director at the Boys & Girls Club while I studied Digital Filming and Video Production at the Art Institute of Atlanta. I actually met a radio host–I was teaching him and his kids how to swim when I still in school–and he just brought me in and helped me get my first job as a Board Technician.

The career path that I started on was that of a television host. I had plans on hosting my own TV show, but the more I got into broadcasting the more I learned that behind the scenes was where all the exciting things take place, both in radio and television

2. Are there many job opportunities in your profession? In what specific areas?

As you work in this profession, you will start to learn other aspects of the business. The longer you work and perfect your craft, the more you are exposed to other parts of the industry and the more you become aware of opportunities in other areas of the business. And there so many areas that you can branch out into. With radio, for instance, you can branch out and advance into on-air talent, program director, or station manager. But it's a very tough field to break into. Sometimes it's who you know. You just have to really be patient and lay some groundwork. Try to get hired as an intern at a local station.

3. What do you wish you had known going into this profession?

The one thing I wish I had known before entering into this profession is how long the hours are. When you're working, because you are constantly busy and have deadlines you need to meet, the time flies by so fast that you feel there's not enough time in a day to complete what you need to do.

4. **How do you see your profession changing in the next five years?**
   In five years or so the profession will change because technology is always evolving. When I started, things such as reel-to-reel tapes were still around– which, in five years, will be considered like eight-track tapes, if they aren't already! Five years from now, this profession with be completely digital. Cameras are getting better every year; audio has completely changed in the five years since I've been in this business, and will change again in five years.

5. **What role will technology play in those changes, and what skills will be required?**
   Broadcast technicians set up, operate, and maintain equipment that regulate the signal strength, clarity, and the range of sounds and colors of radio or television broadcasts. At the least, an associate's degree in broadcast technology, electronics, or computer networking will be required nine out of ten times for these jobs. One of the biggest skills required is the ability to maintain the pace, because radio is so fast. It may sound slow to the listener, but it's very fast.

6. **Do you have any general advice or additional professional insights to share with someone interested in your profession?**

   If you are choosing broadcast technician as a career path, be ready for hard work and dedication. You need to show that you are trustworthy, because you handle millions of dollars worth of equipment. You have to maintain a positive attitude. There will be many times when you feel tired and cranky, but you must never display this attitude. It is a sure way to be fired. You also need to have a love for technology. The people that you will work with, more than likely, will become like a second family. Radio, I hate to say, isn't always the most stable job. People hop from one station to another and they look out for each other.

   There are many times when, as the Technician, the show will ride on you and how fast you cue up music, sound bites, commercials, and the radio host's microphone. Typically, Technicians working in radio are called "Board Operators" or producers. In television, there's not much of a difference in terms of what Broadcast Technicians do. Television is just a little more fast paced and you work in a small, cramped space with five other people, your technical team. In television, Broadcast Technicians are typically called Technical Directors.

7. **Can you suggest a valuable "try this" for students considering a career in your profession?**

   If you'd like to see if Broadcast Technician is something you'd like to do or if you're interested in radio, I would suggest downloading free broadcast software and learning how to operate it. You can also try reading scripts or announcing commercials while staying on cue, on time. You can rip some commercials from YouTube and do a little show with your camera phone. Create a timetable, tape friends doing something, and cue them to finish up in time for the commercials. It's all about the timing. Ten or 20 seconds can be a big deal.

SELECTED SCHOOLS

Many large universities and technical colleges offer programs in broadcast technology. The student can also gain initial training through enrollment in a community college. Below are listed some of the more prominent institutions in this field.

California State University–Northridge
18111 Nordhoff Street
Northridge, CA 91330
818.677.1200
www.csun.edu

Ithaca College
953 Danby Road
Ithaca, NY 14850
607.274.1020
www.ithaca.edu

New England Institute of Technology
1 New England Tech Boulevard
East Greenwich, RI 02818
401.467.7744
www.neit.edu

New York Institute of Technology
Northern Boulevard
Old Westbury, NY 11568
516.686.1000
www.nyit.edu

Rowan University
201 Mullica Hill Road
Glassboro, NJ 08028
856.256.4000
www.rowan.edu

Southern Illinois University
Carbondale, IL 62901
618.453.2121
www.siu.edu

Towson University
800 York Road
Towson, MD 21252
410.704.2000
www.towson.edu

University of Central Florida
4000 Central Florida Boulevard
Orlando, FL 32816
407.823.2000
www.ucf.edu

University of Georgia
Athens, GA 30602
706.542.3000
www.uga.edu

University of Houston
4800 Calhoun Road
Houston, TX 77004
713.743.2255
www.uh.edu

MORE INFORMATION

Broadcast Education Association
1771 N Street, NW
Washington, DC 20036-2891
888.380.7222
www.beaweb.org

International Brotherhood of Electrical Workers
900 Seventh Street, NW
Washington, DC 20001
202.833.7000
www.ibew.org

National Association of Broadcast Employees and Technicians
501 3rd Street, NW
Washington, DC 20001
202.434.1254
www.nabetcwa.org

National Association of Broadcasters
1771 N Street NW
Washington, DC 20036
202.429.5300
www.nab.org

National Systems Contractors Association
3950 River Ridge Drive
Suite B
Cedar Rapids, IA 52402
319.366.6722
www.nsca.org

Society of Broadcast Engineers
9102 North Meridian Street
Suite 150
Indianapolis, IN 46260
317.846.9000
www.sbe.org

Michael Auerbach/Editor

Camera Operator/ Videographer

Snapshot

Career Cluster: Arts, A/V Technology & Communications
Interests: Photography, Broadcasting, Film Production
Earnings (Yearly Average): $42,813
Employment & Outlook: Slower Than Average Growth Expected

OVERVIEW

Sphere of Work

Camera operators record video footage for use in television and film and on the Internet. Camera operators work across all realms of visual media recording, including videography and cinematography. Professional camera operators are traditionally employed by companies specializing in visual media, including news media corporations, television networks, film production companies, and cable television stations. Camera operators are responsible for capturing events across a broad spectrum of subject matter, from live events such as news and

sports competitions to interviews, concerts, wildlife, and documentary and feature films.

Camera-operation professionals work closely with production teams in order to successfully capture the overall visual scope and narrative focus of an event or project. Camera operators must be able to accomplish a variety of filming techniques as specified by project directors, writers, producers, and other creative and technical staff. The numerous interactions and extensive cooperation involved in camera operations requires keen interpersonal communication savvy in concert with extensive technical skills.

Professional camera operators are traditionally broken down into two distinct disciplines: studio operators and field operators.

Work Environment

While the traditional work environment for camera operators is an enclosed studio or set, many work in a variety of external locations and weather conditions. Many camera operators change locations from project to project, meaning that much of their time is spent on the road. Camera-operator crews who specialize in recording live sporting events travel from stadium to stadium to cover events. News camera operators travel to places throughout the world to cover breaking news stories. Similarly, documentary and wildlife camera operators may travel great distances depending on whether their focus is on a particular climate, animal, or natural habitat.

A sense of adaptability and willingness to try new projects is paramount for camera operators, particularly those who are just starting out in the field. Acquiring experience through participation in a variety of different projects can help build the creative and technical skill sets necessary for camera operation.

Occupation Interest

Camera operators enter the field from a variety of creative and dramatic-arts arenas. Many have a foundation of study in traditional arts, including photography, perspective, colorfield exploration, and three-dimensional design. Some enter videography through an interest in drama or narrative arts, including English, theater, and music performance, while others may be drawn to camera work

Profile

Working Conditions: Both Indoors And Outdoors
Physical Strength: Light To Moderate Work
Education Needs: Technical Community College, Apprenticeship On-The-Job Training, Bachelor's Degree
Licensure/Certification: Usually Not Required
Physical Abilities Not Required: No Heavy Work
Opportunities For Experience: Internship, Apprenticeship
Holland Interest Score*: RCS

* See Appendix A

through exposure to reportage, broadcasting, or news journalism. A wide variety of universities offer associate, undergraduate, and postgraduate study in video production, camera operation, and cinematography.

A Day in the Life—Duties and Responsibilities

The day-to-day duties of a camera operator begin with preproduction planning with other technical and creative members of a project's production staff. The scope of production meetings can vary from project to project.

Studio telecasts often entail obtaining footage from fixed camera locations and established camera settings. Other projects, such as live event coverage, feature-film shoots, and documentary filmmaking, can require extensive preparation and a variety of input from several different team members. In concert with production managers and other set technicians, camera operators must also make sure their equipment is in proper working order and secured prior to filming.

The shooting process itself also varies from project to project. While studio operators normally set shooting schedules with more traditional working hours, field camera operators can work during all times of the day, depending on what parameters a particular project entails. If a particular shot or visual component is not captured during initial shooting, camera operators are called upon to reshoot footage.

Duties and Responsibilities

- **Operating various types and sizes of cameras**
- **Overseeing the handling and operation of cameras to be used**
- **Making sure that a scene through the camera lens appears the way it is intended to appear**
- **Evaluating the location to see what type of equipment is necessary**
- **Working with the director, sound engineer and lighting director to make sure everyone has the same idea for a shoot**

OCCUPATION SPECIALTIES

Cinematographers

Cinematographers film motion pictures. They usually have a team of camera operators and assistants working under them. They determine the best angles and types of cameras to capture a shot. They may use stationary cameras that shoot whatever passes in front of them or use a camera mounted on a track and move around the action. Some operators sit on cranes and follow the action. Others carry the camera on their shoulder while they move around the action. Some cinematographers specialize in filming cartoons or special effects.

Studio Camera Operators

Studio Camera Operators work in a broadcast studio and videotape their subjects from a fixed position. There may be one or several cameras in use at a time. Operators normally follow directions that give the order of the shots. They often have time to practice camera movements before shooting begins. If they are shooting a live event, they must be able to make adjustments at a moment's notice and follow the instructions of the show's director.

Videographers

Videographers film or videotape private ceremonies or special events, such as weddings. They also may work with companies and make corporate documentaries on a variety of topics. Some videographers post short videos on websites for businesses. Most videographers edit their own material. Many videographers run their own business or do freelance work. They may submit bids, write contracts, and get permission to shoot on locations that may not be open to the public. They also get copyright protection for their work and keep financial records.

WORK ENVIRONMENT

Physical Environment

Immediate work environments of camera operators vary greatly by discipline. Studio operators work primarily in closed studio locations, while field operators work in a diverse array of locations, from neighborhood street corners to crowded arenas and natural wildlife habitats.

Human Environment

Strong collaborative skills are important for any camera operator, as he or she acts as the eyes for a particular creative or informative vision. Camera operators work in concert with production staff to deliver the most pertinent video that will advance a narrative outline and inform the viewing audience.

Technological Environment

Camera operators must possess a complex set of media-technology skills, ranging from extensive knowledge of video cameras and image-recording technology to basic knowledge of audio and lighting systems. Many camera operators are also versed in video-editing and special-effects software.

Skills and Abilities

Creative/Artistic Skills

- Being skilled in photography or film

Interpersonal/Social Skills

- Being able to work both independently and as part of a team

Organization & Management Skills

- Paying attention to and handling details

Technical Skills

- Familiarity with cameras
- Knowing ways to achieve various lighting effects

Other Skills

- Working under different weather conditions

EDUCATION, TRAINING, AND ADVANCEMENT

High School/Secondary

Students can prepare for a career in camera operation at the high-school level with courses in geometry, visual arts, introductory computer programming, dramatic arts, and broadcast media. In addition to a survey of major dramatic works and theatrical history, participation in the technical aspects of scholastic theatrical productions is also highly encouraged. Many camera operators attain a basic grasp of lighting, audio rigging, and visual display through participation in school plays or on student television networks. Summer study, volunteer work, and internship programs at local cable-access outlets or television news studios can also be a tremendous asset for high-school students eager to gain experience in videography.

Suggested High School Subjects

- Arts
- Audio-Visual
- English
- Graphic Communications
- Journalism
- Photography
- Theatre & Drama

Famous First

The first portable movie cameras came out in 1923, manufactured separately by Kodak and the Victor Animatograph Company of Davenport, IA. Each company claimed to be the first in the field. Such cameras were operated by means of a hand crank that the photographer had to turn twice per second to achieve the desired effect. Within a few years Bell & Howell offered the first "ladies' camera," a thin, lightweight, and handsomely embossed item called the Filmo 75.

College/Postsecondary

Individuals aspiring to a career as a camera operator have a wide variety of postsecondary education opportunity options available at the associate, bachelor, and graduate level. Introductory and certificate-level coursework in camera operation often entails a survey of the basics of the discipline, including routine equipment maintenance, tripod setup, and command of basic camera focus settings.

Undergraduate programs in cinematography cover not only the basics of camera operation but also the historical development of visual arts and the theoretical foundations of contemporary media. Undergraduates also study location recording and computer animation.

Graduate-level study of cinematography includes an in-depth survey of the history of television and film as well as advanced coursework on film theory. Individual conception and production of one or more films is required for students at the graduate level.

Related College Majors

- Commercial Photography
- Film-Video Making/Cinema & Production
- Photography

Adult Job Seekers

Depending on the nature of the programs they are involved in, studio camera operators may often have schedules that involve working in the early morning or late into the evening. Field camera operators are always on the move, either covering events throughout specific regions in tandem with other traveling journalists or traveling to locations far and wide for more specialized projects.

Professional Certification and Licensure

While no specific certification is required to work as a camera operator, affiliation with professional groups or associations, such as the Society of Camera Operators, can boost credentials and present opportunities for networking. Continuing coursework on emerging technologies also helps camera operators stay abreast of contemporary trends in visual media. Cinematographers in the motion-picture industry often obtain professional certification.

Additional Requirements

Patience, cooperation, and attention to detail are qualities that tremendously benefit camera operators across all realms of work. The physical capacity to manipulate large camera equipment is also desirable. Camera operators must possess a sound technical aptitude as well as the ability to adapt to new technologies quickly.

Fun Fact

Over six billion hours of video are watched each month on YouTube, almost an hour for every person on earth.

Source: youtube.com.

EARNINGS AND ADVANCEMENT

Salaries of camera operators depend largely on the type and duration of the project, and the experience, education, and union affiliation of the employee. Median annual earnings for camera operators were $42,813 in 2012. The lowest ten percent earned less than $21,518, and the highest ten percent earned more than $86,146.

Camera operators may receive paid vacations, holidays, and sick days; life and health insurance; and retirement benefits. These are usually paid by the employer.

Metropolitan Areas with the Highest Employment Level in This Occupation

Metropolitan area	Employment[1]	Employment per thousand jobs	Hourly mean wage
New York-White Plains-Wayne, NY-NJ	1,680	0.33	$26.46
Chicago-Joliet-Naperville, IL	630	0.17	$33.17
Seattle-Bellevue-Everett, WA	410	0.29	$24.31
Houston-Sugar Land-Baytown, TX	330	0.12	$15.04
Miami-Miami Beach-Kendall, FL	320	0.32	$16.86
Washington-Arlington-Alexandria, DC-VA-MD-WV	300	0.13	$31.67
Boston-Cambridge-Quincy, MA	290	0.17	$22.71

[1] Does not include self-employed. Source: Bureau of Labor Statistics, 2012

EMPLOYMENT AND OUTLOOK

Camera operators held about 17,000 jobs nationally in 2012. Employment of camera operators is expected to grow slower than the average for all occupations through the year 2020, which means employment is projected to increase about 2 percent. The use of automatic camera systems is reducing the need for camera operators. However, the growing popularity of made-for-the-Internet broadcasts such as live music videos, digital movies, sports features and other entertainment programming could create some job growth.

Employment Trend, Projected 2010–20

Total, All Occupations: 14%

Film and Video Editors: 5%

Film and Video Editors and Camera Operators: 4%

Camera Operators, Television, Video, and Motion Picture: 13%

Note: "All Occupations" includes all occupations in the U.S. Economy. Source: U.S. Bureau of Labor Statistics, Employment Projections Program

Related Occupations

- Cinematographer
- Photographer

Conversation With . . .
PAUL CHIN JR.

Videographer, 3 years

1. What was your individual career path in terms of education, entry-level job, or other significant opportunity?

I received a degree in business and economics and, coming out of school, worked in corporate finance for five years. I wanted to do something more creative with my business degree so I looked into being a commercial photographer and videographer who works with businesses. I loved the idea of making commercials.

I started off freelancing and came up with a business plan to generate work right away. I was looking to continue working and helping businesses so I went in more as a business consultant than a creative. My background in finance helped separate me from other videographers and photographers.

I'm self-taught and don't have any formal training. I took photography in high school and photographed some concerts in college.

2. Are there many job opportunities in your profession? In what specific areas?

The opportunities are amazing now for videographers. Once you develop a niche in your market, you can specifically address that need. It just depends on what you want to create.

3. What do you wish you had known going into this profession?

How to close deals better. I knew about marketing and a little bit about sales. But I was mostly an analyst and hadn't been out in the field, which is going out, meeting people, selling them on an idea you've brought to them. I wish I had known I needed stronger selling skills.

4. How do you see your profession changing in the next five years?

For commercial videography, the next five years are going to get more fast-paced. To get people's attention, you can't be a laggard. You're going to have to look at a client's situation, develop an idea, finish it, and get it out as fast as humanly possible. The first person that gets there with the idea wins. You'll have to understand how to create the most relevant content possible so that it will be seen.

5. What role will technology play in those changes, and what skills will be required?

Technology is everything. It allows me to do what I do, but it's always a source of competition. I always believe in the "blue ocean vs. red ocean" strategy, discussed in *Blue Ocean Strategy: How to Create Uncontested Market Space and Make Competition Irrelevant*, by W. Chan Kim and Renee Mauborgne. There are two ways you can look at things: you can look at the competition as a red ocean – fierce and bloody and everybody trying to get one over on another – or as a blue ocean, with technology being the blue ocean that opens up infinite opportunity and infinite competition. That's the way I see it.

6. Do you have any general advice or additional professional insights to share with someone interested in your profession?

Never get hung up on gear or equipment. What you need are customers.

As a creative you have to learn to balance the work you do for clients and the work you do for yourself. I still do the "48 Hour Film Projects", where you're given random elements to put into a three-to-eight minute film, then work in your region to go to the national or international level. I'm always trying to work with other script writers to do little short films so I can learn and build on my skill set.

If you are interested in being a news gatherer, find feature stories and try to pitch them to the wire services. A lot of local news stations pick up stories that are already put together. There are agencies out there that just produce that stuff. Or go out with very modest gear, shoot the story, and put them on a blog. Depending on the quality of work, it's possible a station will see it.

7. Can you suggest a valuable "try this" for students considering a career in your profession?

Shoot, edit, then edit some more. You're only going to make it professionally if you follow your vision. Think about why you like something and try it. Before freelancing, I was making cooking videos and really elaborate home videos, putting it on YouTube, and getting feedback from anybody. This industry is all about learning by doing.

SELECTED SCHOOLS

Many large universities offer programs in film and video production. The student can also gain initial training through enrollment in an arts program at a liberal arts college or in a film/video production program at a community college. Below are listed some of the more prominent institutions in this field.

Boston University
640 Commonwealth Avenue
Boston, MA 02215
617.353.3450
www.bu.edu

California Institute of the Arts
24700 McBean Parkway
Valencia, CA 91355
661.255.1050
calarts.edu

City College of New York
160 Convent Avenue
New York, NY 10031
212.650.7000
www.ccny.cuny.edu

Florida State University
600 West College Avenue
Tallahassee, FL 32 306
850.644.2525
www.fsu.edu

Loyola Marymount University
1 Loyola Marymount University Drive
Los Angeles, CA 90045
310.338.2700
www.lmu.edu

Syracuse University
900 S. Crouse Avenue
Syracuse, NY 13210
315.443.1870
syr.edu

University of California, Los Angeles
504 Hilgard Avenue
Los Angeles, CA 90095
310.825.4321
www.ucla.edu

University of North Carolina, Winston-Salem
1533 S. Main Street
Winston-Salem, NC 27127
336-770-3399
www.uncsa.edu

University of Southern California
Los Angeles, CA 90089
323.442.1130
www.usc.edu

University of Texas–Austin
100 Inner Campus Drive
Austin, TX 78712
512.475.7387
www.utexas.edu

MORE INFORMATION

American Society of Cinematographers
P.O. Box 2230
Hollywood, CA 90078
800.448.0145
www.theasc.com

International Cinematographers Guild
7755 Sunset Boulevard
Hollywood, CA 90046
323.876.0160
www.cameraguild.com/

National Association of Broadcast Employees and Technicians
501 3rd Street, NW
Washington, DC 20001
202.434.1254
www.nabetcwa.org

Society of Camera Operators
P.O. Box 2006
Toluca Lake, CA 91610
818.382.7070
www.soc.org

John Pritchard/Editor

Cinematographer

Snapshot

Career Cluster: Arts, A/V Technology & Communications
Interests: Art, Filmmaking, Photography, Design, Media & Communications
Earnings (Yearly Average): $63,166
Employment & Outlook: Slower Than Average Growth Expected

OVERVIEW

Sphere of Work

Cinematographers, also known as directors of photography, define and help guide the photographic style or look of a motion picture. Cinematographers ensure that the director's vision for the film, such as its mood and appearance, is achieved. They receive guidance from directors on how photographic shots should be created, and work with other set personnel to design and frame shots appropriately. Cinematographers have a strong knowledge of lighting, special effects, and other important pieces of filmmaking technology that are being used on the set. Many cinematographers are also specialized, and only focus on areas such as special effects or location shots.

Work Environment

Cinematographers work on the movie set, directing the cameras in such a way that the best shot is framed and taken. Such sets are busy and complex, with different groups working together to render a scene. This work environment is often tense, particularly in light of budget concerns and production deadlines. Cinematographers also work in studio offices and production studios, where they coordinate with writers, directors, producers, and other key artistic and technical professionals in the filmmaking process. Cinematographers generally work long and erratic hours. Their work hours may vary based on the production deadlines and the amount of film direction with which they are charged. The work itself can be draining both physically and psychologically, particularly as it may call for multiple shots, angles, and camera mountings in order to achieve the best take.

Profile

Working Conditions: Both Indoors And Outdoors
Physical Strength: Light Work
Education Needs: Bachelor's Degree
Licensure/Certification: Not Required But Sometimes Preferred
Physical Abilities Not Required: No Heavy Physical Work
Opportunities For Experience: Internship, Apprenticeship, Military Service
Holland Interest Score*: AES

* See Appendix A

Occupation Interest

Cinematographers are critical components of the filmmaking field. Cinematographers work closely with film directors and producers to make their artistic dreams a reality. They are also senior-level managers on the set, and must be effective communicators as they direct camera operators and many other production personnel to create the ideal shot. Cinematographers are exceptional students of film, having studied a wide range of past and present techniques and even developing innovative new approaches to filmmaking.

A Day in the Life—Duties and Responsibilities

As the head of a film's camera department, the cinematographer coordinates with the director and producer to determine the best action and blocking (the placement of actors and scene material) for the film. Based on the director's "shot list," the cinematographer determines how the cameras should be positioned, the type of lenses and filters to be used, and how the scene should be lit. After the scene is shot, the cinematographer ensures that the film is processed in accordance with the director's wishes.

In addition, the cinematographer acts as a type of set manager. The cinematographer or director of photography must coordinate the activities of gaffers (set electricians), lighting and audio equipment handlers, and camera operators. This managerial work is critical for ensuring that all film crew members operate according to the director's and/or producer's desires. Furthermore, the cinematographer is frequently at the creative heart of the production. He or she works with scriptwriters, set and costume designers, and even actors to ensure that shots are made according to specifications.

Duties and Responsibilities

- **Setting up lighting**
- **Discussing the interpretation of shots with director**
- **Setting up shots**
- **Checking the scene before shooting**
- **Supervising a support staff**
- **Shooting scenes**
- **Overseeing film processing**

WORK ENVIRONMENT

Physical Environment

Cinematographers and directors of photography work primarily at movie studios and sets. These are complex locations with a wide range of working parts, departments, and individuals. Sets are often in large, enclosed, and ventilated studios and lots, or on location throughout the country and world. Depending on the set and the film needs, a cinematographer may work outdoors in a variety of weather conditions.

Skills and Abilities

Creative/Artistic Skills
- Being skilled in art, film, or photography

Interpersonal/Social Skills
- Cooperating with others
- Coordinating the work of others
- Working independently as well as as a member of a team

Technical Skills
- Making sound decisions
- Managing time and budget
- Meeting goals and deadlines
- Paying attention to and handling details
- Solving problems
- Supervising others as necessary

Other Skills
- Appreciating both the business and the creative sides

Human Environment

Cinematographers are senior-level managers, directing the actions of camera operators and equipment operators on a movie set. They also coordinate directly with other important figures on the set and in the studio, including directors, producers, set and costume designers, special effects crews, screenwriters, and actors.

Technological Environment

Cinematographers interact with many pieces of technical equipment while directing photography on the set. In addition to various cameras, lenses, and filters, they must work with lighting equipment and other set technologies. Off the set, they work with graphics software and related programs and systems. Cinematographers also must keep up with the changing filmmaking technology available on the market.

EDUCATION, TRAINING, AND ADVANCEMENT

High School/Secondary

High school students are encouraged to take classes in photography, film, drama, and art. They must also study communications, computer science, and graphics. Interested high school students should also get involved in school audio-visual departments and clubs.

Suggested High School Subjects

- Applied Communication
- Arts
- Audio-Visual
- English
- Literature
- Mathematics
- Photography
- Theatre & Drama

Famous First

The first full-length documentary film about cinematographers and their work was 1992's *Visions of Light: The Art of Cinematography.* The film garnered several major awards. Other documentaries followed in later decades, including *Cinematographer Style* (2006), *No Subtitles Necessary* (2008), *Cameraman* (2010), and *Side by Side* (2012). The last, hosted by Keanu Reeves, explores the differences between traditional film technology and digital technology—and presents the opinions of several major filmmakers.

College/Postsecondary

Most cinematographers have postsecondary degrees from colleges or film schools. Many colleges offer bachelor's degrees in film studies and in fine arts, while a number of vocational and technical schools offer associate's degrees in specialized fields related to filmmaking. A large number of independent institutions, like the American Film Institute (AFI), offer similar specialized training in cinematography. The majority of the most popular programs are located in cities with thriving film and broadcast industries, such as Los Angeles and New York.

Related College Majors

- Film-Video Making/Cinema & Production
- Photography

Adult Job Seekers

Cinematographers attain their high-level jobs after gaining considerable experience in the film industry. Qualified adults who seek to become cinematographers should therefore be ready to work as a lighting specialist, camera operator, or similar role. This work experience helps build an aspiring cinematographer's qualifications and set-management skills. Cinematographers may also find opportunities by joining and networking through professional associations, such as the American Society of Cinematographers or the International Cinematographers Guild.

Professional Certification and Licensure

There is no licensure requirement for cinematographers. However, many individuals seek additional training and certification in cinematography from accredited universities, such as New York University's Certificate in Cinematography program. Such programs give job candidates highly valuable training that may enhance their job appeal.

Additional Requirements

Cinematographers should have strong artistic vision and capabilities. They must also demonstrate attention to detail and composition. As shooting a scene often requires multiple takes, angles, and camera mounts, a cinematographer should have patience and persistence. As set managers, they should be comfortable working with and directing people on the set. Finally, they must be able to meet the demands of producers and directors.

Fun Fact

Cinematography comes from the Greek *kinema*, which actually means revolution. The correct Greek word is *kinesis*, which means movement, since the intent was for the word to mean "to record movement." Cinesiography, anyone?

Source: allwords.com

EARNINGS AND ADVANCEMENT

Cinematographers may start out as camera operators or set designers. Individuals can advance to cinematographers with experience and talent in utilizing the camera in the most effective ways. Median annual earnings of cinematographers were $63,166 in 2012. Well-known cinematographers in the entertainment industry can earn much more.

Cinematographers may receive paid vacations, holidays, and sick days; life and health insurance; and retirement benefits. These benefits are usually paid by the employer.

EMPLOYMENT AND OUTLOOK

Cinematographers are a specialized category within the group of camera operators and film and video editors. For the latter group, there were about 38,000 jobs held in 2012. Employment of cinematographers is expected to grow slower than the average for all occupations through the year 2020, which means employment is projected to increase 2 percent to 3 percent. While overall job growth in the entertainment industry is expected to be slow, an increase in special effects in motion picture industry may increase the need for these professionals.

Related Occupations

- Camera Operator
- Director/Producer
- Motion Picture Projectionist
- Motion Picture/Radio/TV Art Director
- Photographer

Related Military Occupations

- Audiovisual & Broadcast Director

Conversation With . . .
JEREMY TRAUB
Cinematographer, 24 years

1. What was your individual career path in terms of education, entry-level job, or other significant opportunity?

I got my first camera when I was quite young–a Kodak Instamatic X-15F. It took two weeks to get the pictures back from the drugstore, which felt like an eternity. I also shot a lot of Super 8 mm film, which I enjoyed immensely. We got one of the very first camcorders–a VHS model. In high school, I read every photography book and magazine I could and worked in a camera store. It was a huge help, just being around cameras and talking photography. I had a darkroom, and everything I talk about in a color grading session today goes back to the burning and dodging I did then. I was shooting stills for *Transworld Skateboarding Magazine*, the Associated Press, and the local paper, in addition to portraits, weddings, and events. I bought a few Hasselblads, which encouraged me to slow down and make each exposure count. But mainly I just shot a lot–there's no substitute for shooting–and studied light everywhere. When I saw beautiful light in a great painting, photograph, or just noticed it in real life, I would think about the light.

In college I studied computer science, which turned out to be useful when cameras turned into computers. I did visual effects for a while to learn what's possible. That's an essential part of the job today, because visual effects are used in all types of movies.

2. Are there many job opportunities in your profession? In what specific areas?

It's tough. There's a lot of competition. Focusing on the lighting department as a path makes sense, maybe working on the lighting crew for shorts or features. Get to know the lights and what's possible with them. Spend time in the grip department, too. If you're going to be in charge of these departments, it's important that you've done the jobs yourself. Try to get as much experience as possible as a camera operator. Being able to operate a camera with subtlety and purpose is crucial.

3. What do you wish you had known going into this profession?

Everybody's first movies are terrible. You'll have many, many years of this. The important thing is not to be discouraged. You've got to stick with it until the images you can create are as good as the ones you see in your head. Don't give up.

4. How do you see your profession changing in the next five years?

Cinematography is both an art and a science. The art changes very slowly, but the technology changes every few years. The last five to 10 years have been positively explosive in terms of camera technology. Understanding color spaces, how image sensors see the world, new types of lighting, and new and different ways to move the camera are all important.

5. What role will technology play in those changes, and what skills will be required?

Whatever happens next, technology will play a huge part. Historically, the movie business has been relatively slow to adopt new technologies, but I think that's changing as new technologies prove themselves.

6. Do you have any general advice or additional professional insights to share with someone interested in your profession?

Shoot as much as you can. Watch movies and think about how the camera moves, if at all, and why. In a good movie, there's a story-motivated reason for everything that happens. Notice how the best lighting and camera work underscore the story and characters, without calling attention to themselves. Learn all the technical stuff, then forget it and focus on the feeling.

Start by shooting shorts. You'll meet crew members, learn how a set works, what the jobs of the various departments are, and how they interact. When you shoot, stay close to the director. A good crew works together like a well-oiled machine, and this takes practice.

Experiment with new equipment or techniques on your own, never on an actual job. I learned that when I started in photography, and it has helped me avoid lots of problems.

Spend a lot of time reading, even if you think you already know something. There's always something more to learn.

7. Can you suggest a valuable "try this" for students considering a career in your profession?

Pick a movie scene that you like, and go through it shot by shot. Storyboard the whole scene. Figure out where the cameras were placed–their positions and approximate focal lengths. Try to figure out where every light in the scene is by looking at how it affects everything in the frame, and see why each shot was useful editorially. There's a lot of subtle stuff there that's only noticeable by slowing it down and drawing it out shot by shot yourself. Try to figure out how each camera move was done (Steadicam, dolly, jib, helicopter, etc.), and–more importantly–why. Good movies have a story-based motivation for everything you see and hear.

SELECTED SCHOOLS

Many large universities offer programs in film and video production. The student can also gain initial training through enrollment in an arts program at a liberal arts college or in a film/video production program at a community college. Below are listed some of the more prominent institutions in this field.

California Institute of the Arts
24700 McBean Parkway
Valencia, CA 91355
661.255.1050
calarts.edu

Columbia University
535 W. 116th Street
New York, NY 10027
212.854.1754
www.nyfa.edu

New York Film Academy
100 East 17th Street
New York, NY 10003
212.674.4300
www.nyfa.edu

Northwestern University
633 Clark Street
Evanston, IL 60208
847.491.3741
www.northwestern.edu

University of California, Los Angeles
504 Hilgard Avenue
Los Angeles, CA 90095
310.825.4321
www.ucla.edu

University of Miami
1320 S. Dixie Highway
Coral Gables, FL 33146
305.284.2211
www.miami.edu

University of North Carolina, Winston-Salem
1533 S. Main Street
Winston-Salem NC 27127
336-770-3399
www.uncsa.edu

University of Southern California
Los Angeles, CA 90089
323.442.1130
www.usc.edu

University of Texas, Austin
100 Inner Campus Drive
Austin, TX 78712
512.475.7387
www.utexas.edu

Wesleyan University
45 Willys Avenue
Middletown, CT 06459
860.685.2000
www.wesleyan.edu

MORE INFORMATION

American Society of Cinematographers
P.O. Box 2230
Hollywood, CA 90078
800.448.0145
www.theasc.com

International Cinematographers Guild
7755 Sunset Boulevard
Hollywood, CA 90046
323.876.0160
www.cameraguild.com
Offers the Emerging Cinematographer Awards:
www.ecawards.net
Publishes the ICG Magazine:
www.icgmagazine.com

National Association of Broadcast Employees and Technicians
501 3rd Street NW, Suite 880
Washington, DC 20001
www.nabetcwa.org

Society of Camera Operators
P.O. Box 2006
Toluca Lake, CA 91610
818.382.7070
www.soc.org

Michael Auerbach/Editor

Copywriter

Snapshot

Career Cluster: Arts, Business, Writing & Editing
Interests: Language/Writing, Current Events, Popular Culture, People, Product
Earnings (Yearly Average): $39,602
Employment & Outlook: Slower Than Average Growth Expected

OVERVIEW

Sphere of Work

Copywriters work within the communication and information sectors. They research and prepare the written words that accompany advertising, promotional, and marketing materials. These include brochures, print advertising, press releases, scripts for television and radio commercials, websites, direct mail pieces, and any other communications that call for an ability to write engaging and persuasive content.

Copywriters are often employed by marketing and advertising agencies, but they may also work as independent freelancers. Copywriting is a highly collaborative role, which usually demands working with a team of creative colleagues and supervisors. Copywriters interact with other communication specialists, such as marketers, brand strategists, advertising executives, public relations executives, graphic designers, art directors, multimedia technicians, and editors. They are also likely to work with clients and business specialists across a broad range of industries, topics, products, and services.

Work Environment

Copywriters work in an office environment, although the role is sufficiently flexible to accommodate working from any place where computer and telecommunication technologies are readily available. Freelance copywriters may work remotely, from a home office or other setting.

Full-time copywriters generally work for marketing and advertising agencies or within other communication outlets. A full-time employee may expect to work forty hours per week during normal office hours. He or she may be required to work longer hours, as needed.

Profile

Working Conditions: Office Environment
Physical Strength: Light Work
Education Needs: Bachelor's Degree
Licensure/Certification: Usually Not Required
Physical Abilities Not Required: No Heavy Physical Work
Opportunities For Experience: Internship, Volunteer Work, Part-Time Work
Holland Interest Score*: ASI

* See Appendix A

Occupation Interest

Copywriting attracts graduates and professionals who have a strong grounding in written communications. This occupation suits people with an interest in writing and a flair for creative expression and engaging an audience. Copywriters must be able to write fluently on a broad range of topics and to manage multiple projects concurrently. They usually have a strong interest in trends and markets.

In addition to having excellent writing skills, copywriters must possess strong research and analytical abilities. They must have advanced oral communication and collaboration skills and the ability to produce creative work under pressure. Copywriting demands good organizational, prioritization, and time management skills. Copywriters must also be able to respond positively to constructive criticism and feedback about the work they produce.

Duties and Responsibilities

- **Coming up with creative words and phrases that will sell a product or idea**
- **Developing a central theme for a campaign**
- **Promoting one's work to agencies, clients or upper management**

A Day in the Life—Duties and Responsibilities

The copywriter's day is characterized by periods of independent and collaborative work. As a member of a creative team, copywriters meet with their colleagues, supervisors, and clients on a daily basis to brainstorm and present ideas as well as develop, analyze, and critique creative strategies and solve problems. Copywriters spend solitary time researching, drafting advertising and promotional materials, and revising content as needed. Research may entail activities like referring to consumer surveys or conducting interviews. The solitary aspects of the occupation demand high levels of self-discipline and self-motivation. This is especially important for freelance copywriters who spend much of their time working alone and managing their own workloads.

The copywriter's daily output includes written content and concepts for brochures, print advertising, billboards, press releases, scripts for television and radio commercials, websites, direct mail pieces, and other marketing materials. The copywriter may find that the projects and assignments they work on are subject to tight timeframes and strict deadlines. It is a daily challenge for copywriters to produce high quality creative work under pressure.

Copywriters may be expected to contribute within their workplaces more widely. This may include some administrative duties, such as tracking project hours.

WORK ENVIRONMENT

Physical Environment

Office settings predominate. Copywriters in full-time employment generally work for small to large marketing and advertising firms

Skills and Abilities

Communication Skills
- Expressing thoughts and ideas clearly
- Persuading others
- Writing concisely

Creative/Artistic Skills
- Conceiving interesting ideas
- Participating in creative campaigns

Interpersonal/Social Skills
- Being able to remain calm under pressure
- Being able to work both independently and as part of a team
- Respecting others' opinions

Organization & Management Skills
- Managing time
- Managing multiple tasks/projects
- Meeting goals and deadlines

Other Skills
- Learning about products and customers

or in other corporate contexts. Freelance copywriters often work from home.

Human Environment

Copywriting demands strong collaborative skills. Copywriters interact with other communication and creative specialists, such as marketers, brand strategists, advertising executives, public relations executives, graphic designers, art directors, multimedia technicians, and editors. They are also likely to work with clients and business specialists across a broad range of industries.

Technological Environment

Copywriters use technologies that range from telephone, email, and the Internet to word processing software. Copywriters may also be expected to work with web content management systems and blogging software. Advanced computing skills and an understanding of multimedia, social media, and emerging media technologies are considered an advantage.

EDUCATION, TRAINING, AND ADVANCEMENT

High School/Secondary

High school students can best prepare for a career in copywriting by taking courses in English literature, language and composition, social studies, journalism, and business communications. The creative nature of copywriting may be explored through art and graphic design; the business aspects through business studies, accounting and entrepreneurship; and the technology aspects through computer literacy. Courses such as history and sociology can also prepare the student for synthesizing research into written materials. Psychology and cultural studies may provide an understanding of group and individual responses to written and visual messaging. Extracurricular school activities that involve writing can also provide students with an opportunity to develop their writing skills and learn from others prior to graduation. Such activities might include entering writing competitions and writing for school newspapers or club newsletters.

Suggested High School Subjects

- Applied Communication
- Composition
- English
- Foreign Languages
- Journalism
- Literature
- Psychology
- Social Studies

Famous First

The first commercial jingle heard over the radio was in an ad for Pepsi-Cola in 1940. The jingle ran: "Pepsi-Cola hits the spot / Twelve full ounces, that's a lot / Twice as much for a nickel, too / Pepsi-Cola is the drink for you." Eventually the jingle was translated into 55 languages and ran worldwide.

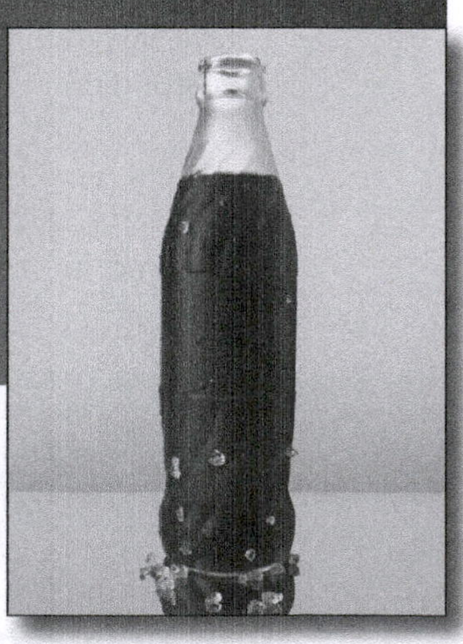

College/Postsecondary

Graduates from a diverse range of disciplines can become copywriters. The most common pathway to copywriting is by obtaining an undergraduate degree in communications, advertising, marketing, or journalism. Coursework in the social sciences can also be helpful preparation for writing persuasive content. A large number of colleges and universities offer courses in copywriting. There are also an increasing number of certified and non-certified copywriting programs, seminars, and workshops offered by private companies, academies, and professional associations.

Postsecondary students interested in a career in copywriting are also encouraged to become involved in extracurricular, club, or volunteer roles where they can develop their writing skills and begin to build a writing portfolio.

Related College Majors

- Advertising
- Communications, General
- English Language & Literature, General
- Liberal Arts & Sciences/Liberal Studies
- Marketing Management & Research
- Public Relations & Organizational Communications
- Social Sciences

Adult Job Seekers

Adults seeking a career transition into copywriting are advised to develop copywriting experience and a portfolio through part-time or volunteer work for a charity, non-profit organization, local club, or association. Writing a personal blog is another way to build a portfolio while also developing the daily discipline of writing.

An increasing number of copywriting opportunities are advertised on non-traditional job sites. The proliferation of web-based freelance writing sites allows people with little or no previous copywriting experience to upload their own articles for sale or bid for writing projects.

Taking writing courses may assist with networking and portfolio development. Self-guided learners may also benefit from reading "how to" books about copywriting or by undertaking short courses, seminars, or workshops.

Professional Certification and Licensure

There are no required professional certifications or licenses for copywriting. Practical experience generally outweighs formal qualifications in this occupation. Some professional associations provide certifications in the field. The American Marketing Association offers the Professional Certified Marketer (PCM) certification, which requires association membership and completion of a written exam. Consult credible professional associations within the field and follow professional debate as to the relevancy and value of any certification program.

Additional Requirements

The most important attribute for prospective copywriters is a love of writing combined with interest in a broad range of topics. In addition to advanced writing skills, copywriters must possess strong social and cultural awareness, an understanding of trends and markets, and the ability to write about products and services in emotionally engaging terms. A portfolio of writing samples is essential.

EARNINGS AND ADVANCEMENT

Copywriters can become copy supervisors or creative supervisors within an organization. Earnings for copywriters vary greatly depending on the specific job and the size, prestige and location of the company. Copywriters working in large organizations in urban areas can demand higher annual earnings. Median annual earnings of copywriters were $39,602 in 2012.

Copywriters may receive paid vacations, holidays, and sick days; life and health insurance; and retirement benefits. These are usually paid by the employer.

Metropolitan Areas with the Highest Concentration of Jobs in this Occupation (Writer)(1)

Metropolitan area	Employment	Employment per thousand jobs	Hourly mean wage
New York-White Plains-Wayne, NY-NJ	5,770	1.12	$40.48
Los Angeles-Long Beach-Glendale, CA	4,160	1.08	$57.47
Washington-Arlington-Alexandria, DC-VA-MD-WV	2,300	0.98	$38.04
Chicago-Joliet-Naperville, IL	1,470	0.40	$32.00
Minneapolis-St. Paul-Bloomington, MN-WI	920	0.53	$24.86
San Francisco-San Mateo-Redwood City, CA	790	0.79	$30.31
Seattle-Bellevue-Everett, WA	760	0.54	$36.56
Philadelphia, PA	750	0.41	$32.74

(1) Includes all writers and authors, exclusive of self-employed writers, technical writers, and public relations specialists. Source: Bureau of Labor Statistics, 2012

Conversation With . . .
DARREN TIBBITS

Copywriter, 15 years

1. What was your individual career path in terms of education, entry-level job, or other significant opportunity?

I went to university to study telecommunications and specialized in film and television production and minored in screen- and television writing, but I had the opportunity to explore advertising. My first job, at a smaller television station, allowed me to write for the local news team, as well as for advertising. Then I moved to Chicago and picked up work as a producer and director, which opened up an opportunity at J. Walter Thompson. They saw somebody who could come in as an effective copywriter who could also produce radio and television.

2. Are there many job opportunities in your profession? In what specific areas?

There are a lot of copywriter positions open throughout the country. It varies from city to city. Client fluctuations tend to push jobs from one agency to another. It just depends on where you are and whether you're willing to relocate.

3. What do you wish you had known going into this profession?

I wish I had known that there was a two-year school for advertising. If I had known this was the profession I wanted to do, that would have been easier, quicker and cheaper to get through. It also would have helped to have had a mentor within the industry to guide me. Be open to allowing a mentor to steer you in different directions without allowing them to dictate your path.

4. How do you see your profession changing in the next five years?

It's on this exponential curve, primarily because of the digital age – and the smart phone age, social networks, the immediacy of news, advertising, comments and opinions, and their ability to infiltrate the internet so quickly. From a copywriting standpoint, I've had to adjust my technique and approach from traditional advertising – print, broadcast, radio and billboards – to write copy for internet, websites, email, and now Facebook posts, social tweets and smartphone apps. You're adjusting writing style and tone. You used to have to write a clever headline with body copy to connect an audience to a brand. Now, the audience is so aware of branding and marketing that you have to approach them from a more personal level. Digital can be anything, including a webpage takeover, a banner, an Instagram page or an email blast. You have to adjust the messaging and interaction of how you are approaching that person. In five years, agencies will be figuring out ways to continue a brand campaign within the new evolving digital medium.

5. What role will technology play in those changes, and what skills will be required?

Whether you're a designer or a copywriter, you're going to be collaborating with a lot of creative minds coming from other backgrounds. Understanding the digital technology and how it applies to new forms of advertising will help round out your talent level. An agency is always about collaborating, about inspiring each other, about pushing each other to elevate beyond what you can do as an individual.

6. Do you have any general advice or additional professional insights to share with someone interested in your profession?

It's great to find other creative outlets to fulfill those nagging needs as a creative person. If you have talent to write and shoot and edit and design and promote a web page, do that. But do it in you free time. Show that you are able to do that and bring that example into an agency culture to elevate the end products.

Also, try to be open-minded about everyone's thoughts, creations and words. Be open to the differences so you don't get too stuck in thinking your way of writing is always the right way. You have to be able to throw out some of your favorite headlines and ideas, to sacrifice to make the project better.

7. Can you suggest a valuable "try this" for students considering a career in your profession?

Look at brands and products you connect with and dissect the reasons why you connect with them. Is it because it's popular? Is it because you like the ad? Do you like the words, the layout, the simplicity? Then look at brands you don't connect with. How would you market that brand to individuals like yourself? How would you change the messaging? Everything you interact with is marketing; everything is branding. Look at the brands you feel emotionally connected with. Understanding how that connection came about, and understanding how other brands are not connecting, will help you from a writing style built with your heart, mind and voice.

EMPLOYMENT AND OUTLOOK

Writers, of which copywriters are a specialty, held about 42,000 jobs nationally in 2012 (This excludes technical writers, public relations specialists, and self-employed writers). About one-half of salaried writers worked in the information sector, which includes advertising; newspaper, periodical, book, and directory publishers; radio and television broadcasting; software publishers; motion picture and sound recording industries; Internet service providers, web search portals, and data processing services; and Internet publishing and broadcasting.

Employment is expected to grow slower than the average for all occupations through the year 2020, which means employment is projected to increase 5 percent to 6 percent. Turnover is relatively high in this occupation. Freelancers often leave the field because they cannot earn enough money.

Employment Trend, Projected 2010–20

Total, All Occupations: 14%

Media and Communication Workers: 13%

Writers and Authors: 6%

Note: "All Occupations" includes all occupations in the U.S. Economy. Source: U.S. Bureau of Labor Statistics, 2012.

Related Occupations

- Advertising & Marketing Manager
- Advertising Director
- Advertising Sales Agent
- Electronic Commerce Specialist
- Journalist
- Public Relations Specialist
- Radio/TV Announcer and Newscaster
- Technical Writer
- Writer & Editor

SELECTED SCHOOLS

Many colleges and universities offer bachelor's degree programs in English/writing as well as in business communications. The student can also gain initial training through enrollment at a community college. Below are listed some of the more prominent institutions in this field.

American University
4400 Massachusetts Avenue NW
Washington, DC 20016
202.885.1000
www.american.edu

Arizona State University
411 N. Central Avenue
Phoenix, AZ85004
602.496.4636
www.asu.edu

Baruch College
55 Lexington Avenue
New York, NY 10010
646.312.1000
www.baruch.cuny.edu

California State University, Fullerton
800 N. State College Boulevard
Fullerton, CA 92831
657.278.2011
www.fullerton.edu

Indiana University, Bloomington
Bloomington, IN 47408
812.856.4648
www.indiana.edu

University of Michigan, Ann Arbor
Ann Arbor, MI 48109
734.764.1817
www.umich.edu

University of South Carolina
1600 Hampton Street
Columbia, SC 29208
803.777.7000
www.sc.edu

University of Southern California
Los Angeles, CA 90089
213.442.2000
www.usc.edu

Temple University
1801 N. Broad Street
Philadelphia, PA 19122
215.204.7000
www.temple.edu

University of Texas, Austin
100 Inner Campus Drive
Austin, TX 78712
512.475.7387
www.utexas.edu

MORE INFORMATION

Advertising Research Foundation
432 Park Avenue South, 6th Floor
New York, NY 10016-8013
212.751.5656
thearf.org

Advertising Women of New York
25 West 45th Street, Suite 403
New York, NY 10036
212.221.7969
www.awny.org

American Advertising Federation
1101 Vermont Avenue NW, Suite 500
Washington, DC 20005-6306
202.898.0089
www.aaf.org

National Student Advertising Competition
www.aaf.org/default.asp?id=122

Most Promising Minority Students
www.aaf.org/default.asp?id=213

American Association of Advertising Agencies
405 Lexington Avenue, 18th Floor
New York, NY 10174-1801
212.682.2500
www.aaaa.org
4A's Scholarship Funds
http://www.aaaa.org/careers/scholarships/Pages/default.aspx
High School of Innovation in Advertising and Media
http://www.aaaa.org/careers/IAM/Pages/default.aspx

American Marketing Association
311 South Wacker Drive, Suite 5800
Chicago, IL 60606
800.262.1150
www.marketingpower.com

American Society of Magazine Editors
810 Seventh Avenue, 24th Floor
New York, NY 10019
212.872.3700
www.magazine.org

Association of National Advertisers
708 3rd Avenue, 33rd Floor
New York, NY 10017
212.697.5950
www.ana.net

International Association of Business Communicators
601 Montgomery Street, Suite 1900
San Francisco, CA 94111
415.544.4700
www.iabc.com

Kylie Grimshaw Hughes/Editor

Desktop Publisher

Snapshot

Career Cluster: Arts, Computer Systems/Technology, Media & Communications
Interests: Art, Graphic Design, Printing, Writing
Earnings (Yearly Average): $38,804
Employment & Outlook: Decline Expected

OVERVIEW

Sphere of Work

Desktop publishers use digital word-processing and design software to arrange and prepare design layouts for newspapers, books, magazines, and other materials for print or online publication. Desktop publishers may also work as graphic designers, creating and modifying graphics for publication. Desktop publishers typically work closely with editors, designers, graphic artists, and computer programmers in the design of web-based or printed publications. Depending on their area of employment, desktop publishers may spend time editing and writing text for publication in addition to supervising layout and design. Desktop publishing is utilized by a variety of companies, from traditional print publishers

to the many businesses that produce web-based publications for advertising and informational purposes.

Work Environment

Desktop publishers work closely with writers, editors, and designers to complete projects for publication. Those who work on web-based publications may work with web designers or computer programmers to create websites for online publication. They may also work with graphic designers to create and refine fonts, images, and other graphics. Desktop publishing can be performed in a standard office, using a desktop or laptop computer. Some desktop-publishing specialists may be able to complete part of their work off-site in a home office.

Profile

Working Conditions: Office Environment
Physical Strength: Light Work
Education Needs: On-The-Job Training
Technical/Community College
Bachelor's Degree
Licensure/Certification: Usually Not Required
Physical Abilities Not Required: No Heavy Work
Opportunities For Experience: Apprenticeship, Part-Time Work
Holland Interest Score*: CRE, RCE, RCS

* See Appendix A

Occupation Interest

Desktop publishing attracts individuals interested in graphic design, printing, and technical artistry. Many desktop publishers have backgrounds in art or writing. A strong knowledge of both subjects is helpful to anyone interested in the field. Digital design for web publications has become an important facet in the field of publishing, and demand is increasing for desktop-publishing specialists with experience and expertise in web design, digital art, and computer programming.

A Day in the Life—Duties and Responsibilities

The printing process is typically divided into three stages: prepress, printing, and postpress activities. Desktop publishers are generally considered part of the prepress team, and they may also spend time working with professionals during the printing process.

Desktop publishers usually work full time during regular business hours, though overtime or alternate schedules are sometimes necessary during seasonal peak periods or when working on time-sensitive projects. For example, newspapers may require night workers to prepare for early-morning publication. Holidays and special events may also require employees to work extra hours. In some cases, desktop publishers work part-time hours or during varying schedules depending on the deadlines for upcoming projects. Some desktop publishers are able to work from a home office, but this requires frequent communication and collaboration with other individuals involved in various parts of a project.

During a typical day, a desktop publisher communicates with writers, editors, project managers, and designers about ongoing and upcoming projects. They also gather pictures or artwork from various sources and then arrange the images into a cohesive and attractive layout for publication. Desktop publishers write, edit, proofread, and arrange text and work with various typefaces. Desktop publishers also merge files from design and publishing programs and therefore need to have extensive knowledge of a variety of digital design, writing, editing, and image-processing programs.

Duties and Responsibilities

- **Placing text and graphics into desktop publishing software programs**
- **Locating and editing graphics, such as illustrations and photographs**
- **Working with designers and writers to create printed or online pieces**
- **Checking layouts for errors and making corrections**

WORK ENVIRONMENT

Physical Environment

Offices and workspaces for desktop publishers tend to be quiet, indoor environments comprised of desks and worktables for laying out print samples. Most desktop publishers work at a desk or worktable with a computer, and they also spend time in a printing room or print shop checking on projects.

In some cases, desktop publishers work in offices that are attached to industrial printing presses as is the case with many large-scale magazines, newspapers, and book publishers. Desktop publishers do not typically work in a printing room environment but may visit the printing press to examine printed examples of their projects to ensure that the digital layout transitions well to the printed copy.

Human Environment

Desktop publishers are part of a creative team and work closely with writers, editors, and various design professionals to complete projects. In some cases, companies hire desktop publishers to work on interoffice or professional publications specific to their industry, which often requires publishing professionals to work closely with industry specialists. A pharmaceutical company interested in publishing printed or web-based information about a specific medication, for instance, would expect a desktop publisher to work closely with their in-house sales team as well as with physicians and pharmacists to ensure the information was accurate and clear. In some small companies, there is less interaction between groups since desktop publishers tend to work independently and are responsible for the writing, editing, and graphic design duties in addition to organizing layouts for publication.

Skills and Abilities

Communication Skills
- Writing clearly and concisely

Creative/Artistic Skills
- Having an eye for layout and graphic design elements

Interpersonal/Social Skills
- Being able to work independently as well as on a team

Organization & Management Skills
- Following instructions
- Managing time
- Meeting goals and deadlines
- Paying attention to and handling details

Technical Skills
- Performing technical work using computer software
- Working with text and graphics
- Working with technology/ hardware

Other Skills
- Understanding printing terms and measurements

Technological Environment

Desktop publishers use specific digital publishing software and other computer programs to create and manage their projects. The digital design software programs produced by Adobe Systems have become one of the industry standards in this field, but it is important for desktop publishing professionals to have experience in a variety of digital composition and graphic design software programs. Desktop publishing professionals must also understand computer operation and technical maintenance. Continued education is necessary in order to stay abreast of software changes or new programs relevant to the field. Many of the skills and technologies employed by desktop publishers are made use of in non-print environments such as e-books and other digital formats.

EDUCATION, TRAINING, AND ADVANCEMENT

High School/Secondary

High school students can prepare for a career in desktop publishing by taking classes in journalism, composition, art, and drafting. Some high schools offer graphic design programs and train students in the use of printing and publishing software. In addition, desktop publishers should be knowledgeable about grammar, spelling, and editing procedures, as they typically must check and revise their work prior to printing. Basic English skills developed through a high school education are essential for those pursuing work in the publishing field.

Suggested High School Subjects

- Algebra
- Applied Communication
- Applied Math
- Arts
- Composition
- English
- Graphic Communications
- Keyboarding
- Machining Technology
- Photography

Famous First

The first desktop publishing application, PageMaker, came out in 1985. It was created by Paul Brainerd, co-founder of Aldus Corporation. The software was designed for use with a Macintosh computer linked to an Apple Laser-Writer printer. Brainerd, in fact, coined the term "desktop publishing."

Postsecondary

Community colleges and technical institutes sometimes offer courses and programs in the field of desktop publishing. Typically, desktop publishers hold associate's degrees in journalism or graphic design. Individuals can also enter the publishing field by pursuing a bachelor's degree or higher certification in graphic design, graphic arts, or a specific print-oriented program. Journalism and technical writing programs are viable avenues into desktop publishing when supplemented with courses in computers, computer software, and graphic design.

Related College Majors

- Desktop/Electronic Publishing
- Digital Imaging
- Graphic Communications
- Typography & Composition

Adult Job Seekers

Adults interested in pursuing desktop publishing as a career are advised to seek out community college or technical certification programs in their area. Individuals with a background in manual or computer design may have a competitive advantage in transitioning to the desktop publishing field.

Professional Certification and Licensure

Desktop publishers are not legally required to hold a professional certificate or license; however, some employers may require workers to undergo specific training. Some technical institutes, community colleges, and universities offer certification courses in the software programs used in desktop publishing as well as training programs in other aspects of computer-aided programming and design. Desktop publishers typically receive on-the-job training while working under experienced professionals. Some independent desktop publishing specialists work as freelancers or independent contractors and work for several different clients.

Additional Requirements

Desktop publishers must possess attention to detail and the interest and ability to make aesthetic judgments that combine artistic sensibility with technical precision. Because exact measurements are needed, desktop publishers also benefit from experience with basic mathematics and geometry since exact measurements are used when developing and creating projects.

EARNINGS AND ADVANCEMENT

Earnings depend on the type, size, geographic location, and union affiliation of the employer, and the employee's experience and skills. Median annual earnings of desktop publishers were $38,804 in 2012. The lowest ten percent earned less than $23,062, and the highest ten percent earned more than $62,881.

Desktop publishers may receive paid vacations, holidays, and sick days; life and health insurance, and retirement benefits. These are usually paid by the employer.

Metropolitan Areas with the Highest Concentration of Jobs in this Occupation

Metropolitan area	Employment	Employment per thousand jobs	Hourly mean wage
New York-White Plains-Wayne, NY-NJ	630	0.12	$26.16
Chicago-Joliet-Naperville, IL	600	0.16	$21.37
Boston-Cambridge-Quincy, MA	430	0.25	$21.95
Philadelphia, PA	380	0.21	$21.54
Washington-Arlington-Alexandria, DC-VA-MD-WV	380	0.16	$21.82
St. Louis, MO-IL	370	0.29	$15.90
Los Angeles-Long Beach-Glendale, CA	360	0.09	$20.22
Minneapolis-St. Paul-Bloomington, MN-WI	320	0.18	$23.02

(1) Does not include self-employed. Source: Bureau of Labor Statistics, 2012

EMPLOYMENT AND OUTLOOK

There were approximately 16,000 desktop publishers employed nationally in 2012. Employment is expected to decline through the year 2020. Improvements in printing technology will result in the rising productivity of desktop publishers and the ability for non-printing professionals to create their own printed and online materials, resulting in less demand for these workers.

Employment Trend, Projected 2010–20

Total, All Occupations: 14%

Arts, Designing, Entertainment, Sports and Media Occupations: 13%

Art Directors: 9%

Note: "All Occupations" includes all occupations in the U.S. Economy. Source: U.S. Bureau of Labor Statistics, Employment Projections Program

Related Occupations

- Photoengraver & Lithographer
- Prepress Technician
- Printing Machine Operator

Conversation With . . .
STEPHANIE CHAMBERS

Asset Production Specialist,
17 years in the profession

1. What was your individual career path in terms of education, entry-level job, or other significant opportunity?

I graduated with a bachelor of science degree with a major in journalism and a minor in speech communication. I focused on news writing and while I enjoyed that, I didn't really have the personality that you need to go out and interview people and chase stories. While in college, I took graphic design courses, so that's the route I pursued when I left school. My first job out of college was with an insurance company, designing brochures and other internal marketing pieces. From there, I moved onto a marketing job for another company, discovered I didn't like marketing, and went back to desktop publishing, this time working for a company that published industrial catalogs for large retailers, such as Home Depot and Lowe's. My job required that I program code to create, automate, and lay out these catalogs. That's not the usual path into this field. Most people do layouts and design; I ended up in the programming aspect of it. In my current job, I'm the middle person who takes written content and prepares it to go into a content management system. That then goes to the engineering department, which produces the content online.

2. Are there many job opportunities in your profession? In what specific areas?

The publishing industry is evolving so fast it is hard to imagine what is next. Instead of hiring permanent employees, publishing companies are tending to hire temporary and contract help. Hardware and software engineers and project managers are in demand.

3. What do you wish you had known going into this profession?

I wish I had a crystal ball so I could have seen the technological advances that were going to transform the publishing industry. It would have been nice to know that it would become harder to be able to create books and that the Internet was going to revolutionize the need for digital content and the reuse of that content to such a variety of platforms.

4. **How do you see your profession changing in the next five years?**

I think that publishing technology is going to get faster, harder, more complex, and more platforms and devices will emerge. Open source, community-driven efforts are going to continue to revolutionize how publishing companies store, reuse and publish their content. It's very exciting to see how these efforts are providing alternatives to the software programs that have always been the industry standard, such as Adobe's inDesign and Photoshop.

5. **What role will technology play in those changes, and what skills will be required?**

Technology will be key to changes in the publishing industry. Our layout editors and copy editors have had to learn XML, which stands for extensible markup language. In addition to their regular editing duties, they're responsible for inserting the XML tags that allow the text to be stored, retrieved, and used in different ways for different formats and platforms, such as eBooks, smart boards, iPads, and mobile devices. It's a good idea to keep an open mind because the skills that you need for a particular desktop publishing position are likely to grow to include ones that you hadn't even thought of, just because of the need to stay on top of the technological changes

6. **Do you have any general advice or additional professional insights to share with someone interested in your profession?**

I strongly encourage anyone interested in publishing to also pursue a degree in engineering or computer science. It's important to understand the backend programs that fuel the content that we see and read. Learn as much as you can about computers and how things work behind the scenes, not just what the end user sees. Ask yourself, what makes this program work this way? Think globally and if something scares you, challenge yourself to figure it out.

7. **Can you suggest a valuable "try this" for students considering a career in your profession?**

For someone interested in working in publishing technology I would suggest they try to create their own web page using CSS and HTML. A good exercise would be to take a web page, view its source file and figure out how different scripting languages are used to build a web page. Try to improve the web page's functionality and/or learn to add new interactive features. If you think this exercise is fun, you may want to pursue this as a career.

SELECTED SCHOOLS

A variety of colleges and universities offer programs in graphic communications with a concentration in desktop/electronic publishing. This includes many community/technical colleges. Below are listed some of the more prominent institutions in this field.

Black Hills State University
1200 University Street
Spearfish, SD 57799
800.255.2478
www.bhsu.edu

California Polytechnic State University
San Louis Obispo, CA 93407
805.756.1111
www.calpoly.edu

Carroll University
100 N. East Avenue
Waukesha, WI 53186
262.547.1211
www.carroll.edu

Ferris State University
1201 S. State Street
Big Rapids, MI 49307
231.591.2000
www.ferris.edu

Idaho State University
921 S. 8th Street
Pocatello, ID 83209
208.282.0211
www.isu.edu

Rochester Institute of Technology
1 Lomb Memorial Drive
Rochester, NY 14623
585.475.2411
www.rit.edu

St. Mary's University of Minnesota
700 Terrace Heights
Winona, MN 55987
507.457.6987
www.smumn.edu

Texas State University, San Marcos
601 University Drive
San Marcos, TX 78666
512.245.2111
www.txstate.edu

University of Houston
4800 Calhoun Road
Houston, TX 77004
713.743.2255
www.uh.edu

Western Illinois University
1 University Circle
Macomb, IL 61455
309.298.1414
www.wiu.edu

MORE INFORMATION

Graphic Arts Education and Research Foundation
1899 Preston White Drive
Reston, VA 20191
703.264.7200
www.gaerf.org

National Association of Schools of Art and Design
11250 Roger Bacon Drive, Suite 21
Reston, VA 20190-5248
703.437.0700
www.nasad.arts-accredit.org

Printing Industries of America
200 Deer Run Road
Sewickley, PA 15143
800.910.4283
printing@printing.org
www.printing.org

Society for Technical Communication
9401 Lee Highway, Suite 300
Fairfax, VA 22031
703.522.4114
www.stc.org

Type Directors Club
347 W 36th Street, Suite 603
New York, NY 10018
212.633.8943
www.tdc.org

Micah Issitt/Editor

Director/Producer

Snapshot

Career Cluster: Arts, A/V Technology & Communications, Entertainment
Interests: Theater, Film, Event Planning, Business Management
Earnings (Yearly Average): $72,546
Employment & Outlook: Average Growth Expected

OVERVIEW

Sphere of Work

Directors and producers oversee all aspects of a film or theatrical production. Directors plan, coordinate, and manage the creative aspects of the production, including interpreting scripts, casting talent, approving artistic designs, and directing the work of actors, cinematographers, set designers, wardrobe designers, and other members of the cast and crew. Producers plan, coordinate, and manage the business side of a production, which includes raising money, approving and developing the script, and performing any related administrative tasks. In most cases, directors and producers must both report to the executive producer (usually the

person or entity who finances the project), who must approve all final decisions.

Work Environment

Like actors, directors and producers must be willing to work an irregular schedule with long hours and evening and weekend work, punctuated by frequent periods of unemployment. Productions may last from one day to several months, and during that time, directors and producers are expected to be on call and available to solve problems that arise before, during, and after a production has finished. They may also be away from home, or "on location," for extended periods. The irregular hours and intense competition in these occupations can result in stress, fatigue, and frustration. Most directors and producers must work day jobs or other employment unrelated to entertainment.

Profile

Working Conditions: Work Indoors (Primarily)
Physical Strength: Light Work
Education Needs: Prior Experience
College And/Or Bachelor's Degree
Apprenticeship
Licensure/Certification: Usually Not Required
Physical Abilities Not Required: No Heavy Work
Opportunities For Experience: Internship, Apprenticeship, Military Service, Part-Time Work
Holland Interest Score*: ESA, SEC, SEI

* See Appendix A

Occupation Interest

Prospective directors should be highly creative, confident, and possess a strong desire to tell stories. They must be extremely organized, be natural leaders, and understand all aspects of coordinating a theatrical or film production, including the role that each cast and crew member plays in the successful completion of a production. Prospective producers should be detail-oriented people who have a desire to take on both small and large tasks. Producers should enjoy planning, coordinating, and organizing an event from start to finish and should be willing to handle and resolve any issues that arise.

A Day in the Life—Duties and Responsibilities

There are many different styles of directing films and plays, just as there are many different styles of acting. Directors are ultimately responsible for the appearance, stylistic and emotional tone, and aesthetic organization of a dramatic production. A film studio or independent producer normally hires a director through the director's agent or manager. Before production begins, a director auditions and chooses actors, holds rehearsals, and prepares the cast for production. He or she also consults with set designers, choreographers, cinematographers, music supervisors, and other creative personnel to plan and develop a successful production. During production, a director guides and oversees the entire creative execution of a project, often with help from assistant directors and production assistants. Once production is finished, a director oversees any postproduction responsibilities, such as video and sound editing, graphic design, and music selection.

Producers are responsible for handling the business aspects of a production. They secure funds, set budget limitations, coordinate schedules, and ensure smooth management of the whole project. Producers also work with directors to approve their decisions regarding talent, locations, and other creative choices, as well as to ensure that deadlines are met and money is spent according to financier instructions. Larger productions usually require the services of associate or line producers to assist the producer with his or her duties.

Duties and Responsibilities

- **Judging and motivating acting talent**
- **Making artistic interpretations of scripts**
- **Making optimum use of taping and production equipment**
- **Working with union representatives**
- **Managing contractual obligations**
- **Maintaining strict production time schedules**

OCCUPATION SPECIALTIES

Stage Directors

Stage Directors interpret scripts, direct technicians, and conduct rehearsals to create stage presentations.

Motion Picture Directors

Motion Picture Directors read and interpret scripts, conduct rehearsals, and direct the activities of cast and technical crews for motion picture films.

Television Directors

Television Directors interpret scripts, conduct rehearsals, and direct television programs.

Radio Directors

Radio Directors direct radio rehearsals and broadcasts.

Casting Directors

Casting Directors audition and interview performers for specific parts.

Motion Picture Producers

Motion Picture Producers initiate and manage all the business needs of a motion picture production.

WORK ENVIRONMENT

Physical Environment

Most directors and producers work on set during the production of a theatrical project. Set locations vary greatly and may be indoors or outdoors in any weather conditions. Some productions are held in different locations across the country or around the world. Before production begins (during "preproduction") and after a production finishes (during "postproduction"), directors and producers may work from an office or home studio.

Human Environment

Directors and producers constantly interact with other cast and crew members. Their coworkers typically include executive producers, actors, production staff, set designers, costume and makeup personnel, and assistants. Producers regularly work with external vendors, such as caterers, insurance representatives, and establishment owners.

Skills and Abilities

Communication Skills
- Describing motivations and feelings (to actors)
- Expressing thoughts and ideas clearly
- Persuading others

Creative/Artistic Skills
- Creating ideas
- Understanding narrative and its power

Interpersonal/Social Skills
- Asserting oneself
- Being sensitive to others
- Cooperating with others
- Working as a member of a team

Organization & Management Skills
- Managing conflict
- Managing time
- Organizing information or materials
- Paying attention to and handling details
- Performing duties which change frequently

Technological Environment

Directors and producers employ a wide variety of tools and equipment to assist them in the completion of their daily tasks. Directors use video cameras, lighting and sound equipment, two-way radios, cell phones, audiovisual editing equipment and software, and the Internet. Producers use schedules, budgets, contracts, e-mail and the Internet, laptops, cell phones, and other devices.

EDUCATION, TRAINING, AND ADVANCEMENT

High School/Secondary

High school students who wish to become directors or producers should have an inherent interest in the dramatic arts and should foster that interest by pursuing academic study in English literature, theater, public speaking, communications, and cinema. They should also learn as much as they can about management, business, and event planning. Involvement in school groups or extracurricular activities, such as drama clubs, plays, musical productions, dance performances, film clubs, and photography clubs, can provide a solid background in the arts. They should also enroll in a basic acting class to become familiar with the fundamentals of acting, dramatic literature, and theater production.

Suggested High School Subjects

- Accounting
- Arts
- Audio-Visual
- Business
- College Preparatory
- English
- Literature
- Mathematics
- Speech
- Theatre & Drama

Famous First

The first blockbuster movie was D. W. Griffith's *Birth of a Nation*, which premiered in 1915. A silent epic, it told the story of the South in the aftermath of the Civil War. Although innovative in its cinematic techniques and strong in its emotional impact, it was protested by the NAACP for its stereotypical depiction of blacks. Three years later, the first African American director, Oscar Micheaux, released his *Within Our Gates* as a rejoinder to Griffith's film.

Postsecondary

Although an undergraduate degree is not necessarily required for one to become a director or producer, many people consider it essential to have received some formal training at the postsecondary level. Many universities and colleges offer bachelor's degree programs in the dramatic arts. Some directors find it beneficial to have studied directing, filmmaking, writing, acting, designing, radio broadcasting, film history, or public speech at the college level. Producers can benefit by taking undergraduate business courses in marketing, public relations, management, and finance.

After obtaining a bachelor's degree, some directors and producers earn a master of fine arts degree (MFA) in directing, producing, acting, or screenwriting. Some conservatories, like the American Film Institute (AFI) in Los Angeles, offer MFA programs that teach students the practical skills needed to start a career in filmmaking. Often, students are required to complete a thesis film as part of their coursework, designed to simulate a large-scale production. Producers and directors must raise money, find talent, and promote their thesis films.

Related College Majors
- Acting & Directing
- Business Management
- Drama/Theater Arts, General
- Film-Video Making/Cinema & Production
- Film/Cinema Studies
- Playwriting & Screenwriting
- Radio & Television Broadcasting

Adult Job Seekers

Prospective directors and producers possess varying levels of experience. Those who attend conservatories often make valuable connections with faculty and other students, which eventually lead to production work. Others become apprentices, interns, or assistants for established directors or producers. Some job seekers begin by taking other employment positions in the entertainment industry and working their way up to director or producer positions through networking and industry contacts.

Many directors and producers are members of professional organizations, such as the Producers Guild of America and the Directors Guild of America, which protect the rights of the producers and provide networking opportunities.

Professional Certification and Licensure

Directors and producers are not required to receive any kind of professional certification or licensure in dramatic production. There is no official training for producers, but many directors train or take classes in directing and cinematography.

Additional Requirements

Directing and producing are highly competitive fields, and few people are able to achieve financial stability through these occupations. Candidates must be able to handle criticism well, demonstrate emotional and physical stamina, and remain incredibly driven to succeed. Being talented is not enough to make one successful in these fields—directors and producers must not give up easily, especially after experiencing rejection. They should be self-promoters who are passionate about their work and use every opportunity to meet potential investors, employers, and talent. Long hours and demanding or difficult employers or work conditions are common in these occupations.

EARNINGS AND ADVANCEMENT

Due to the entrepreneurial nature of directing and producing, earnings vary according to the success of the productions in progress. Earnings of directors and producers also vary greatly due to the type of production they are producing or directing, location, project budget, and personal reputation. Median annual earnings of directors and producers were $72,546 in 2012. The lowest ten percent earned less than $34,068, and the highest ten percent earned more than $176,384. Median annual earnings were $98,389 in motion picture and video industries and $57,367 in radio and television broadcasting.

Fringe benefits for directors are typically provided according to union guidelines, but vary according to the size and financial scope of a given production. Producers, being entrepreneurs, are responsible for their own fringe benefits.

Metropolitan Areas with the Highest Concentration of Jobs in this Occupation

Metropolitan area	Employment	Employment per thousand jobs	Hourly mean wage
Los Angeles-Long Beach-Glendale, CA	19,570	5.06	$66.13
New York-White Plains-Wayne, NY-NJ	14,150	2.74	$55.71
Washington-Arlington-Alexandria, DC-VA-MD-WV	2,210	0.94	$42.93
Chicago-Joliet-Naperville, IL	1,780	0.49	$34.17
Atlanta-Sandy Springs-Marietta, GA	1,770	0.78	$33.51
Philadelphia, PA	1,580	0.86	$41.78
Boston-Cambridge-Quincy, MA	1,450	0.85	$34.98
Seattle-Bellevue-Everett, WA	1,400	1.00	$28.31

(1) Does not include self-employed. Source: Bureau of Labor Statistics, 2012

EMPLOYMENT AND OUTLOOK

Directors and producers held about 87,000 jobs in motion pictures, stage plays, television and radio in 2012. Employment of directors and producers is expected to grow about as fast as the average for all occupations through the year 2020, which means employment is projected to increase about 11 percent. Expanding cable and satellite television operations, increasing production and distribution of major studio and independent films, and continued growth and development of interactive media, online movies and mobile content for cell phones and other portable devices, should increase demand.

Employment Trend, Projected 2010–20

Total, All Occupations: 14%

Arts, Designing, Entertainment, Sports and Media Occupations: 13%

Art Directors: 9%

Note: "All Occupations" includes all occupations in the U.S. Economy. Source: U.S. Bureau of Labor Statistics, Employment Projections Program

Related Occupations

- Actor
- Cinematographer
- Dancer/Choreographer
- Motion Picture/TV/Radio Art Director

Related Occupations

- Audiovisual & Broadcast Director
- Audiovisual & Broadcast Technician

Conversation With . . .
CAROLINE BATH

Network News Producer

7 years in the profession

1. What was your individual career path in terms of education, entry-level job, or other significant opportunity?

In high school I was the subject of a story for a national broadcast news magazine. I learned during the shoot that I hated being on camera, but I loved watching what went on behind the scenes. I was already a news hound but that experience pointed me towards broadcast news.

I stayed in touch with the story's producer, then reached out to him my junior year of college, where I studied journalism and history, and was hired as an intern at his network's morning show. I used that internship to learn more about the industry and to lay the groundwork for a job out of college. I met with producers and studied the network's technical and editorial systems so when I applied for a production assistant job I was able to say, "I can hit the ground running."

If you are entering broadcast news at a national level, the entry-level position is typically a production assistant. It varies from show to show, but at my show I was running Teleprompter, delivering scripts, greeting on-air guests, and filling in on associate producer jobs.

After about a year as a production assistant, I was promoted to the graphics associate producer position, where I managed all the show's graphics to ensure they were editorially correct and looked good. After two years as graphics AP, I became a segment producer. Every day I was assigned a guest or two who would come on the show to discuss a current event ranging from elections to accidents. I would research the subject, talk to the guest on the phone, and then draft five questions I thought our anchor should ask during a live interview.

I'm still segment producing, now seven years out of college, and I just picked up tape producing. Tape producing, or field producing, means you come up with a story idea (say, a behind-the-scenes tour at a candy factory), film the story, and then write and edit the piece.

2. **Are there many job opportunities in your profession? In what specific areas?**

My industry looks for experience, ideally internships, for all jobs. This is not an industry you can casually enter because you are interested in being on-air. There are two routes you can take: technical and editorial. If editing, directing, filming, or graphics appeal to you, the technical path is a good option. If you love writing, investigating, and telling a good story, then the editorial side is a good fit.

You also need to decide whether you would like to go down the local news route, or the national news route. If you go the local route, you can start off as a producer at a small station and will write and produce entire half-hour shows. The entry-level jobs at the national level require a lot more busy work such as answering the phone or delivering scripts. You might not write a script until you hit the producer level, but then you can cover major stories that have implications for millions. Some local-producers may find the small-town stories tiresome after a few years. Others love it, especially the freedom to essentially pick where you want to work in the country. At the national level you are generally stuck with New York, Washington, and Los Angeles.

3. **What do you wish you had known going into this profession?**

It can take over your life! It's an addicting job and your work-life balance can get out of whack.

4. **How do you see your profession changing in the next five years?**

As cameras become smaller and more user-friendly, networks want their producers to be able to shoot and edit video themselves. There's also a push for online interactivity. Producers and reporters must be social-network savvy: that's where the feedback comes from, and that's how you can find some of the best stories.

5. **What role will technology play in those changes, and what skills will be required?**

Producers are now expected to shoot some footage themselves. Shooting and editing skills are must-haves for producer positions.

6. **Do you have any general advice or additional professional insights to share with someone interested in your profession?**

I have found that the people who succeed in my industry are the go-getters. Sure, delivering scripts isn't the most exciting job on the planet, but you better act like those scripts are the Magna Carta. You don't need to be a genius to succeed, but if you don't have a sense of urgency, if you don't exude passion for news, you are going to be found out quick, or just be miserable.

7. Can you suggest a valuable "try this" for students considering a career in your profession?

Watch your local TV broadcast with a watch and a timer. "Log" the show – write down the time each story started, and how long the story lasted. Example:
6:01: Apartment Fire – 2min
6:03: Pet Adoption Story – 1min 30secs
If you can, record a competing station's broadcast, then log how they handled their day's broadcast. Compare logs. What was their "lead" (first) story? How did they cover stories differently? Compare the logs to the local newspaper. Did the broadcasts miss any stories? It's a great way to familiarize yourself with a broadcast and get a sense as to how the producers prioritized the news coming into their station.

SELECTED SCHOOLS

Many colleges and universities offer bachelor's degree programs in the arts; some have programs in theater, film, and television production as well. The student may also gain initial training through enrollment at a community college. Below are listed some of the more prominent institutions in this field.

Columbia University
116th Street and Broadway
New York, NY 10027
212.854.1754
www.columbia.edu

Emerson College
120 Boylston Street
Boston, MA 02116
617.824.8500
www.emerson.edu

Loyola Marymount
1 Loyola Marymount University Drive
Los Angeles, CA 90045
310.338.2700
www.lmu.edu

New York University
70 Washington Square S.
New York, NY 10012
212.998.1212
www.nyu.edu

Purdue University
610 Purdue Mall
West Lafayette, IN 47907
765.494.4600
www.purdue.edu

University of Arizona
1401 E. University Boulevard
Tucson, AZ 85721
520.621.2211
www.arizona.edu

University of California, Los Angeles
405 Hilgard Avenue
Los Angeles, CA 90095
310.825.4321
www.ucla.edu

University of Colorado, Denver
Boulder, CO 80309
303.492.1411
www.colorado.edu

University of Southern California
Los Angeles, CA 90089
323.442.1130
www.usc.edu

University of Texas, Austin
110 Inner Campus Drive
Austin, TX 78712
512.471.3434
www.utexas.edu

MORE INFORMATION

American Film Institute
2021 North Western Avenue
Los Angeles, CA 90027-1657
323.856.7600
www.afi.com

Association of Independent Commercial Producers
3 West 18th Street, 5th Floor
New York, NY 10011
212.929.3000
www.aicp.com

Directors Guild of America
7920 Sunset Boulevard
Los Angeles, California 90046
310.289.2000
www.dga.org

National Association of Schools of Theatre
11250 Roger Bacon Drive, Suite 21
Reston, VA 20190-5248
703.437.0700
nast.arts-accredit.org

Producers Guild of America
8530 Wilshire Boulevard, Suite 450
Beverly Hills, CA 90211
310.358.9020
www.producersguild.org

Stage Directors and Choreographers Society
1501 Broadway, Suite 1701
New York, NY 10036
800.541.5204
www.sdcweb.org

Briana Nadeau/Editor

Graphic Designer & Illustrator

Snapshot

Career Cluster: Arts, A/V Technology & Communications, Business, Management & Administration, Information Technology
Interests: Visual Arts, Advertising, Communications, Media
Earnings (Yearly Average): $46,110
Employment & Outlook: Average Growth Expected

OVERVIEW

Sphere of Work

Graphic designers and illustrators create visually appealing products and illustrative materials that range from simple logos or business cards to picture books and entire corporate branding campaigns. Their work is intended to convey a commercial or educational message or otherwise draw attention to an idea, which they accomplish mostly with sophisticated graphic design and illustration techniques. Traditional artistic mediums, such as printmaking or painting, continue to be used, but sporadically. A designer interested

in a long-term career must also learn skills in animation, digital video production, and web design, or collaborate frequently with people who possess these skill sets or perform these job functions.

Work Environment

Graphic designers and illustrators work mostly in the publishing, advertising, and marketing industries, but some work for graphic design firms or government agencies. Many are self-employed. They spend much of their time working on computers, but may also have access to a full art studio. If self-employed, they interact heavily with clients. If employed in a design firm or design department, they interact with a team of professionals and staff and have less direct contact with clients; however, some customer service is necessary when choosing the final design—a process that can take anywhere from a couple of days to several weeks.

Profile

Working Conditions: Office/Studio Environment
Physical Strength: Light Work
Education Needs: Bachelor's Degree
Licensure/Certification: Usually Not Required
Physical Abilities Not Required: No Heavy Work
Opportunities For Experience: Apprenticeship, Part-Time Work
Holland Interest Score*: AES

* See Appendix A

Occupation Interest

People who are attracted to graphic design and illustration tend to be creative thinkers who are interested in solving problems with images or in making the world more visually interesting. They are artistic and have a good eye for detail, but are also capable of seeing the big picture and being flexible in their presentation of multiple design or pictorial ideas for a single project. They must have excellent interpersonal and communication skills since they almost always work closely with members of a team. They must be able to handle criticism and work under pressure to meet deadlines.

A Day in the Life—Duties and Responsibilities

Graphic designers and illustrators are responsible for planning and carrying out projects that fulfill their clients' needs. A major specialty today, for example, is branding, in which the designer works with a team of writers, artists, market researchers, and others to create a company's image, including a recognizable logo, stylized advertisements, catchy slogans, and high-tech trade show displays. The designer will suggest colors, images, fonts, and other artistic elements, then create several sample designs for each element of the branding campaign.

Graphic designers and illustrators create the covers and interior layouts for magazines, books, brochures, newspapers, and other print materials. Typically, they work with editors to acquire the articles and advertisements, and then fit them into the allotted space in the most appealing manner. Graphic designers select fonts, graphics, and other design elements (in collaboration with the client or author if the project is a book) and also design internal advertisements that are presented with the final product.

Study of graphic design and illustration includes the option to learn website design skills, so some designers/illustrators specialize in web design and are able to earn a living without working on any print design projects. Some graphic designers/illustrators collaborate with programmers to create video games, with authors to create graphic novels, and even with interior decorators and architects to design building spaces.

Self-employed graphic designers/illustrators must also spend some of their time marketing their services, billing customers, preparing contracts, and handling other administrative and business management tasks.

Duties and Responsibilities

- **Designing images that convey a message or identify a product or organization**
- **Creating designs or illustrations by hand or using computer software**
- **Meeting with clients to determine their needs**
- **Deciding on the message that a design or illustration should portray**
- **Giving advice to clients on ways to reach an audience through visual means**

OCCUPATION SPECIALTIES

Cartoonists

Cartoonists draw political cartoons, newspaper comics, or comic books. Their work is used in commercial applications, as well. They may work with animators in creating digital productions

Drafters

Drafters use software to convert the designs of engineers and architects into technical drawings and plans.

Fashion Artists

Fashion Artists draw stylish illustrations of new clothing fashions for newspapers or related advertisements.

Illustrators

Illustrators create pictures for books, magazines, billboards, posters, and CD/DVD packages. They may work with multimedia artists in creating digital productions.

Medical and Scientific Illustrators

Medical and Scientific Illustrators draw precise illustrations of machines, plants, animals or parts of the human body or animal bodies for business and educational purposes.

Typographers

Typographers create type fonts for use in print and online publications. One major use is in signage, including "wayfinding" signs for drivers and other travelers.

WORK ENVIRONMENT

Physical Environment

Graphic designers and illustrators usually work in studios or offices surrounded by art samples and design reference materials. If a project has a tight deadline, the designer/illustrator can expect to work some evening hours or work on the design from their home computer until the project is done.

Human Environment

In larger design firms and departments, a graphic designer or illustrator is often one member of a creative team comprised of photographers, multimedia artists, web developers, and others who collaborate on projects under the supervision of a creative director. Designers/illustrators may also work with market researchers, architects, interior designers, content editors, clients, authors, and other professionals outside the firm.

Technological Environment

Graphic designers most often use Adobe Creative Suite software (Photoshop, Illustrator, and InDesign) for cover design, manipulating and creating illustrations, page layout design, editing and placing digital photographs, and other purposes. They also use digital photography and video cameras, scanners, printmaking equipment, printing and publishing equipment, and other tools. Each design project

Skills and Abilities

Communication Skills
- Expressing thoughts and ideas clearly
- Speaking and writing effectively

Creative/Artistic Skills
- Being able to create new ideas
- Being skilled in art and design

Interpersonal/Social Skills
- Being able to work independently and as part of a team
- Understanding others' wishes

Organization & Management Skills
- Managing time
- Meeting goals and deadlines

Technical Skills
- Applying technology to a task
- Performing technical work
- Working with different tools and media

is different and may require different resources, so graphic designers should enjoy learning new skills. Illustrators make use of computer software and traditional art materials in creating their works.

EDUCATION, TRAINING, AND ADVANCEMENT

High School/Secondary

Students should pursue a comprehensive college-preparatory program that includes courses in art, graphic design, computer science, and the social sciences. Other relevant courses include film, new media, photography, and industrial arts. Awareness of contemporary graphic design, web design, and animation software programs is extremely important. Most college admissions programs require a portfolio of artistic work, which might include digital designs, as well as hand-drawn sketches or paintings, sculpture, and other sample work.

Suggested High School Subjects

- Applied Communication
- Applied Math
- Arts
- Composition
- Computer Science
- Drawing & Painting
- English
- Graphic Communications
- Industrial Arts

Famous First

The first graphic design to receive a patent was a typeface designed by George Bruce of New York in 1842. The typeface was used in printed school primers. The first company logo to receive a trademark was that of the Bass brewery of England, which still uses its distinctive red triangle on its label.

College/Postsecondary

Most entry-level positions require a bachelor's degree from an art school or program. Graphic design programs include courses in studio art, design, computer graphics, printing, and other graphic design specialties. Programs should include the option to work an internship. A general awareness of contemporary design is also helpful. Illustration programs focus more on drawing, painting, and other manual methods while not excluding digital technologies. In either case, the development of a portfolio for use in future job searches is essential, so many graphic design and illustration students make an effort to obtain freelance work.

Related College Majors

- Design & Visual Communications
- Drawing & Painting
- Commercial Art & Illustration
- Graphic Design
- Industrial Design

Adult Job Seekers

Adults with a background in fine art, illustration, photography, typography, or another creative discipline can learn the fundamentals of graphic design and illustration and update their skills by taking graphic arts courses, which some schools offer in the evenings and on weekends to accommodate adult professionals. A portfolio can be assembled independently and/or in conjunction with classes.

Advancement for graphic designers and illustrators comes with experience or taking classes in new software or techniques to supplement current skills. Some designers/illustrators choose to establish their own firms. Advanced degrees can help experienced artists begin to obtain work in a different specialty, such as web animation.

Professional Certification and Licensure

There are no state licenses or nationally recognized certificates required for graphic designers or illustrators; however, the idea of professional certification has gained popularity, so it is advisable to follow the issue as it progresses. Getting certified on the use of a particular software program or type of equipment, for example, may be in order as one's career advances.

Additional Requirements

Graphic artists and illustrators must have a good eye for aesthetics, be extremely creative, enjoy art and design, and find satisfaction in continuing professional development. They should be willing to follow trends in advertising, web media, design, and illustration and should enjoy brainstorming for a single project. Although creativity is a plus, graphic designers/illustrators must be able to distance themselves from their work enough to accept a client's criticism and revisions of their ideas. Excellent people skills are a must in this collaborative field, which can be highly competitive and requires the ability to make and maintain good contacts with clients and colleagues.

Fun Fact

The typical client/graphic designer relationship lasts, on average, three years. In addition, it takes six months to a year (or more) from first contact to closing the deal.

Source: www.graphicdesign.com.

EARNINGS AND ADVANCEMENT

Earnings for self-employed graphic designers and illustrators vary widely. Those struggling to gain experience and a reputation may be forced to charge less for their work. Well-established freelancers may earn much more than salaried artists. Median annual earnings of graphic designers/illustrators were $46,110 in 2012. The lowest ten percent earned less than $27,772, and the highest ten percent earned more than $81,525.

Graphic designers and illustrators on salary may receive paid vacations, holidays, and sick days; life and health insurance; and retirement benefits. These are paid by the employer. Self-employed graphic designers must arrange for their own ways of meeting these costs.

Metropolitan Areas with the Highest Concentration of Jobs in this Occupation

Metropolitan area	Employment	Employment per thousand jobs	Hourly mean wage
New York-White Plains-Wayne, NY-NJ	14,260	2.77	$30.37
Los Angeles-Long Beach-Glendale, CA	9,260	2.39	$27.80
Chicago-Joliet-Naperville, IL	8,100	2.23	$24.63
Minneapolis-St. Paul-Bloomington, MN-WI	4,460	2.55	$23.84
Washington-Arlington-Alexandria, DC-VA-MD-WV	4,390	1.87	$30.85
Atlanta-Sandy Springs-Marietta, GA	3,750	1.66	$23.67
Philadelphia, PA	3,630	1.99	$24.60
Boston-Cambridge-Quincy, MA	3,190	1.87	$26.79

[1] Does not include self-employed. Source: Bureau of Labor Statistics, 2012

EMPLOYMENT AND OUTLOOK

Graphic designers and illustrators held about 191,000 jobs nationally in 2012. Some designers/illustrators do freelance work on the side while holding down a salaried position in the field or in another occupation. Employment of graphic designers/illustrators is expected to grow about as fast as the average for all occupations through the year 2020, which means employment is projected to increase about 13 percent. Demand for graphic designers and illustrators should increase because of the rapidly expanding demand for interactive media for mobile devices, websites, electronic publications and video entertainment. Advertising firms will also need designers and illustrators to create Web-based and print materials to promote the growing number of products and services available to consumers.

Employment Trend, Projected 2010–20

Total, All Occupations: 14%

Graphic Designers and Illustrators: 13%

Arts, Design, Entertainment, Sports, and Media Occupations: 13%

Note: "All Occupations" includes all occupations in the U.S. Economy. Source: U.S. Bureau of Labor Statistics, Employment Projections Program

Related Occupations

- Art Director
- Designer
- Desktop Publisher
- Drafter
- Industrial Designer
- Medical & Scientific Illustrator
- Multimedia Artist & Animator
- Web Developer

Related Occupations

- Graphic Designer & Illustrator

Conversation With . . . *NICK COMPARONE*

Graphic Designer, 7 years

1. What was your individual career path in terms of education, entry-level job, or other significant opportunity?

I went to school for graphic design; I got a bachelor's degree from Central Connecticut State University. I'd always done a lot of art and for me, design seemed a more feasible career path than fine art. Our design department had an in-house design firm, portfolio-reviewed, where four people per semester worked. I did that one semester, and I also designed for the college, for on-campus events and promotions, a paid, part-time position. Design firms recruited entry-level people and I interviewed at a local firm and was working there part-time by my last semester. After I graduated, they hired me full-time. When the firm dissolved, I took the majority of clients I was already working with and started freelancing.

2. Are there many job opportunities in your profession? In what specific areas?

As with anything, if you're good at what you do and work hard, you're going to be able to find a job. Always being on top of whatever the new thing is – that is always going to be helpful.

3. What do you wish you had known going into this profession?

We had a tough program in college and a lot of people felt like it was a lot of work and a lot of pressure. One of the biggest things I realized getting out of school is that the actual industry is more intensive. It's fast-paced with a quick turnaround. If you don't have a passion to do it, graphic design might not be the best direction to go in.

4. How do you see your profession changing in the next five years?

You're always going to have different trends, aesthetically. It depends on your demographic audience. But if you are gearing your work toward the up-and-coming generation, these are people who are used to constant, multiple messages. If you don't grab people's attention with a couple of seconds, you're done.

5. **What role will technology play in those changes, and what skills will be required?**

   The whole in-your-hands-device technology in our culture is definitely big, and how we manufacture apps and devices in the future will continue to be big. It's information on the go, and being able to develop and design things to get into people's hands. All your bigger companies and industries need a mobile version of what they're doing.

   A lot of people who may be versed in web design are going into app development. It's not as static; you are designing things that are more interactive. A lot of people think print's going to disappear; it's not. People are always going to need catalogs and brochures, and any of your higher-end companies are still going to use a lot of print stuff. You get a really nice piece in your hand, you feel the paper and see the ink. You can't do that on a computer screen. But there are always new technologies with print; digital presses let small businesses start up and have lower costs. A lot of designers are talking about 3D printing. That's going to be huge. You can print out mechanical things.

6. **Do you have any general advice or additional professional insights to share with someone interested in your profession?**

   You're going to be working long hours, so it's really got to be something you know you can spend the time with and enjoy. It's also one of those fun professions where you can play around with things and get your hands dirty and see if you like it.

7. **Can you suggest a valuable "try this" for students considering a career in your profession?**

   Redesign something – your favorite book cover or movie poster – and see how you feel about it.

SELECTED SCHOOLS

Many colleges and universities offer programs in graphic design and illustration. The student may also gain initial training at a technical/community college. Below are listed some of the more prominent institutions in this field.

Art Center College of Design
1700 Lida Street
Pasadena, CA 91103
626.396.2200
www.artcenter.edu

California Institute of the Arts
24700 McBean Parkway
Valencia, CA 91355
661.255.1050
www.calarts.edu

Carnegie Mellon University
5000 Forbes Avenue
Pittsburgh, PA 15213
412.268.2000
www.cmu.edu

Cranbrook Academy of Art
39221 Woodward Avenue
Bloomfield Hills, MI 48303
248.645.3300
www.cranbrookart.edu

Maryland Institute College of Art
1300 W. Mount Royale Avenue
Baltimore, MD 21217
410.669.9200
www.mica.edu

Pratt Institute
200 Willoughby Avenue
Brooklyn, NY 11205
718.636.3600
www.pratt.edu

Rhode Island School of Design
2 College Street
Providence, RI 02903
401.454.6100
www.risd.edu

School of Visual Arts
209 E. 23rd Street
New York, NY 10010
212.592.2100
www.sva.edu

Virginia Commonwealth University
821 W. Franklin Street
Richmond, VA 23284
804.828.0100
www.vcu.edu

Yale University
New Haven, CT 06520
203.432.4771
www.yale.edu

MORE INFORMATION

American Institute of Graphic Arts
164 Fifth Avenue
New York, NY 10010
212.807.1990
www.aiga.org

Association of Independent Colleges of Art and Design
236 Hope Street
Providence, RI 02906
401.270.5991
www.aicad.org

Graphic Artists Guild
32 Broadway, Suite 1114
New York, NY 10004-1612
212.791.3400
www.graphicartistsguild.org

National Art Education Association
1806 Robert Fulton Drive, Suite 300
Reston, VA 20191-1590
703.860.8000
www.naea-reston.org

National Association of Schools of Art & Design
11250 Roger Bacon Drive, Suite 21
Reston, VA 20190-5248
703.437.0700
nasad.arts-accredit.org/index.jsp

Society for Environmental Graphic Design
1000 Vermont Avenue NW, Suite 400
Washington, DC 20005
202.638.5555
www.segd.org

Society of Illustrators
128 E. 63rd Street
New York, NY 10065
212.838.2560
www.societyillustrators.org

Society of Publication Designers
27 Union Square W., Suite 207
New York, NY 10003
212.223.3332
www.spd.org/

Briana Nadeau/Editor

Interpreter & Translator

Snapshot

Career Cluster: Business Communications, Government & Diplomacy, Hospitality & Tourism, Writing & Editing
Interests: Languages, Foreign Cultures, World Literature
Earnings (Yearly Average): $45,893
Employment & Outlook: Faster Than Average Growth Expected

OVERVIEW

Sphere of Work

Interpreters and translators facilitate communication between people who speak different languages or between hearing and deaf people. While the terms are commonly thought to be interchangeable, translators and interpreters work in different media. A translator translates written materials, usually into his or her native language, while an interpreter translates oral communication and may switch between languages. Some do both types of work. Among the most popular languages being translated into

English today are Spanish, Arabic, Chinese, and American Sign Language (ASL).

Work Environment

Translators often work by themselves at home, where they receive assignments via the Internet or mail. Interpreters work in a variety of settings, such as hospitals, courtrooms, schools, airports, and government offices. They may work alone with just their clients or with partners. In some cases, a translator or interpreter might work the night shift or odd hours, especially when communicating with people who live and work in other time zones. Some interpreters work with reporters in combat zones, risking their lives to do so.

Profile

Working Conditions: Work Indoors And Outdoors
Physical Strength: Light Work
Education Needs: Bachelor's Degree Master's Degree
Licensure/Certification: Recommended
Physical Abilities Not Required: No Heavy Work
Opportunities For Experience: Foreign Exchange Programs, Military Service, Overseas Travel, Volunteer Work
Holland Interest Score*: ESA, ISC, SCE

* See Appendix A

Occupation Interest

Interpreting and translating attract those who are linguistically gifted and enjoy foreign cultures. Translators tend to be introverts who enjoy reading and writing and prefer solitary work, while interpreters tend to be extroverts who love being around people, have excellent hearing and listening skills, and are quick thinkers. Translators must manage deadlines while interpreters comply with variable schedules. In either case, the work demands strong cognitive skills and a sharp memory. Sign language interpreters also need excellent hand dexterity.

A Day in the Life—Duties and Responsibilities

A translator spends most of his or her day translating documents at a computer. A job might be as simple as a few paragraphs in a blog, to a book or transcript hundreds of pages long. The translator takes time to reflect on what he or she reads. The translator then tries to communicate the message with as much of its natural rhythm and nuances intact as possible. Such work requires full knowledge of each

Duties and Responsibilities

- **Listening directly or through earphones to what is being said**
- **Taking notes on what is being said**
- **Translating orally, possibly using a microphone**
- **Preparing written translations**
- **Editing translations for correctness of grammar and punctuation**
- **Reviewing finished translations for accuracy and completeness**
- **Reading a document in one language and then rewriting it into another following rules of grammar and punctuation**

language, including slang, subject-specific jargon, colloquialisms, as well as a deep understanding of each culture. Usually a translator has several dictionaries and style guides at his or her disposal, as grammar and punctuation are extremely important.

Interpreters work closely with their clients, in person or via phone, videophone, or microphone. Interpretation may be simultaneous or consecutive. Simultaneous interpreting involves listening to a speaker and translating orally, or signing, at the same time. In some cases, the interpreter is given a written speech or paper to consult in advance for general ideas and language. In other cases, there is no time to think! Consecutive interpreting involves listening to a speaker complete a few words or a sentence and then translating it orally. Depending on the speaker's pace, the interpreter might have time to consider various interpretations of a word or phrase.

Interpreters at United Nations conventions or other types of conferences often sit in the audience and whisper their translations into a microphone. Sign language interpreters sometimes use videophones and a computer to communicate with the deaf.

Self-employed translators and interpreters spend part of the day keeping up with marketing, billing, and other administrative tasks.

OCCUPATION SPECIALTIES

The services of interpreters and translators are needed in a number of different subject areas. Although these professionals often do not specialize in any particular field or industry, many do focus on one area of expertise. The following are examples of occupational specialties.

Conference Interpreters

Conference interpreters work at conferences that have non-English-speaking attendees. The work is often in the field of international business or diplomacy, although conference interpreters can interpret for any organization that works with speakers of foreign languages. Employers prefer high-level interpreters who have the ability to translate from at least two languages into one native language—for example, the ability to interpret from Spanish and French into English. For some positions, such as those with the United Nations, this qualification is required.

Guide or Escort Interpreters

Guide or escort interpreters accompany either U.S. visitors abroad or foreign visitors in the United States to ensure that they are able to communicate during their stay. These specialists interpret informally and on a professional level. Frequent travel for these workers is common.

Health or Medical Interpreters and Translators

Health or medical interpreters and translators typically work in healthcare settings and help patients communicate with doctors, nurses, and other medical staff. Both interpreters and translators must have a strong grasp of medical terminology and the common words for those medical terms in both languages.

Legal or Judiciary Interpreters and Translators

Legal or judiciary interpreters and translators typically work in courts and other legal settings. At hearings, arraignments, depositions, and trials, they help people who have limited English proficiency. They must understand legal terminology. Many court interpreters must sometimes read documents aloud in a language other than that in which they were written, a task known as sight translation.

Literary Translators

Literary translators rewrite journal articles, books, poetry, and short stories from one language into another language. They strive to keep the author's tone and style intact as well as his or her meaning. Whenever possible, literary translators work closely with authors to capture their intended meaning and literary characteristics.

Localization Translators

Localization translators adapt text for a product or service from one language into another. Localization specialists strive to make it appear as though the product originated in the country where it will be sold. They must know not only both languages, but they must also understand the technical information they are working with and must understand the culture of the people who will be using the product or service.

Sign Language Interpreters

Sign language interpreters help people who are deaf or hard of hearing and people who can hear communicate with each other. Sign language interpreters must be fluent in English and in American Sign Language (ASL), which combines signing, finger spelling, and specific body language. ASL is a separate language from English with its own grammar.

WORK ENVIRONMENT

Physical Environment

Interpreters tend to work in diverse interior and exterior environmental conditions, including potentially dangerous or unhealthy job sites. Travel is often required. Translators, on the other hand, work in offices with less variable conditions or at home.

Skills and Abilities

Communication Skills

- Listening to and understanding speakers in a foreign language
- Expressing thoughts and ideas clearly
- Speaking and writing effectively

Interpersonal/Social Skills

- Appreciating cultural differences
- Cooperating with others
- Working as a member of a team

Organization & Management Skills

- Attending/scheduling meetings
- Developing evaluation strategies
- Making decisions

Other Skills

- Expertise in a foreign language

Human Environment

Unless self-employed, translators and interpreters report to supervisors or directors and usually interact with various office staff and professionals. Their clients may change from day to day. Interpreters also interact with the public at conventions or while touring cities with their clients.

Technological Environment

A translator uses translation software on a computer and might use a transcription machine. An interpreter sometimes uses a microphone and might rely on a smart phone, tablet computer, or laptop to access the Internet or a digital dictionary. Some sign language interpreters use a videophone along with a video relay service (VRS) or video interpreting service.

EDUCATION, TRAINING, AND ADVANCEMENT

High School/Secondary

Achieving proficiency in a foreign language takes many years. A college-preparatory program with four years of at least one foreign language, along with courses in English, speech, and the social sciences (political science, anthropology, and world cultures), will provide the best foundation for a career in interpretation or translation. Those students interested in translating technical material should consider additional courses in science and technology. Foreign exchange programs and travel, volunteer work with ethnic organizations, and other independent educational experiences can prove invaluable.

Suggested High School Subjects

- College Preparatory
- Composition
- English
- Foreign Languages
- Literature
- Speech

Famous First

The first U.S. college course in Chinese language and literature opened at Yale University in 1877. The lecturer was Samuel Wells Williams, who earlier had served as interpreter and secretary to Commodore Matthew C. Perry in Japan during the diplomatic effort to "open" that country to the West. (Williams spoke both Japanese and Chinese.)

College/Postsecondary

While a bachelor's degree is the minimum requirement for most jobs, the selection of a major is a personal decision based on the type of work desired. Students might consider double majoring in a foreign language and in another subject, such as English literature, history, or a social science, or in two foreign languages, such as Spanish and French. Some translators and interpreters need an advanced degree to translate subject-specific concepts and vocabulary.

Study abroad programs, foreign travel, and participation in international clubs are some ways to gain important hands-on experience. An internship might be needed for some jobs; some employers offer on-the-job-training.

Related College Majors

- Anthropology
- Linguistics
- Literature
- Sign Language Interpretation

Adult Job Seekers

Bilingual adults should be able to transition well into an interpreting or translating career, especially with relevant experience. For example, a bilingual nurse would have an advantage translating or interpreting in a medical setting. Continuing education courses can refresh or teach new skills. Prospective interpreters and translators should expect to be tested in their language abilities as a prerequisite for employment.

Advancement is highly dependent on experience. Advancement opportunities might include better work hours, higher pay, or more interesting assignments. Those with experience may also consider moving into editorial positions or starting their own companies.

Professional Certification and Licensure

States do not license interpreters or translators. Professional certification is voluntary, although many employers only hire those who are certified in a particular subject or specialty. Professional associations, such as the American Translators Association and the International Association of Conference Interpreters, offer certification. Translators typically must pass a written examination.

Additional Requirements

Interpreters and translators who wish to work for government agencies must pass a civil service exam while freelancers need good business skills as well as experience in the field. Interpreters and translators should consider membership in professional associations, which often provide opportunities for networking and professional development. Work experience or certification is required for membership in some organizations.

EARNINGS AND ADVANCEMENT

Earnings of interpreters and translators depend on the type of work done and the language spoken, as well as the education, experience and skill of the individual. Median annual earnings of interpreters and translators were $45,893 in 2012. The lowest ten percent earned less than $24,327, and the highest ten percent earned more than $91,595.

Full-time interpreters and translators employed by multinational companies may receive paid vacations, holidays, and sick days; life and health insurance; and retirement benefits. These are usually paid by the employer. Interpreters working for the United Nations earn tax-free salaries. In addition, international organizations often pay supplementary living and family allowances. Freelance work in this field offers less in fringe benefits.

Metropolitan Areas with the Highest Concentration of Jobs in this Occupation

Metropolitan area	Employment	Employment per thousand jobs	Hourly mean wage
Washington-Arlington-Alexandria, DC-VA-MD-WV	3,680	1.57	$44.42
New York-White Plains-Wayne, NY-NJ	2,510	0.49	$30.26
Los Angeles-Long Beach-Glendale, CA	2,160	0.56	$30.09
Chicago-Joliet-Naperville, IL	1,210	0.33	$19.44
Boston-Cambridge-Quincy, MA	1,210	0.71	$30.53
Dallas-Plano-Irving, TX	990	0.47	$17.07
Columbus, OH	950	1.04	$27.18
Atlanta-Sandy Springs-Marietta, GA	930	0.41	$19.16

(1) Does not include self-employed. Source: Bureau of Labor Statistics, 2012

Conversation With . . .
RIA OLSEN

Freelance English-Dutch Translator

35 years

1. **What was your individual career path in terms of education, entry-level job, or other significant opportunity?**

   I was always interested in languages and visiting/working in other countries, so I enrolled at the University of Antwerp (my hometown in Belgium) to get a graduate degree in translation. After I graduated, I worked for a few years as a secretary/translator in Italy and France. Later I worked at the United Nations in New York City as a secretary. I could not work there as a translator because they require fluency in their 6 official languages. In the US, I got a Master's in Linguistics from City University, New York. For many years I have worked at home as a freelancer. I get work from translation agencies which in turn get projects from major corporations.

2. **Are there many job opportunities in your profession? In what specific areas?**

   There have been for many years but the profession is changing because software programs increasingly are relied on to do much of the work. I have worked as a freelancer for over 30 years and have never been out of work. My areas of specialty include those that require accuracy, often for safety's sake such as heavy equipment (manuals for cranes, tractors, excavators etc.) and medical translation (manuals for surgical equipment, drug inserts, informed consent forms, medical trial documents, etc.). I also translate a lot of employee surveys.

3. **What do you wish you had known going into this profession?**

   I was lucky to have professors at the University of Antwerp who told us from the start that literary translation is done by authors and poets, and that most professional translators work in specialized fields. We were trained in various areas, including technical and legal translation, besides attending very intensive language courses, for 4 years.

4. **How do you see your profession changing in the next five years?**

Major changes are underway due to automatic translation services. At this point I use translation software programs for assistance but I expect that at one point automatic translation will be good enough and the output will only require editing, especially in technical fields. Some other areas, in particular legal and medical, may remain the domain of human translators because the output has to be extremely accurate.

5. **What role will technology play in those changes, and what skills will be required?**

Use of translation programs, of which there are many. Skills in searching the internet for reference material. Clients often want me to reproduce the text as it looks on a PDF, which takes extra skills and time on my part, such as layout skills. In brief, computer skills.

6. **Do you have any general advice or additional professional insights to share with someone interested in your profession?**

It is important to love language and to understand language. Often I have to explain why something is translated one way and not another. It is important to be able to explain the subtleties of language, not just in terms of terminology but also of grammar.

Thanks to my two degrees (Translation and Linguistics) I can justify my choices when questioned by the client. More and more, source texts are written very poorly and I have to turn these texts into useable texts in Dutch. Since these are often for medical equipment or products (like drugs), or highly-engineered products such as cranes, that must be safely used or operated, it concerns me that the grammar is so poor. Thanks to my knowledge of grammar and language structure, I can usually figure out what the author means and/or propose how a text should be improved.

7. **Can you suggest a valuable "try this" for students considering a career in your profession?**

Find an area of interest and try translating. Many products have instructions in many languages so it's possible to get some training by reading labels or inserts.

EMPLOYMENT AND OUTLOOK

There were about 50,000 interpreters and translators employed nationally in 2012. Interpreters and translators are employed in a variety of industries, reflecting the diversity of employment options in the field. About one-fourth worked in public and private educational institutions, such as schools, colleges, and universities; about one-tenth worked in healthcare and social assistance, such as in hospitals and other health care facilities; and about another one-tenth worked in government, such as in federal, state and local courts. Other employers included publishing companies, telephone companies; airlines and interpreting and translating agencies. Another 12,000 were self-employed.

Employment Trend, Projected 2010–20

Interpreters and Translators: 42%

Total, All Occupations: 14%

Media and Communication Workers: 13%

Note: "All Occupations" includes all occupations in the U.S. Economy. Source: U.S. Bureau of Labor Statistics, Employment Projections Program

Employment of interpreters and translators is expected to grow much faster than the average for all occupations through the year 2020, which means employment is projected to increase as much as 42 percent. This is a result of the broadening of international ties and the increase in foreign language speakers in the United States. Both of these trends are expected to continue, contributing to relatively rapid growth in the number of jobs for interpreters and translators. Demand will remain strong for translators of the languages referred to as PFIGS—Portuguese, French, Italian, German, and Spanish—and the principal Asian languages (Chinese, Japanese, and Korean). In addition, current events and changing political environments, often difficult to foresee, will increase the need for persons who can work with other languages. For example, homeland security needs are expected to drive increasing demand for interpreters and translators of Arabic and other Middle Eastern languages, primarily in Federal Government agencies. In addition, demand for American Sign Language interpreters will grow due to the increasing use of video relay services that provide video calls using a sign language interpreter over an Internet connection.

Related Military Occupations

- Intelligence Officer
- Interpreter & Translator
- Radio Intelligence Officer

SELECTED SCHOOLS

Many colleges and universities offer programs in foreign languages. The student may also gain initial training in selected languages at a community college. Below are listed some of the more prominent institutions in this field.

American University
4400 Massachusetts Avenue, NW
Washington, DC 20016
202.885.1000
www.american.edu

Boston University
1 Silber Way
Boston, MA 02215
617.353.2000
www.bu.edu

Florida International University
11200 SW 8th Street
Miami, FL 33199
305.348.2000
www.fiu.edu

Gallaudet University
800 Florida Avenue NE
Washington, DC 20002
202.651.5000
www.gallaudet.edu

Georgia State University
33 Gilmer Street SE
Atlanta, GA 30303
404.413.2000
www.gsu.edu

Kent State University
800 E. Summit Street
Kent, OH 44240
330.672.3000
www.kent.edu

Monterey Institute of International Studies
460 Pierce Street
Monterey, CA 93940
831.647.4123
www.miis.edu

New York University
70 Washington Square S.
New York, NY 10012
212.998.1212
www.nyu.edu

State University of New York, Binghamton
4400 Vestal Parkway East
Binghamton, NY 13902
607.777.2000
www.binghamton.edu

University of Texas, Dallas
800 W. Campbell Road
Richardson, TX 75080
972.883.2111
www.utdallas.edu

MORE INFORMATION

American Association of Language Specialists
P.O. Box 27306
Washington, DC 20038
www.taals.net

American Literary Translators Association
The University of Texas at Dallas
800 W. Campbell Road
Richardson, TX 75080
972.883.2092
www.utdallas.edu/alta

American Translators Association
225 Reinekers Lane, Suite 590
Alexandria, VA 22314
703.683.6100
www.atanet.org

National Security Education Program
P.O. Box 20010
Arlington, VA 22219
703.696.1991
www.nsep.gov

Registry of Interpreters for the Deaf
333 Commerce Street
Alexandria, VA 22314
703.838.0030
www.rid.org

Sally Driscoll/Editor

Journalist

Snapshot

Career Cluster: Broadcasting, Media & Communications, Publishing, Writing & Editing
Interests: Writing, Research, Story-Telling, News
Earnings (Yearly Average): $36,602
Employment & Outlook: Decline Expected

OVERVIEW

Sphere of Work

The field of journalism involves reporting news, events, and ideas to a wide audience through various media, including print (newspapers and magazines), broadcasting (television and radio), or the Internet (news websites and blogs). Journalists usually start out as reporters, covering anything from sports and weather to business, crime, politics, and consumer affairs. Later, they may become editors, helping to direct the process of gathering and presenting stories.

Journalists can operate on many different levels local, regional, national, or international. It is common for a journalist to start out working on the local or regional level and then move up the ladder as his or her career progresses. Journalists spend the bulk of their time investigating and composing stories, observing events, interviewing people, taking notes, taking photographs, shooting videos, and preparing their material for publication or broadcast. This work can happen in a matter of minutes, or it can take days or weeks to gather information and build a story.

Work Environment

A journalist's work environment is fast-paced and competitive, subject to tight and changing deadlines, irregular work hours, and pressure to get breaking news on the air or on-line before other news organizations. Journalists covering "hard news"—current events that directly affect people's lives, such as crime, politics, or natural disasters—typically work with stories that are moving and changing constantly; their challenge is to present as much relevant and verifiable information as possible under the circumstances. Journalists covering less pressing subjects, like economic and social trends, popular culture, or "human interest" stories, are subject to less immediate time pressures, but are under no less of an obligation to get their facts straight.

Journalists must therefore be able to adapt to unfamiliar places and a variety of people. They must be accustomed to interruptions and have the ability to pick up and process new information at all times.

Profile

Working Conditions: Work Both Indoors And Outdoors
Physical Strength: Light Work
Education Needs: Bachelor's Degree Master's Degree
Licensure/Certification: Usually Not Required
Physical Abilities Not Required: No Strenuous Labor
Opportunities For Experience: Internship, Apprenticeship, Military Service, Volunteer Work, Part-Time Work
Holland Interest Score*: EAS

* See Appendix A

Occupation Interest

Successful journalists are curious by nature and can work comfortably with a wide variety of subjects. They enjoy writing and presenting stories, and they have a great respect for principals that define a free society. These principals include the public's right to know and to question government, business, and social institutions. They also respect an individual's desire to feel connected to what is going on in society. Journalists have to be adept at dealing with people, and successful journalists often have a competitive nature that drives them to try to get the "scoop" before other journalists.

Journalism can be multifaceted work—it can be a low-key, local position for a community newspaper, or it can involve travel and a myriad of settings. Reporting can be a fast-paced in- or out-of-office experience driven by publication editors or broadcast producers.

Finally, journalists have to exhibit tenacity and a tough skin, able to pursue a story to its natural end with a commitment to fair and accurate reporting, even when dealing with controversial topics or evasive interview subjects.

A Day in the Life—Duties and Responsibilities

On any given day, journalists are researching and developing story ideas, checking facts, writing articles for publication, all on a tight deadline. Journalists uncover news, information, statistics, and trends that they incorporate into news stories, broadcasts, feature stories, and editorials. They meet regularly with editors and get assignments based on the day's or week's happenings. Depending where a journalist works, a typical day can vary.

Duties and Responsibilities

- **Researching public records**
- **Interviewing people**
- **Writing news stories**
- **Specializing in one or more fields of news**
- **Covering news in a particular location**
- **Taking photographs**
- **Writing headlines**
- **Laying out pages**
- **Editing wire service copy**
- **Writing editorials**
- **Investigating leads and news tips**

Daily newspapers and newswire services, with very short lead times, have journalists working at all times, around the clock, following ongoing news stories. Weekly newspapers, and weekly and monthly magazines, have longer lead times, and so deadlines are less frequent.

Some journalists work in the field as correspondents, perhaps traveling with a camera crew and conducting "man-on-the-street" interviews, or gathering information about rapidly developing events, which they then submit electronically to newspaper editors or radio or television producers. Since the rise of the Internet, the distinction between print and broadcast journalism has become less sharp: newspaper websites today often include video feeds, and television news stations have websites where their stories appear in text form.

The most important part of a journalist's job is making sure that the stories he or she presents are based on solid, verifiable facts, rather than rumors or misinformation. Inaccuracies can creep into news stories in many ways. Honest mistakes, the reporter's own conscious or unconscious biases, and sources attempting to deceive the public are just a few. For this reason, journalists must invest a good deal of time in making sure their stories are correct before they reach the public.

OCCUPATION SPECIALTIES

News Writers

News Writers write news stories from notes recorded by reporters after evaluating and verifying the information, supplementing it with other material, and organizing stories to fit formats.

Reporters and Correspondents

Reporters and Correspondents gather and assess information, organize it, and write news stories in prescribed style and format. They may also take photographs for stories and give broadcast reports, or report live from the site of events.

Investigative Journalists

Investigative Journalists dig deeply into a single topic of interest, often involving crime, political corruption, or corporate wrongdoing.

News Analysts

News Analysts examine and interpret news. They may write commentaries, columns, or scripts, or they may serve as an anchor on a broadcast news programs.

Editors

Editors manage sections—such as business, sports, and features—or other components of a news publication. They assign reporters to stories and oversee their work.

Producers

Producers function in much the same way as Editors do but in the context of broadcast news.

WORK ENVIRONMENT

Physical Environment

A journalist's work environment can be anywhere, from a crime scene to a press conference to a desk in an office. News outlets usually house journalists in large, well-lit rooms filled with work stations, computer equipment, and the sounds of keyboards and printers. "Boots-on-the-ground" reporting can take a journalist anywhere, though: embedded war correspondents may travel with a military unit right into battle; a journalist reporting on the fishing industry may spend several days on a fishing boat at sea; the next week, that same journalist may tour a farm or a factory or a school to get the next story.

Skills and Abilities

Analytical Skills
- Identifying key elements/players in an unfolding event
- Understanding the impact of human actions

Communication Skills
- Speaking effectively
- Writing concisely

Interpersonal/Social Skills
- Being flexible
- Being persistent
- Cooperating with others
- Working as a member of a team
- Using tact

Organization & Management Skills
- Managing time
- Meeting goals and deadlines
- Paying attention to and handling details

Research & Planning Skills
- Gathering and analyzing information
- Solving problem

Other Skills
- Expertise in a foreign language

Human Environment

Journalists deal with people. They are constantly interviewing people and collecting and analyzing information; therefore, they can usually be found speaking with anyone who has something to do with the story at hand, be it politicians, company officials, protesters, or an average person.

Technological Environment

Today, journalists submit their stories electronically and can therefore be anywhere in the world, collecting information. They often carry their technology on their back, with just a laptop or tablet computer and camera, or travel with a crew of broadcast professionals who can put the journalist on the air live at any time.

EDUCATION, TRAINING, AND ADVANCEMENT

High School/Secondary

High school students can prepare to be a journalist by working for the school newspaper or yearbook, volunteering with local broadcasting stations, and participating in internships with news organizations. Coursework should include a strong focus on writing and communication, through classes such as English, social studies, political science, history, and psychology. Knowledge of foreign languages can also be highly useful in many journalism jobs.

Practical experience is highly valued and can be found through part-time or summer jobs, summer journalism camps, work at college broadcasting stations, and professional organizations. Work in these areas can help in obtaining scholarships, fellowships, and assistantships for college journalism majors.

Local television stations and newspapers often offer internship opportunities for up-and-coming journalists to improve their craft by reporting on town hall meetings or writing obituaries and human-interest stories.

Suggested High School Subjects

- Business
- College Preparatory
- Composition
- Computer Science
- Economics
- English
- Government
- Journalism
- Literature
- Photography
- Political Science
- Social Studies
- Speech

Famous First

The first war correspondent was George Wilkins Kendall of the *New Orleans Picayune* (which he co-founded). Kendall participated with the American army during the Mexican War of 1846–50, and began filing reports carried by pony express. Wounded, he later embarked on a different career and became known as the father of Texas sheep ranching.

College/Postsecondary

Most, but not all, journalists have a bachelor's degree in journalism, English, or another liberal arts–related field. There are many journalism schools within colleges and universities across the country. Many schools also offer master's and doctoral degrees, which are especially useful for those interested in journalistic research and teaching.

Bachelor degree program coursework should include broad liberal arts subjects, a general overview of journalism, and then specialty courses that correspond with the highly important requirements for good writing and communication. These can include classes in social media, broadcast writing, news editorial writing, magazine writing, copy editing, interviewing, media ethics, blogging, feature writing, news reporting, and news photography.

All college and university students should make the effort to use career centers, academic counselors, and professors when seeking opportunities for advancement through volunteering or interning.

Related College Majors

- Broadcast Journalism
- Journalism

Adult Job Seekers

Almost anyone can become a journalist if they can find a local newspaper willing to let them try writing a story. (Of course, it helps to have a background in writing.) Adults can seek continuing journalism education and ongoing opportunities to volunteer in various capacities, perhaps by writing guest newspaper columns, or helping produce a local newsletter, or writing for a blog. These options mean it is entirely viable to seek journalism jobs after having been out of the workplace for a while. Prospective journalists will need to have updated resumes, preferably with portfolios showing relevant work.

More experience leads to more specialized and challenging assignments. Large publications and news stations prefer journalists with several years of experience. With more experience, journalists can advance to become columnists, correspondents, announcers, reporters, or publishing industry managers.

Becoming adept at freelancing—where reporters work independently by selling stories to any interested media outlet—is another way to stay involved in the journalism field.

Professional Certification and Licensure

In the United States, professional certification is not necessary to be a journalist; however, involvement in the Society of Professional Journalists or other professional organizations can help journalists network and raise their profile.

Additional Requirements

It is useful in some cases for journalists to have experience with computer graphics and digital publishing/desktop skills, as well as proficiency in all forms of multimedia. Familiarity with databases and knowledge of news photography is an added plus.

Fun Fact

Younger generations are following the news less than their elders. According to a 2012 Pew Research national poll, the Silent generation (67-84 years) spent 84 minutes a day watching, reading or listening to the news. Baby Boomers (48-66 years) spent 77 minutes per day, Gen Xers (33-48 years) 66 minutes, and Millennials (?-32) only 46 minutes per day following the news.

EARNINGS AND ADVANCEMENT

Median annual earnings of journalists were $36,602 in 2012. The lowest ten percent earned less than $21,168, and the highest ten percent earned more than $79,744.

Journalists may receive paid vacations, holidays, and sick days; life and health insurance; and retirement benefits. These are usually paid by the employer.

Metropolitan Areas with the Highest Employment Level in this Occupation

Metropolitan area	Employment	Employment per thousand jobs	Hourly mean wage
New York-White Plains-Wayne, NY-NJ	3,620	0.70	$31.79
Washington-Arlington-Alexandria, DC-VA-MD-WV	2,320	0.99	$34.05
Los Angeles-Long Beach-Glendale, CA	1,450	0.37	$25.19
Chicago-Joliet-Naperville, IL	1,220	0.34	$30.61
San Francisco-San Mateo-Redwood City, CA	1,050	1.05	$25.95
Boston-Cambridge-Quincy, MA	750	0.44	$30.58
Phoenix-Mesa-Glendale, AZ	640	0.37	$23.61
Atlanta-Sandy Springs-Marietta, GA	530	0.24	$38.15

(1) Does not include self-employed. Source: Bureau of Labor Statistics, 2012

EMPLOYMENT AND OUTLOOK

Journalists held about 46,000 jobs nationally in 2012. About one-half worked for newspaper, magazine and book publishers, and nearly another one-half worked in radio and television broadcasting; the remainder worked in other settings. Employment of journalists is expected to decline through the year 2020. Many factors will contribute to the limited job growth in this occupation. Consolidation and convergence should continue in the publishing and broadcasting industries. As a result, companies will be better able to allocate their journalists to cover news stories. Constantly improving technology also is allowing workers to do their jobs more efficiently, another factor that will limit the number of journalists needed to cover a story or certain type of news. However, the continued demand for news will create some job opportunities. For example, some job growth is expected in new media areas, such as online newspapers and magazines. There is high turnover in this field, as the work is hectic and stressful. Talented writers who can handle highly specialized scientific or technical subjects will be at an advantage in the job market.

Employment Trend, Projected 2010–20

Total, All Occupations: 14%

Broadcast News Analysts: 10%

Reporters, Correspondents, and Broadcast News Analysts: -6%

Reporters and Correspondents: -8%

Note: "All Occupations" includes all occupations in the U.S. Economy. Source: U.S. Bureau of Labor Statistics, Employment Projections Program

Related Occupations

- Copywriter
- Radio/TV Announcer and Newscaster
- Technical Writer
- Writer & Editor

Conversation With . . .
DAN CASEY

Journalist, 29 years in the profession

1. What was your individual career path in terms of education, entry-level job, or other significant opportunity?

I wasn't your typical college student. It took me eight years to earn a four-year degree. One of the jobs I had was working as a bicycle messenger in Washington, D.C. A majority of our clients were newspapers, wire services, public relations companies. It was exciting work, especially on certain days – such as when John Hinckley tried to assassinate President Reagan, or when a jetliner loaded with people crashed into the 14th Street bridge during an ice storm. That excitement totally hooked me on the news business and its importance in our daily lives. When I finally managed to earn a college degree (in English) I took a job for $210/week at a weekly newspaper in the Washington suburbs. I got some good stories then moved on to a bigger paper six months later.

The messenger job had focused me on a career path, but every job I've had since age 11 has helped me in this business. I delivered newspapers, washed dishes, made pizzas, did roofing, jockeyed gasoline, sold shoes, and performed maintenance and repairs at a large apartment complex. Experiences like those helped me understand how things worked in the world, and how to relate to people from all walks of life.

2. Are there many job opportunities in your profession? In what specific areas?

The job opportunities in newspapers are fading quickly. But that's not true of the larger media. There's plenty of opportunity and growth in online news media especially - sites such as Talking Points Memo, and Raw Story. Basic skills such as gathering information fast and being able to present it coherently are more in demand than ever because the traditional news cycle is shorter than ever.

3. What do you wish you had known going into this profession?

This is generally a low-paid profession, with no law degree or medical license or scientific credentials necessary. Publishers take advantage of that, wage-wise.

They'll try to hire you as inexpensively as possible and keep your wages low. This doesn't mean you can't make a decent living or even a lot of money working in news. You can, if you're willing to work hard, get good stories, and jump to newer, higher-paying jobs as quickly as you can. Don't spend more than two years in one place. Do this early in your career and you'll have a lot more satisfaction later on.

4. How do you see your profession changing in the next five years?

Traditional newspapers and magazines are quickly on their way out. Whatever you do, DON'T plan a career in them. If you want to work in news, it's OK to get some experience at a paper or magazine, but get out as fast as you can and head for online news outlets.

5. What role will technology play in those changes, and what skills will be required?

The traditional skills in the news business are 1) news-gathering ability and 2) writing, in that order. As the media morphs more and more into online only, those will remain very important. But they're not nearly enough. Skills in photography, video, online presentation and social media will be at least as important.

6. Do you have any general advice or additional professional insights to share with someone interested in your profession?

The biggest trap I've witnessed many reporters fall into is losing sight of who their client is. The client is ALWAYS your reader. It is NEVER your sources. Still, a lot of people in this profession spend great deals of time trying hardest to please their sources, as if they fear their ability to gather information will dry up if they make their sources unhappy. The truth is, your sources need you more than you need them.

7. Can you suggest a valuable "try this" for students considering a career in your profession?

Few people naturally have a writer's voice. Those are developed, not ingrained. So develop yours. Find a variety of writers whose voices you admire and read them a lot. Analyze passages you particularly admire. What makes this passage so good? And then play around, outside the confines of writing on deadline. Ask yourself: How would Hemingway, or Hunter Thompson or Mike Royko (or whoever) write this story? What lead would they write? Do it over and over again. Eventually you'll find your own voice.

SELECTED SCHOOLS

Many colleges and universities offer bachelor's degree programs in journalism. The student may also gain initial training through enrollment at a community college. Below are listed some of the more prominent institutions in this field.

Columbia University
535 W. 116th Street
New York, NY 10027
212.854.1754
www.columbia.edu

Indiana University, Bloomington
107 S. Indiana Avenue
Bloomington, IN 47405
812.855.4848
www.iub.edu

New York University
70 Washington Square S
New York, NY 10012
212.998.1212
www.nyu.edu

Northwestern University
633 Clark Street
Evanston, IL 60208
847.491.3741
www.northwestern.edu

Penn State University
201 Old Main
University Park, PA 16802
814.865.4700
www.psu.edu

University of Colorado, Boulder
Boulder, CO 80309
303.492.80309
www.colorado.edu

University of Kansas
1450 Jayhawk Boulevard
Lawrence, KS 66045
785.864.2700
www.ku.edu

University of Minnesota, Twin Cities
231 Pillsbury Drive, SE
Minneapolis, MN 55455
612.625.2008
www1.umn.edu

University of Missouri, Columbia
230 Jesse Hall
Columbia, MO 65211
573.882.7786
www.missouri.edu

West Virginia University
1550 University Avenue
Morgantown, WV 26506
304.293.0111
www.wvu.edu

MORE INFORMATION

Accrediting Council on Education in Journalism & Mass Comm.
University of Kansas
Stauffer-Flint Hall
1435 Jayhawk Boulevard
Lawrence, KS 66045-7575
785.864.3973
www2.ku.edu/~acejmc

Dow Jones Newspaper Fund, Inc.
P.O. Box 300
Princeton, NJ 08543-0300
609.452.2820
www.newsfund.org

National Association of Broadcasters
1771 N Street NW
Washington, DC 20036
202.429.5300
www.nab.org

National Federation of Press Women
P.O. Box 34798
Alexandria, VA 22334-0798
800.780.2715
www.nfpw.org

National Newspaper Association
P.O. Box 7540
Columbia, MO 65205-7540
800.829.4662
www.nnpa.org

National Press Club
529 14th Street NW, 13th Floor
Washington, DC 20045
202.662.7500
www.press.org

Newspaper Association of America
4401 Wilson Boulevard, Suite 900
Arlington, VA 22203-1867
571.366.1000
www.naa.org

Newspaper Guild-CWA Research and Information Department
501 Third Street NW, 6th Floor
Washington, DC 20001-2797
202.434.7177
www.newsguild.org

Poynter Institute
801 3rd Street S.
St. Petersburg, FL 33701
727.821.9494
www.poynter.org

Society of Professional Journalists
Eugene S. Pulliam National Journalism Center
3909 N. Meridian Street
Indianapolis, IN 46208
317.927.8000
www.spj.org

Medical and Scientific Illustrator

Snapshot

Career Cluster: Arts, Health Science, Science, Technology, Engineering & Mathematics
Interests: Art, Illustration, Medicine, Science
Earnings (Yearly Average): $47,535
Employment & Outlook: Average Growth Expected

OVERVIEW

Sphere of Work

Medical and scientific illustrators are professional artists with training in the arts and the relevant sciences. Medical illustrators draw human anatomy, three-dimensional forms, and steps in the surgical process, while scientific illustrators draw animals and plants as well as molecular, planetary, and geological forms. Medical and scientific illustrators use a wide variety of media to create their work, including pencil, ink, paint, and digital tools such as computer animation. They

Detail of an editorial-style medical illustration demonstrating various bicycling-related injuries and relevant anatomy. See page 171 for interview with Cassio Lynm. Image: © Cassio Lynm.

often use photography and video to capture or record their subjects, and may also make models from plaster or wax to use as the source or inspiration for their illustrations. Medical and scientific illustrations are used in teaching, publications, and legal matters.

Work Environment

Medical and scientific illustrators are often self-employed or employed on a contract basis to produce a limited set of illustrations. They may work days, evenings, or weekends, depending on the scope and urgency of the project.

Occupation Interest

Individuals drawn to the profession of medical or scientific illustrator tend to be artistic, intelligent, and detail oriented. Those most successful at the job display traits such as good eyesight, hand-eye coordination, focus, and artistic sensibility. Medical and scientific illustrators should have an interest in medical or scientific subjects, be willing to conduct independent research, and should be skilled in a wide range of artistic techniques.

Profile

Working Conditions: Office/Studio Environment
Physical Strength: Light Work
Education Needs: Bachelor's Degree
Licensure/Certification: Usually Not Required
Physical Abilities Not Required: No Heavy Work
Opportunities For Experience: Internship, Apprenticeship
Holland Interest Score*: AIE

* See Appendix A

A Day in the Life—Duties and Responsibilities

The daily occupational duties and responsibilities of medical and scientific illustrators will be determined by the individual's area of job specialization and work environment. Areas of specialization include subject matter specialties such as surgery, botany, animal science, or ophthalmology; media specialties such as model making or computer animation; and production specialties such as textbooks, exhibits, advertising, instructional videos, or stock image production.

A medical or scientific illustrator should keep his or her tools, including pencil, ink, paint, paper, plaster, wax, cameras, video cameras, and computers, ready and in good working order. During

Duties and Responsibilities

- **Preparing various kinds of illustrations and computer animations**
- **Making three-dimensional models of wax, plaster, plastics, or other materials**
- **Drawing, painting, modeling, and diagramming**
- **Taking photographs or motion pictures during surgery**

the course of a day, a medical or scientific illustrator may attend surgical procedures or physical examinations, use microscopes or other equipment in medical laboratory settings, read scientific papers, or meet with relevant experts in order to obtain information and source material for their work. A medical or scientific illustrator may be tasked with creating a traditional illustration, a computer animation, or a three-dimensional model for veterinary textbooks and schools; medical textbooks, journals, or advertising campaigns; visual aids, filmstrips, transparencies, and videos to be used for teaching purposes; or court cases. He or she may also write the text to accompany a medical or scientific illustration in a publication, or create medical illustrations that depict best practices for patient care or laboratory procedures.

In addition to the tasks described above, medical and scientific illustrators will benefit from promoting their illustration services to medical and scientific publishing communities and engaging in professional development with physicians, scientists, and other medical and scientific illustrators.

WORK ENVIRONMENT

Physical Environment

The immediate physical environment of medical and scientific illustrators varies based on their employer and specialization. They may work in art studios, medical schools, hospitals, medical offices

Skills and Abilities

Communication Skills
- Expressing thoughts and ideas

Creative/Artistic Skills
- Being skilled in art

Interpersonal/Social Skills
- Listening to others
- Working independently and as part of a team

Research & Planning Skills
- Examining subjects and creating ideas

Technical Skills
- Performing scientific, mathematical, and technical work
- Working with accuracy and precision

Other Skills
- Appreciating both the artistic and technical sides

and clinics, medical laboratories, medical libraries, or art-related businesses such as advertising companies or stock image companies.

Human Environment

Medical and scientific illustrators generally work in isolation but should be comfortable interacting with physicians, scientists, lab workers, publishers, teachers, lawyers, and art business professionals, through virtual or face-to-face means, to discuss illustration subjects and contracts.

Technological Environment

Medical and scientific illustrators use a wide variety of tools and equipment to complete their work, including pencil, ink, paint, paper, plaster, wax, cameras, video cameras, computers, scanners, and printers.

EDUCATION, TRAINING, AND ADVANCEMENT

High School/Secondary

High school students interested in pursuing a career as a medical and scientific illustrator should prepare themselves by studying sciences such as anatomy, biology, chemistry, physics, and physiology, and by taking as many art classes as possible. College preparatory programs may be helpful in this regard.

Suggested High School Subjects

- Applied Math
- Arts
- Biology
- Chemistry
- Computer Science
- Drafting
- English
- Health Science Technology
- Mechanical Drawing
- Photography
- Physiology

Famous First

The first anatomy book, *A Compendious System of Anatomy*, was published in Philadelphia in 1792. Its contents, however, were drawn directly from the *Encyclopaedia Britannica*. The first original anatomy book was Caspar Wistar's *A System of Anatomy*, published in two volumes between 1811 and 1814.

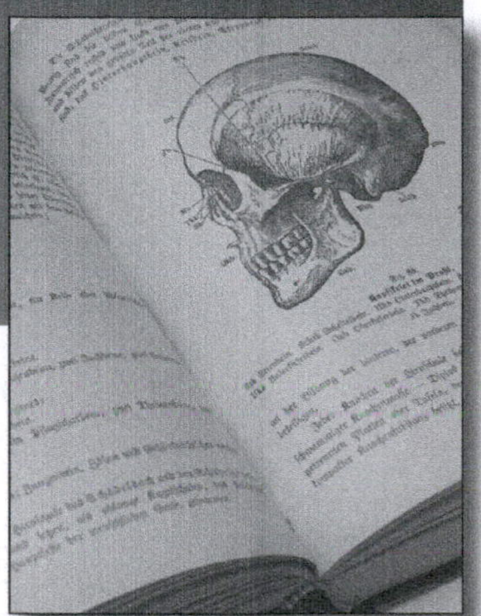

College/Postsecondary

Postsecondary students interested in becoming medical or scientific illustrators should work toward a bachelor's degree combining art or graphic design with science and/or premedical courses, or a master's degree in medical and scientific illustration from a program accredited by the Commission on Accreditation of Allied Health Education Programs (CAAHEP). Coursework in photography and web design may also prove useful in their future work. Postsecondary students can gain work experience by securing internships or part-time employment in visual art or medical settings.

Related College Majors

- Graphic Design, Commercial Art & Illustration
- Medical Illustrating

Adult Job Seekers

Adult job seekers may find employment as medical or scientific illustrators without a degree, but having a formal education will greatly increase their opportunities. Some universities and institutions offer informal or certificate programs. A portfolio of work examples is essential. Adult job seekers will benefit from joining professional associations to help with networking and job searching. Professional illustration associations, such as the Association of Medical Illustrators and the Guild of Natural Science Illustrators, generally offer career workshops and maintain lists of available jobs.

Professional Certification and Licensure

Certification is not legally required for medical or scientific illustrators but may be required as a condition of employment or promotion. The Board of Certification of Medical Illustrators awards the voluntary Certified Medical Illustrator credential to medical illustrators who have completed a training program, undergone a portfolio review, and passed a national exam on illustration skills, best business practices, ethics, and biomedical science. The Certified Medical Illustrator credential requires ongoing continuing education credits and recertification. State licensing is not required for medical or scientific illustrators.

Additional Requirements

High levels of integrity and professional ethics are required of medical and scientific illustrators, as professionals in this role create materials that have a profound effect on patients, medical students, juries, and the public at large. Membership in professional medical and scientific illustration associations is encouraged among all medical and scientific illustrators as a means of building status within the professional community and networking.

EARNINGS AND ADVANCEMENT

Medical and scientific illustrators advance as their work circulates and they establish a reputation for a particular style. The best medical and scientific illustrators continue to grow in ideas, and their work constantly evolves over time. Many medical and scientific illustrators supplement their income by freelancing. Median annual earnings of medical and scientific illustrators were $47,535 in 2012.

Medical and scientific illustrators, when holding a permanent position, may receive paid vacations, holidays, and sick days; life and health insurance; and retirement benefits.

Metropolitan Areas with the Highest Employment Level in this Occupation

Metropolitan area	Employment	Employment per thousand jobs	Hourly mean wage
Los Angeles-Long Beach-Glendale, CA	3,080	0.80	$32.45
New York-White Plains-Wayne, NY-NJ	1,150	0.22	$33.42
Seattle-Bellevue-Everett, WA	550	0.39	$33.86
Orlando-Kissimmee-Sanford, FL	370	0.36	$17.80
Chicago-Joliet-Naperville, IL	320	0.09	$24.99
Boston-Cambridge-Quincy, MA	260	0.15	$19.20
San Francisco-San Mateo-Redwood City, CA	210	0.21	$28.49
Bridgeport-Stamford-Norwalk, CT	190	0.46	$27.08

(1) Does not include self-employed. Source: Bureau of Labor Statistics, 2012

EMPLOYMENT AND OUTLOOK

Fine artists, of whom medical and scientific illustrators are considered a part, held about 12,000 jobs nationally in 2012. Medical and scientific illustrators usually worked for medical centers and publishers. Some freelance for pharmaceutical companies and advertising agencies. It is also possible for those with a background in graphic arts to create medical and scientific illustrations for basic applications. Employment in the field is expected to grow slower than the average for all occupations through the year 2020, which means employment is projected to increase about 8 percent. As medical research and new technologies evolve, the need for illustrators who can record and communicate these advancements will grow.

Employment Trend, Projected 2010–20

Total, All Occupations: 14%

Fine Artists, Including Painters, Sculptors, and Illustrators: 8%

Craft Artists: 7%

Craft and Fine Artists: 5%

Artists and Related Workers, All Other: 1%

Note: "All Occupations" includes all occupations in the U.S. Economy. Source: U.S. Bureau of Labor Statistics, Employment Projections Program

Related Occupations

- Art Director
- Graphic Designer & Illustrator
- Multimedia Artist & Animator

Conversation With . . .
CASSIO LYNM

Senior Medical Illustrator,
13 years in the profession

1. What was your individual career path in terms of education, entry-level job, or other significant opportunity?

I learned about the field of medical illustration on a high school trip to the anatomy department at Wake Forest Baptist Medical Center in Winston-Salem, NC. At the University of North Carolina/Chapel Hill, I concentrated on bachelor's degrees in biology and studio art. I worked part-time, then full-time, with a local artist, doing a variety of work from large-scale murals to design, illustration, and book layout. I began investigating medical illustration jobs, but many required a master's. I was accepted into the two-year program at The Department of Art as Applied to Medicine at The Johns Hopkins University School of Medicine. Thereafter, I accepted the first full-time Medical Illustrator position at the Journal of the American Medical Association (JAMA). I am also an adjunct faculty member of the University of Illinois at Chicago.

2. Are there many job opportunities in your profession? In what specific areas?

Medical illustration now includes medical animation and video, website design, medical device and patents, prosthetics, online media, medical models and simulation, and even gaming and app development.

3. What do you wish you had known going into this profession?

Aside from a good grounding in sciences and visual arts, good communication is one of the most useful, yet least remarked-upon, skills. From pitching ideas to seeking answers to negotiating contracts, having a solid ability to express your ideas in written and spoken form is essential.

Good ideas take time. Deadlines can make for creative decision-making, but it's better to budget extra time and allow yourself time for thinking and exploration.

Be flexible and open–minded. The work we do requires focus, but too much concentration on the details can mean missing larger connections. Also, inspiration can come from unlikely sources.

Wherever possible, use projects to challenge yourself technically. Keep your hands and mind sharp by attending seminars or doing online tutorials.

Develop an understanding of copyright and of your work as intellectual property. It will help you gauge your work's worth.

Reach out to other professionals for advice.

4. How do you see your profession changing in the next five years?

I believe that the next few years will bring growth in areas involving patient information and public awareness of advancements in medicine and science. We already team up with hospitals, physicians, and allied health care professionals for this purpose, but I believe our collaborations will expand to biotechnology and advanced clinical imaging.

Furthermore, I imagine that Medical Illustrators will be sought out by film and television for their unique blend of expertise in science and art.

One thing that will remain fairly constant is that Medical Illustrators will continue to connect the expert and novice, the scholar and student, or the physician and patient.

5. What role will technology play in those changes, and what skills will be required?

Developments in medical technology and the devices that drive care and research will generate new material that medical illustrators will be called upon to convey.

Advances in equipment used for the creative process will influence the manner in which we produce. Many Medical Illustrators still sketch and compose on paper but finish in 2D painting and rendering programs or 3D modeling and sculpting programs. Digital touch- and/or pressure-sensitive devices have made creating work incredibly efficient and as close to the feeling of traditional materials as we can get. Technology will never be a substitute for good drafting and conceptualization skills, but computer proficiency will certainly be required.

6. Do you have any general advice or additional professional insights to share with someone interested in your profession?

Most successful Medical Illustrators hold a master's degree from an accredited graduate program in medical illustration. My experience at the Hopkins' graduate program was rewarding and, I believe, instrumental in landing initial job interviews and preparing me for this type of specialized profession. Students considering the field should take as many classes as possible in art and science, with the intention of majoring or having a minor in art and a biological science. The Association of Medical Illustrators (www.ami.org) is a valuable resource.

7. Can you suggest a valuable "try this" for students considering a career in your profession?

Choose a simple concept in biology or anatomy and phrase it as a question, like "What layers of skin are injured in different types of burns?" Imagine that you have to explain it to an audience unfamiliar with the subject. Speak with people who represent this audience (for example, fellow students), and ask what they find difficult to understand about the subject or want to know more about. Think about what viewpoints you will have to take to show the main parts of the concept. What labels or words will you need to use? Research how the subject has been depicted and evaluate what is successful about existing depictions compared to the idea forming in your mind and to any photos you uncover. It's easy to make a pretty image, but accuracy, the information that it contains, and how it is presented are more important considerations.

SELECTED SCHOOLS

Many colleges and universities offer bachelor's degree programs in the visual arts; some have programs in illustration. The student may also gain basic training through enrollment at a community college. Below are listed some of the more prominent institutions in this field.

Arcadia University
450 S. Easton Road
Glenside, PA 19038
215.572.2900
www.arcadia.edu

Cleveland Institute of Art
11141 East Boulevard
Cleveland, OH 44106
800.233.4700
www.cia.edu

Iowa State University
2229 Lincoln Way
Ames, IA 50011
515.294.4111
www.iastate.edu

Northern Illinois University
1425 W. Lincoln Highway
DeKalb, IL 60115
815.753.1000
www.niu.edu

Rochester Institute of Technology
1 Lomb Memorial Drive
Rochester, NY 14623
585.475.2411
www.rit.edu

Sheridan College
1430 Trafalgar Road
Oakville, Ontario, Canada L6H 2L1
905.845.9430
www.sheridancollege.ca

University of Florida
226 Tigert Hall
Gainesville, FL 32611
352.392.3261
www.ufl.edu

University of Georgia
10 Green Street
Athens, GA 30601
706.542.3000
www.uga.edu

University of Illinois, Chicago
2035 W. Taylor Street
Chicago, IL 60612
312.996.6620
www.uic.edu

Virginia Commonwealth University
821 W. Franklin Street
Richmond, VA 23284
804.828.0100
www.vcu.edu

MORE INFORMATION

American Society of Botanical Artists
The New York Botanical Garden
2900 Southern Boulevard
Bronx, NY 10458
212.691.9080
www.asba-art.org

Association of Independent Colleges of Art and Design
236 Hope Street
Providence, RI 02906
401.270.5991
www.aicad.org

Association of Medical Illustrators
201 E. Main Street, Suite 1405
Lexington, KY 40507
866.393.4264
www.ami.org

Guild of Natural Science Illustrators
P.O. Box 652
Ben Franklin Station
Washington, DC 20044
301.309.1514
www.gnsi.org

International Association of Astronomical Artists
P.O. Box 4592
Carmel-by-the-Sea, CA 93921
iaaa.org

Simone Isadora Flynn/Editor

Motion Picture/ Radio/TV Art Director

Snapshot

Career Cluster: Arts, A/V Technology & Communication, Business, Management & Administration
Interests: Set Design, Marketing & Advertising, Management, Art, IllustrationTechniques, Film Production
Earnings (Yearly Average): $85,468
Employment & Outlook: Average Growth Expected

OVERVIEW

Sphere of Work

Art directors for motion pictures, radio, and television work in collaboration with producers, writers, and directors to bring concepts from the page to the screen or airwaves. They oversee a studio's art department and typically play a major role in hiring the creative staff, which can include artists, graphic designers, model makers, and set builders. Sometimes known as production designers, they often directly assist in the construction of sets and props. Motion picture, radio, and television art directors are also responsible for the management and allocation of the art department's budget, ensuring that the work performed on a given project stays within the production's overall financial framework. In addition, they are frequently called upon to assist in the marketing and advertisement of their projects.

Work Environment

Motion picture, radio, and television art directors commonly work in studios and sound stages that allow for little contact with individuals not involved in the production. Studios are busy locations in which many different working groups operate in concert with one another, so art directors should be comfortable interacting with others on a regular basis. Some art directors also spend a great deal of time in an office environment, working on advertising and marketing plans and designing sets. Frequently, art directors travel to off-site locations to scout filming or recording spots and must be prepared to encounter potentially unpleasant weather and climate conditions. Art directors often work irregular hours, particularly when working on a production set, but may work fewer and more consistent hours during pre-production periods prior to the start of shooting or recording. Due to the expectations of producers and directors to stay on schedule and within budget, art directors in the entertainment industry may experience work-related stress.

Profile

Working Conditions: Office/Production Studio Some Out Side Work
Physical Strength: Light To Moderate Work
Education Needs: Technical/ Community College Bachelor's Degree
Licensure/Certification: Recommended
Physical Abilities Not Required: No Strenuous Work
Opportunities For Experience: Apprenticeship, Military Service Volunteer Work, Part-Time Work
Holland Interest Score*: RCE

* See Appendix A

Occupation Interest

Art direction is a critical facet of the entertainment industry, and the seniority afforded by the position allows the art director creative input into the ways in which films, television programs, and radio shows are made and marketed. As such, this career attracts those who have a strong interest in the behind-the-scenes workings of media. The nature of the work requires that a large number of diverse responsibilities be managed simultaneously, so art directors are frequently masters of organization, leadership and delegation, and multitasking.

A Day in the Life—Duties and Responsibilities

Art directors are responsible for bringing the collective creative vision of producers, directors, and writers to life. They begin by meeting and consulting with these individuals during the pre-production stage, months in advance of shooting or recording. Using computer technologies as well as their own artistic abilities, they design set blueprints, present sketches and illustrations, and when applicable, conduct research on architectural styles to ensure historical accuracy. In addition to designing and building project-specific sets, they scout potential shooting or recording locations in both outdoor and indoor environments. Art directors also work with advertising managers to create a marketing strategy for the film, program, or show.

During the shoot or recording session, art directors assist in set building and design and in directing artists, model makers, and other members of the crew in accordance with the director and producer's desires. They often contribute to the design of costumes, makeup, lighting effects, and other aspects of the production. Art directors must also manage the internal operations of the art department, including establishing departmental budgets; hiring, training, and terminating team members; and monitoring individual assignments to ensure that the department is operating efficiently, on time, and within budget parameters.

In contrast, smaller stations frequently have few or no specialized technicians. Consequently, broadcast technicians working in these environments are often generalists, responsible for lights, sound, transmitters, and all other aspects of the station's technical systems.

Duties and Responsibilities

- **Designing set blueprints and creating all visual elements**
- **Consulting with writers, producers and directors**
- **Supervising design staff**
- **Assisting in the marketing and advertising of products**
- **Managing budgets and ensuring that projects meet budget requirements**

WORK ENVIRONMENT

Skills and Abilities

Communication Skills
- Speaking and writing effectively
- Describing visual elements to others

Creative/Artistic Skills
- Being skilled in art, music, or dance
- Creating ideas
- Translating ideas into concrete forms

Interpersonal/Social Skills
- Following instructions
- Paying attention to and handling details

Organization & Management Skills
- Coordinating tasks
- Managing people/groups
- Managing time
- Meeting goals and deadlines

Research & Planning Skil
- Researching subjects in art and architecture

Physical Environment

Motion picture, radio, and television art directors typically work in studios and office environments, which are generally well organized and highly controlled to ensure no interference from uninvolved individuals. They also work on location, which can either be an existing structure, such as a hotel, museum, or office building, or an outdoor setting, which can be remote and susceptible to various weather conditions.

Human Environment

Art directors work with and oversee a wide range of crew and cast members, including actors and extras, directors, producers, writers, creative directors, electricians, painters, construction crews, lighting and sound crews, unit publicists, camera operators, costume designers, and makeup artists. Therefore, they must have excellent interpersonal skills and the ability to work past any personality conflicts.

Technological Environment

Art directors must use a wide range of technologies. Off the set, they rely on many computer-based systems, including software devoted to computer-aided design (CAD), animation, graphic design, and special effects. On the set, they may use hand tools, photography and filming equipment, lighting systems, and sound recording equipment

EDUCATION, TRAINING, AND ADVANCEMENT

High School/Secondary

High school students should study theater as well as explore the technical and creative arts through mechanical drawing, graphics, drafting, photography, and audio-visual courses. English, art history, the industrial arts, and mathematics are also highly useful for aspiring art directors. High school students can also gain experience in art direction through participation in school- or community-based theater and media productions

Suggested High School Subjects

- Arts
- Audio-Visual
- Drafting
- English
- Graphic Communications
- Industrial Arts
- Mathematics
- Mechanical Drawing
- Photography
- Theatre & Drama

Famous First

The first theater designed expressly for dance performances was Ted Shawn's theater at Jacob's Pillow in Becket, Mass. Opening in 1942, the space featured a large, smooth maple floor inside a pinewood building. Since that time the annual dance festival held there has become one of the largest and most respected venues of its kind.

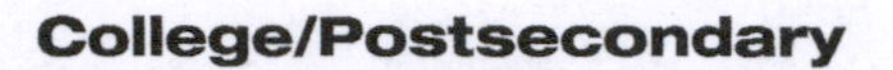

College/Postsecondary

Art directors for motion pictures, radio, and television generally have a bachelor's degree in fine arts, theater, or a similar field. During postsecondary schooling, many aspiring art directors assemble a portfolio of their work, which can be used to fulfill the admission requirements for specialized undergraduate and graduate art programs that provide training in photography, graphic design, design, and other relevant fields. A strong portfolio also demonstrates the future art director's knowledge and skill to prospective employers. Students can gain practical experience and build a portfolio by participating in school-based or independent film, radio, and television productions.

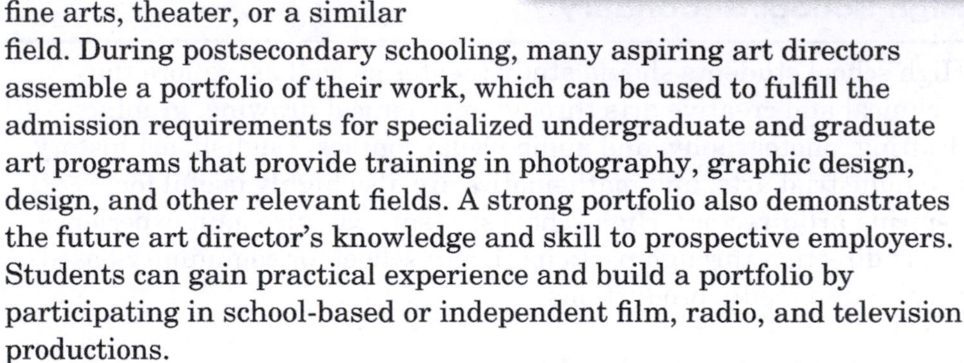

Related College Majors

- Advertising
- Design & Visual Communications
- Graphic Design, Commercial Art & Illustration
- Studio Production
- Theater & Drama

Adult Job Seekers

The film, radio, and television job market is very competitive. While some individuals find work through placement offices at art schools or colleges, most art directors attain their positions after having acquired and worked in lower-level jobs within an art department. Internships, frequently unpaid, serve as a common entry point into the industry. Aspiring art directors can build their portfolios by working on commercials, independent film projects, and music videos, as well as through employment with entertainment-oriented advertising and marketing firms. As with many other entertainment careers, networking is essential.

Professional Certification and Licensure

No certification is required to work as a motion picture, radio, and television art director. Some art directors, however, may pursue voluntary certification in specialized areas, such as design, digital technology, and art direction. As with any voluntary certification process, it is beneficial to consult credible professional associations within the field and follow professional debate as to the relevancy and value of any certification program.

Additional Requirements

Motion picture, television, and radio art directors should be excellent communicators and managers. They must be creative and detail oriented, and they should possess strong computer and budgeting skills. In order to succeed in this fast-paced environment, art directors must be decisive and able to handle stressful situations.

EARNINGS AND ADVANCEMENT

People who have become art directors do so after acquiring much experience in the advertising field. Salaries and job opportunities depend on the size and geographic location of the employer and the individual's experience and ability.

Median annual earnings of motion picture, radio and television art directors were $85,468 in 2012. The lowest ten percent earned less than $45,410, and the highest ten percent earned more than $173,236. Art directors may receive paid vacations, holidays, and sick days; life and health insurance; and retirement benefits. These are usually paid by the employer.

Metropolitan Areas with the Highest Employment Level in This Occupation

Metropolitan area	Employment[1]	Employment per thousand jobs	Hourly mean wage
New York-White Plains-Wayne, NY-NJ	5,940	1.15	$62.83
Los Angeles-Long Beach-Glendale, CA	2,830	0.73	$57.01
Chicago-Joliet-Naperville, IL	1,650	0.45	$38.67
Boston-Cambridge-Quincy, MA	1,010	0.59	$45.34
San Francisco-San Mateo-Redwood City, CA	970	0.96	$59.28
Minneapolis-St. Paul-Bloomington, MN-WI	730	0.42	$39.45
Seattle-Bellevue-Everett, WA	630	0.45	$48.69
Washington-Arlington-Alexandria, DC-VA-MD-WV	590	0.25	$40.97

[1] Includes all art directors, not only those employed in the motion picture/radio/television industry. Does not include self-employed Source: Bureau of Labor Statistics, 2012

EMPLOYMENT AND OUTLOOK

Art directors of all varieties (including those outside of the entertainment industry) held about 32,000 jobs nationally in 2012. Employment is expected to grow slower than the average for all occupations through the year 2020, which means employment is projected to increase up to 9 percent. Producers of information, goods and services will continue to place increased emphasis on visual appeal in product design, advertising, marketing and television. Competition for good jobs will be strong.

Employment Trend, Projected 2010–20

Total, All Occupations: 14%

Arts, Design, Entertainment, Sports, and Media: 13%

Art Directors: 9%

Note: "All Occupations" includes all occupations in the U.S. Economy Source: U.S. Bureau of Labor Statistics, Employment Projections Program

Related Occupations

- Advertising Director
- Art Director
- Cinematographer
- Photographer

Conversation With . . .
CHARLES E. MCCARRY

Motion Picture / Television Art Director

30 years in the profession

1. What was your individual career path in terms of education, entry-level job, or other significant opportunity?

I was always one of the kids who hung around the art room in high school and helped backstage with plays. I selected a college which had a very robust graduate theater program in my hometown of Philadelphia. I received a bachelor's of science degree. In a way I'm glad I didn't simply concentrate in theater. I always advise my college students, don't forget to go to college while you're here! Get as broad an education as possible. You need to know about the world.

By my sophomore year of college is was clear to me that I had an interest in design – creating the environment for theater productions. A faculty member endorsed me for a number of different jobs as scenic designer at small theaters around town. I did that for two years, then, with a nice portfolio of my work, moved to New York. That got me into a number of professional studios as an assistant and I had opportunities to work on quite a number of interesting and fairly sizeable Broadway shows. Some of them won Tony awards for scenic design, and I was part of that.

After a few years I was accepted into Yale School of Drama, concentrating in scenic drama. It was a three-year M.F.A. program. I got into film when I was asked to create the film sequence for the Broadway musical *City of Angels*, which is about Hollywood. I thought, I could do that for real and began looking for opportunities to work in film.

2. Are there many job opportunities in your profession? In what specific areas?

There are never any job opportunities and there are always lots of job opportunities. In the arts, that's pretty much the way it is. There are absolutely always opportunities for someone who is committed and well rounded and willing to work hard and willing to learn. You need to be completely prepared and then you need to locate yourself in a place where opportunity might knock. If you aspire to be a production designer in film or an art director on a network, you should probably be in New York or Los Angeles. Possibly Chicago, Washington, or Boston.

Union membership is important. I'm a member of United Scenic Artists Local 829.

3. What do you wish you had known going into this profession?

I wish I had known the critical importance of the social side of the profession. Never pass up an opportunity to have lunch with someone. Never pass up an opportunity to go to a reception or a gathering. It's entirely people based. It's who you know.

4. How do you see your profession changing in the next five years?

With the digital revolution, anything is possible now. Creating gaming environments is a rich area of opportunity for the kids coming up nowadays. There's also a blending of gaming environments with other areas of production design. The very nature of a "show" is changing, with the television networks dying off and Netflix, Hulu Plus and the like replacing them. And the delivery of the product is absolutely changing. I will often watch a movie on my laptop or on my television set in my living room instead of going to the movie theater.

Yet, as a production designer and art director I use exactly the same skills as always. These digital tools are just entering a centuries-old profession and being seamlessly integrated.

5. What role will technology play in those changes, and what skills will be required?

Twenty to 30 years ago, we would make a little model out of foam core and now that model might exist on a laptop, but it's essentially the same work. Any young person entering the profession at the very least needs to be familiar with Google SketchUp and possibly Vectorworks, and always, a pencil, pencil, pencil. You need to be able to present your visual ideas. The easiest way to do that at lunch with the director is to sketch it on a napkin and that will never change. And then you can open your laptop.

6. Do you have any general advice or additional professional insights to share with someone interested in your profession?

The most important word in our line of work is "collaborate." So, ask yourself if you enjoy collaborating. For someone who has a real comfort level with working with others and can bring strong, visual ideas to the table while being mindful of checking your ego at the door, then you're a good fit for this profession. If you're more of a loner, someone much more happy working in a studio on sculpture or a painting, then this is not your line of work.

7. Can you suggest a valuable "try this" for students considering a career in your profession?

Get involved with the shows at school and see if that floats your boat. By involved, I mean the collaboration. Be part of a situation where a day might consist of a lofty conversation about characters and motivation one moment, and a how many sheets of plywood you need the next. A high school drama club can sometimes be a clique, so if you're not comfortable with that, seek out other opportunities in community theater.

SELECTED SCHOOLS

Many colleges and universities offer bachelor's degree programs in the arts; some have programs in theater, film, and television production as well. The student may also gain initial training through enrollment at a community college. Below are listed some of the more prominent institutions in this field.

Art Center College of Design
1700 Lida Street
Pasadena, CA 91103
626.396.2200
www.artcenter.edu

Carnegie-Mellon University
5000 Forbes Avenue
Pittsburgh, PA 15213
412.268.2000
www.cmu.edu

Columbia University
116th Street and Broadway
New York, NY 10027
212.854.1754
www.columbia.edu

Loyola Marymount
1 Loyola Marymount University Drive
Los Angeles, CA 90045
310.338.2700
www.lmu.edu

New York University
70 Washington Square S.
New York, NY 10012
212.998.1212
www.nyu.edu

Parsons The New School for Design
66 5th Avenue
New York, NY 10011
212.229.8900
www.newschool.edu/parsons

Pratt Institute
2000 Willoughby Avenue
Brooklyn, NY 11205
718.636.3600
www.pratt.edu

Rhode Island School of Design
2 College Street
Providence, RI 02903
401.454.6100
www.risd.edu

University of Southern California
Los Angeles, CA 90089
323.442.1130
www.usc.edu

University of Texas–Austin
110 Inner Campus Drive
Austin, TX 78712
512.471.3434
www.utexas.edu

MORE INFORMATION

Art Directors Club
106 West 29th Street
New York, NY 10001
212.643.1440
www.adcglobal.org

Art Directors Guild
11969 Ventura Boulevard, 2nd Floor
Studio City, CA 91604
818.762.9995
www.adg.org

Association of Independent Colleges of Art and Design
236 Hope Street
Providence, RI 02906
401.270.5991
www.aicad.org

National Association of Broadcasters
1771 N Street NW
Washington, DC 20036
202.429.5300
www.nab.org

Set Decorators Society of America
7100 Tujunga Avenue, Suite A
North Hollywood, CA 91605
818.255.2425
www.setdecorators.org

Michael Auerbach/Editor

Multimedia Artist & Animator

Snapshot

Career Cluster: Arts, A/V Technology & Communications
Interests: Art, Illustration, Web Design, Cartooning
Earnings (Yearly Average): $62,021
Employment & Outlook: Slower Than Average Growth Expected

OVERVIEW

Sphere of Work

Multimedia artists and animators create visual effects and animations for television, movies, video games, and other media. They create two- and three-dimensional models and animations. They may be involved in the creation of media advertisements and other marketing campaigns, or create illustrations for websites, online magazines, and other forms of media. Some are self-employed, working from home offices, while others work for film, television, and video production companies of varying sizes.

Work Environment

Multimedia artists and animators often work in studio environments that are generally clean and comfortable, or they work in a home office/studio. Their hours vary based on the size and scope of the project on which they are working, as well as the time constraints established in a contract. Smaller companies and independent, self-employed artists tend to work longer hours to manage not only their projects but also the issues associated with running a small business.

Profile

Working Conditions: Office/Production Studio Some Out Side Work
Physical Strength: Light To Moderate Work
Education Needs: Technical/ Community College Bachelor's Degree
Licensure/Certification: Recommended
Physical Abilities Not Required: No Strenuous Work
Opportunities For Experience: Apprenticeship, Military Service Volunteer Work, Part-Time Work
Holland Interest Score*: RCE

* See Appendix A

Occupation Interest

Multimedia artists and animators must combine a talent for art and creative thinking with good research and communication skills, close attention to detail, and the ability to meet deadlines and work in a competitive atmosphere, all while remaining true to the needs of the client. They should be aware of general public attitudes and keep up with current trends. Many independent commercial artists set their own hours and act as small business entrepreneurs as well as creative artists.

A Day in the Life—Duties and Responsibilities

The duties and responsibilities of multimedia artists and animators vary based on the area and the size of the business in which they work. These artists may specialize in video games or animated movies, or they may create visual effects for television shows or online venues. They can further specialize in particular elements, such as characters or scenery or pieces that contribute to the overall look and feel of a digital production.

In general, multimedia artists and animators first confer with clients or supervisors to establish the preferred design approach, budget, and anything else that needs to be taken into account. They then develop the requested design, often showing samples to the client at different points in the process. The artist may work independently, or as part of a team overseen by an art director. In a team setting, the art director's job is to assign tasks, give the artists advice and feedback, and approve and present the final product.

Duties and Responsibilities

- **Conferring with clients, other artists, and directors to determine budgets and timelines**
- **Creating graphics and animations using computer programs**
- **Developing storyboards that lay out the main scenes in a production**
- **Editing and refining the work in response to feedback**

WORK ENVIRONMENT

Skills and Abilities

Communication Skills
- Expressing thoughts and ideas
- Understanding others' wishes

Creative/Artistic Skills
- Creating ideas
- Translating ideas into concrete forms

Interpersonal/Social Skills
- Respecting others' opinions
- Working as part of a team

Organization & Management Skills
- Adhering to time schedules
- Making decisions
- Paying attention to and handling details

Technical Skills
- Performing technical work using computer programs

Physical Environment

Multimedia artists and animators work primarily in video production firms, studios, or office spaces in film and television companies. These environments are well lit and well ventilated, with computers and other production and display technologies. Many artists/animators are independent consultants who work from studios and office spaces in their own private residences.

Human Environment

Depending on their areas of expertise, multimedia artists and animators meet and interact with a wide range of individuals. These parties include creative professionals, business executives, editors, designers, and other specialized commercial artists.

Technological Environment

Multimedia artists and animators might not only use computer programs in their work but also may be required to write programming code in order to create or mount their art.. For this reason a solid grounding in digital graphics technology is a must. Some animation studios have their own software and computer applications that they use to create films. They give workers on-the-job training to use this software.

EDUCATION, TRAINING, AND ADVANCEMENT

High School/Secondary

High school students should study art, including drawing, photography, and design; math, including geometry; and computer science, including graphic design and drafting. They should also take advantage of any subject areas of interest to them as artists; for example, future animators are advised to take cartooning and media classes.

Suggested High School Subjects

- Applied Math
- Arts
- Cartooning
- Computer Science
- Crafts
- Drafting
- English
- Graphic Communications
- Photography
- Web Design

Famous First

The first entirely computer-animated film was *Toy Story,* released in 1995. It was produced by Pixar Studios under the control of Walt Disney Pictures. The film was an "instant classic," garnering $300 million in its first year and spawning legions of toys, video games, theme-park attractions, and other spin-offs—including two sequels.

Postsecondary

Aspiring multimedia artists and animators may pursue a bachelor's degree in graphic art, design, computer graphics, or a similar field. Alternatively, they may enroll in art or design institutes for programs with more studio time and a greater focus on graphic design, digital imaging, or illustration. Further education may be warranted depending on how an artist chooses to specialize. For example, a prospective art director may also study management or art administration, while somebody interested in animation would be well served by specialist programs in that field.

Related College Majors

- Art, General
- Computer Graphics
- Educational/Instructional Media Design
- Educational/Instructional Media Technology
- Fine/Studio Arts
- Graphic Design/Commercial Art & Illustration
- Illustration
- Multimedia Production
- Visual & Performing Arts
- Web Design

Adult Job Seekers

An internship or apprenticeship is a good way to gain necessary experience. Individuals looking for work can apply directly to the art or advertising director of a particular company, and may also find opportunities through professional organizations such as the American Institute of Graphic Arts (now known as AIGA). Any potential commercial artist must have a portfolio showing his or her best work.

Professional Certification and Licensure

Some organizations provide certification programs to help multimedia artists and animators become specialists in their particular fields. Such certification can provide a competitive edge for job candidates.

Additional Requirements

Multimedia artists and animators should be both creative and extremely knowledgeable of the wide range of media options available to them to meet a client's needs. They should be willing to listen to and communicate with clients who may or may not agree with their ideas. Such artists must have self-discipline and a strong work ethic, especially in light of the fact that many are self-employed.

Fun Fact

In 1920, Walter Elias Disney, at 19 years old, started working in animation at the Kansas City Slide Company.

Source: http://www.arenamalleswaram.com/animation_facts.html

EARNINGS AND ADVANCEMENT

Earnings of multimedia artists and animators depend on skill, education, and the type, size, and geographic location of the employer. Earnings of freelance multimedia artists and animators may vary with the artists' individual fees and reputation, as well as the nature and amount of work sold.

Median annual earnings of salaried multimedia artists and animators were $62,021 in 2012. The lowest ten percent earned less than $35,870, and the highest ten percent earned more than $105,820.

Earnings for self-employed multimedia artists and animators vary widely. Those struggling to gain experience and build a reputation may be forced to charge only small fees for their work. Well-established free-lancers may earn much more than salaried artists.

Multimedia artists and animators may receive paid vacations, holidays, and sick days; life and health insurance; and retirement benefits. These are usually paid for by the employer.

Metropolitan Areas with the Highest Employment Level in This Occupation

Metropolitan area	Employment[1]	Employment per thousand jobs	Hourly mean wage
Los Angeles-Long Beach-Glendale, CA	5,730	1.48	$43.11
Seattle-Bellevue-Everett, WA	2,330	1.65	$33.17
New York-White Plains-Wayne, NY-NJ	2,280	0.44	$35.03
San Francisco-San Mateo-Redwood City, CA	1,050	1.05	$34.33
Bridgeport-Stamford-Norwalk, CT	850	2.05	(8)
Chicago-Joliet-Naperville, IL	810	0.22	$30.52
Atlanta-Sandy Springs-Marietta, GA	790	0.35	$27.18
Oakland-Fremont-Hayward, CA	750	0.78	$41.83

[1] Does not include self-employed Source: Bureau of Labor Statistics, 2012

EMPLOYMENT AND OUTLOOK

Nationally, there were approximately 30,000 multimedia artists and animators employed in 2012. Employment is expected to grow slower than the average for all occupations through the year 2020, which means employment is projected to increase about 8 percent. Multimedia artists and animators should have better job opportunities than other artists, but still will experience competition. Demand for these workers will increase as consumers continue to require more realistic video games, movie and television special effects, and 3-D animated movies. Additional job openings will arise from the growth of computer graphics in the increasing number of mobile technologies. However, job growth will be limited by companies sending animation work overseas where workers can be paid less than in the United States.

Employment Trend, Projected 2010–20

Total, All Occupations: 14%

Art and Design Workers: 10%

Multimedia Artists and Animators: 8%

Note: "All Occupations" includes all occupations in the U.S. Economy Source: U.S. Bureau of Labor Statistics, Employment Projections Program

Related Occupations

- Art Director
- Designer
- Graphic Designer & Illustrator
- Industrial Designer
- Medical & Scientific Illustrator
- Photographer
- Software Developer
- Web Developer

Related Military Occupations

- Graphic Designer & Illustrator

Conversation With . . .
TYLER NAUGLE
MTV Production Assistant and Freelance Animator, 2 years

1. What was your individual career path in terms of education, entry-level job, or other significant opportunity?

At Maryland Institute, College of Art (MICA) I majored in 2D Animation with a concentration in Video. After my junior year I was fortunate to get an internship with MTV's On-Air Design department. Shortly before my 2011 graduation, I received a call from my previous supervisor at MTV who offered me Production Assistant position. I accepted the position and started working at MTV full-time a few weeks after graduation. I work on different projects: it could be animating, it could be editing. Something called a "lower third" is a big thing we work on; it pops out from the corner of the screen and gives information about a show coming out and directs the viewer toward something. I've also done some freelance jobs in my free time.

2. Are there many job opportunities in your profession? In what specific areas?

Animation is a big industry with a lot of opportunities. Corporations, independent film makers, small companies trying to show people what they're about...people are willing to pay for motion graphics. There is no shortage of people looking for motion graphics or animation in general.

I focus in 2D Animation and there are an assortment of positions available (Key Artist, In-betweener, Background Artist, Effects Artist, Motion Designer). At MTV, I'm specifically in motion graphics. Work assignments are mainly elements for TV, and more subdued than what I do in my spare time, which is very character-based, usually revolving around humor, and much more manic.

3. What do you wish you had known going into this profession?

I wish that I had known more about negotiating pay. That is a topic that's only very briefly touched on in school and is a huge part of working as an artist.

4. How do you see your profession changing in the next five years?

I may be wrong, but it think animation is going toward a more graphic-based presentation even though there is always going to be a market for more experimental animation. Also, independents use Kickstarter. Outside the commercial side of things, that's where all the independent animation is going to be flourishing. That's where people should focus if they just want to do their own projects.

5. What role will technology play in those changes, and what skills will be required?

Technology is huge in the animation industry. Programs are constantly changing so you have to pay attention to what's new and what's being phased out. Depending on what you want to do, your toolkit could be completely different from your fellow animators. For example, I use mostly Flash and After Effects and edit in Premiere. There are people I know who use Toon Boom and edit in Final Cut. We end up with a similar product but how we each get there is completely different.

6. Do you have any general advice or additional professional insights to share with someone interested in your profession?

To work professionally as an animator is to essentially sell your abilities as a product and you need to be able to sell the product successfully. Being confident in your work and knowing what your abilities are worth is very important. Too many animators sell their abilities for way less than they are worth. This is a problem that I have found affects recent graduates more than any other group. It's something that a lot of people are uncomfortable talking about, and though pay varies depending on the type of job you're doing and the client that it's for, it's a good idea to talk about it with your peers to make sure that you're not getting taken advantage of.

7. Can you suggest a valuable "try this" for students considering a career in your profession?

Anyone wanting to go into animation should work with others as often as possible. Commercial animation requires you to work closely with peers. That's quite different from other fields within art and it's an aspect of the industry that some people might find difficult or unusual. Practicing that level of cooperation in school could be particularly useful; it has the potential to provide contacts that could be mutually beneficial in later years.

SELECTED SCHOOLS

A variety of colleges and universities offer bachelor's degree programs in graphic arts; some have programs in digital media and animation. The student may also gain initial training through enrollment at a community college. Below are listed some of the more prominent institutions in this field. stitutions in this field.

California State University, Fullerton
800 N. State College Boulevard
Fullerton, CA 92831
657.278.1600
www.fullerton.edu

City University of New York
535 E. 80th Street
New York, NY 10075
212.794.5555
www.cuny.edu

Drexel University
3141 Chestnut Street
Philadelphia, PA 19104
215.895.2000
www.drexel.edu
Emerson College

120 Boylston Street
Boston, MA 02116
617.824.8500
www.emerson.edu

Florida State University
600 W. College Avenue
Tallahassee, FL 32308
850.644.2525
www.fsu.edu

Lesley University
29 Everett Street
Cambridge, MA 02138
617.868.9600
www.lesley.edu

Louisiana State University
3357 Highland Road
Baton Rouge, LA 70802
225.578.3202
www.lsu.edu

North Carolina State University
2200 Hillsborough
Raleigh, NC 27695
919.515.2011
www.ncsu.edu

Syracuse University
900 S. Crouse Avenue
Syracuse, NY 13210
315.443.1870
syr.edu

University of Colorado, Denver
1250 14th Street
Denver, CO 80202
303.556.2400
www.ucdenver.edu

MORE INFORMATION

Association of Independent Colleges of Art and Design
236 Hope Street
Providence, RI 02906
401.270.5991
www.aicad.org

Computer Graphics Society
134 Gilbert Street
Adelaide, SA, 5000
AUSTRALIA
61.8.82128255
www.cgsociety.org

International Digital Media and Arts Association
P.O. Box 622
Agoura Hills, CA 91376
818.564.7898
idmaa.org

National Art Education Association
1806 Robert Fulton Drive, Suite 300
Reston, VA 20191-1590
703.860.8000
info@arteducators.org
www.naea-reston.org

Michael Auerbach/Editor

Photographer

Snapshot

Career Cluster: Arts, A/V Technology & Communications
Interests: Photography, Art, Photojournalism, Media, Technology
Earnings (Yearly Average): $30,867
Employment & Outlook: Average Growth Expected

OVERVIEW

Sphere of Work

Photographers capture images of various objects, people, and events using a film or digital camera. They must exhibit a solid understanding of technical camera operation and the fundamental processes behind photography, lighting, and the composition of an image. Most photographers focus on one area of photographic specialty. Photographic specialties include news, portrait, commercial and industrial, scientific, and fine arts photography. Because their profession is based on choosing image composition and creating unique images, creativity is a trait common among all types of photographers regardless of their area of specialization.

Work Environment

A photographer's work environment depends primarily on his or her area of photographic specialty. Some photographers, such as those who take studio portraits of children and families, work primarily out of comfortable, well-lit, indoor studios. Other photographers work outside in a multitude of environments and are subject to various weather conditions. Photographers who work for the government, advertising agencies, or private companies frequently maintain a forty-hour week. Freelance and newspaper photographers, or photojournalists, generally work irregular hours, travel often, and are expected to be on-call for last-minute projects or emergency events.

Profile

Working Conditions: Work Both Indoors And Outdoors
Physical Strength: Light to Medium Work
Education Needs: On-The-Job Training, High School Diploma or GED, Apprenticeship, Some College
Licensure/Certification: Usually Not Required
Physical Abilities Not Required: No Strenuous Work
Opportunities For Experience: Internship, Apprenticeship, Military Service, Volunteer Work, Part-Time Work
Holland Interest Score*: AES, ESA, RIC, RSE, SRC

* See Appendix A

Occupation Interest

Potential photographers should demonstrate a passion for artistic creation. They should be compelled to tell stories through photographs and possess a deep desire to analyze, present, and offer a unique perspective on their photographic subjects. They should express a definitive opinion through their photographs, and that opinion should be easily discernible to an audience examining their photography. They should be able to lead and work with different types of people and personalities.

A Day in the Life—Duties and Responsibilities

Most photographers purchase and maintain their own camera equipment, lenses, and accessories, which can be costly at the outset. Photographers usually work independently or with an assistant. They are responsible for the physical positioning of subjects as well as the arrangement of lighting and camera angles. If the photographs are taken with film (which is increasingly rare), the photographer develops the film and prints in either a darkroom or printing facility. Digital photographs may be edited and retouched prior to publishing or printing.

Photographers' specialties determine what they photograph and how those images are used. Portrait photographers specialize in photographing people or groups of people. They are generally self-employed and often travel to various locations for special events like weddings, school functions, and other special ceremonies. Commercial and industrial photographers travel to various locations to photograph landscapes, buildings, and merchandise. Their photographs are usually published in books, advertisements, catalogs, or other media. Scientific photographers make a photographic record of objects or events related to science and medicine. These photographers usually have technical training in the sciences as well as the arts. News photographers, or photojournalists, take pictures of relevant people or events for publication in regular newspapers or periodicals. Fine arts photographers are usually highly technically proficient, and may display their photographs in museums, art galleries, or private art shows.

Self-employed and freelance photographers must perform business and administrative tasks in addition to their creative work. Such tasks might include managing employees, handling billing and payments, setting appointments, and obtaining licenses, copyrights, contracts, and other legal documents as needed. They must also arrange their own advertising, marketing campaigns, and self-promotion.

OCCUPATION SPECIALTIES

Aerial Photographers

Aerial Photographers photograph segments of earth and other subject material from aircraft.

Scientific Photographers

Scientific Photographers use specialized equipment to illustrate and record scientific phenomena.

Studio Photographers

Studio Photographers photograph subjects in formal studios or similar settings, and use a variety of accessories. They normally specialize

Duties and Responsibilities

- **Composing subjects using distance, angle, and lighting**
- **Deciding on camera settings**
- **Using, lights, reflectors, screens and props**
- **Capturing subjects on film or in digital images**
- **Editing, printing, and publishing photographic images**
- **Marketing and advertising services to prospective clients**
- **Maintaining a professional portfolio**

in a particular area of photography, such as illustrative, fashion, or portrait.

Photojournalists

Photojournalists photograph newsworthy events, locations, people, or other illustrative and educational material for use in publications or telecasts, using a still camera.

Fine Arts Photographers

Fine Arts Photographers create photographs for sale as art.

Other Photographic Specialties

Other notable photographic specialties include: Architectural Photography, Forensic Photography, Landscape/Nature/Wildlife Photography, Sports Photography, and Wedding Photography.

WORK ENVIRONMENT

Physical Environment

A photographer's working conditions vary greatly depending on his or her specialty. Some photographers can work in clean, comfortable, well-ventilated studios. Others work in unpleasant or

Skills and Abilities

Communication Skills
- Speaking effectively

Creative/Artistic Skills
- Being skilled in art or photography
- Having a good eye for identifying and capturing subjects
- Displaying a sensitivity to color, light, and shadow

Interpersonal/Social Skills
- Listening to clients
- Cooperating with others
- Working independently and as a member of a team

Organization & Management Skills
- Handling challenging situations
- Paying attention to and handling details
- Promoting one's work to potential clients

Technical Skills
- Operating camera equipment
- Using digital editing software
- Working in a darkroom (film development)

dangerous outdoor environments. Photographers regularly travel to and from photographic sites. Those who process film and prints, especially in a darkroom, are exposed to potentially harmful chemicals.

Human Environment

Photographers work with numerous clients, customers, and subjects. They must interact easily with others, and they should be comfortable directing, evaluating, and occasionally comforting their photographic subjects. Photographers sometimes collaborate with graphic designers, journalists, reporters, and editors. Some may report to a supervisor or direct an assistant.

Technological Environment

Photographers must learn how to operate camera equipment in order to be successful. To create a photograph, photographers use film and digital cameras, film, digital memory and storage devices, tripods, lenses and filters, floodlights, reflectors, light meters, and electronic flash units. Image processing may require computers, imaging and editing software, printers and scanners, photographic paper, darkroom equipment, and chemicals for developing film and prints from film.

EDUCATION, TRAINING, AND ADVANCEMENT

High School/Secondary

High school students interested in becoming photographers should devote time to the study of communications, computers, art, photography, and media. Aspiring photographers should also engage in extracurricular activities (like the school newspaper or yearbook) that allow them to practice taking pictures, editing their work, and posting or printing their best photographs. Interested students should pursue part-time work with a photographer or store and consider applying to postsecondary photography programs.

Famous First

The first photograph to be sent via satellite from one location to another was an image of President Dwight D. Eisenhower taken in 1960. The picture was transmitted as a wirephoto from Cedar Rapids, Iowa, bounced off the Echo I satellite, and received in Dallas, Texas. One year before that, the first photograph of the earth taken in space was transmitted by the Explorer 6 satellite to a NASA unit in Hawaii.

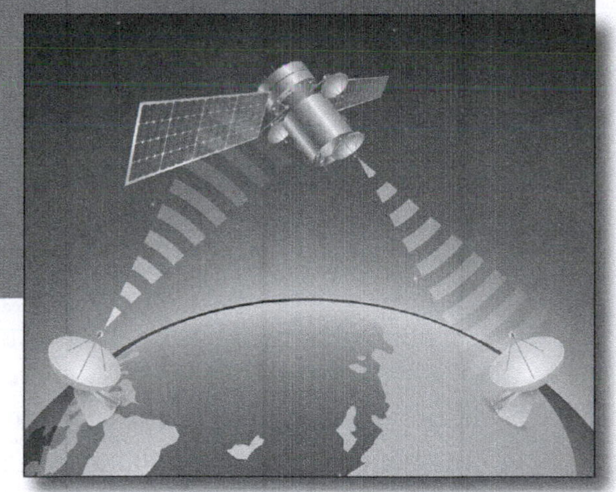

Suggested High School Subjects

- Arts
- Communications
- Computers & Digital Imaging
- Media Studies
- Photography

Photographer

Most photographers find it helpful to have an undergraduate degree or certificate in photography from a university, community college, private art school, or vocational institute. Many vocational education programs offer courses in visual imaging technology as well as in the fundamentals of photography. Other postsecondary programs teach students the practical and technical aspects of photography. Coursework may include the history of photography and cinema, camera maintenance, photojournalism, composition, color printing and print finishing, lighting, retouching, and other related subjects. Prospective freelance photographers may benefit from studying courses in business, including marketing, public relations, and business management.

Related College Majors

- Commercial Photography
- Digital Imaging
- Educational/Instructional Media Design
- Educational/Instructional Media Technology
- Fine/Studio Arts
- Photography

Adult Job Seekers

Many prospective photographers find positions as assistants to local, professional photographers after receiving their formal education. Assistants gain valuable technical experience, on-the-job training, and the practical skills needed to start their own businesses. Other job seekers apply for full- or part-time positions at camera shops, local newspapers, or photography studios. Candidates can also participate in apprenticeships, mentorships, or internships through their schools or photography training programs.

Many photographers subscribe to photography newsletters and magazines in order to make contacts in the industry. Networking, mentoring, and professional development opportunities are also frequently available through professional photographer associations.

Professional Certification and Licensure

Photographers are usually not required to obtain professional certification or licensure in their field; to an extent, this is because the work is highly visual, so photographers can easily provide samples of their work to others. Some professional photography organizations offer voluntary certifications, which may enhance a photographer's marketing and job-seeking efforts. To become a Certified Professional Photographer (CPP) through the Professional Photographers of America, candidates must pass a written exam and provide images for critique. Continuing education is typically required for certification renewal.

Additional Requirements

Photography is a well- respected form of artistic expression. Therefore, aspiring and professional photographers should be naturally artistic and able to understand the fundamentals of photographic composition. Because the field is intrinsically subjective, photographers should maintain the integrity and conviction necessary to present effective artwork and subject analysis, without reacting negatively to criticism. Photographers should be patient, have great eyesight, possess boundless imagination, and demonstrate impeccable communication skills when dealing with clients and subjects.

EARNINGS AND ADVANCEMENT

Earnings of photographers depend on geographic location, type of photographic specialty, number of hours worked, photographic skills and marketing ability. Most salaried photographers work full-time and earn more than the majority of self-employed photographers who usually work part-time, but some self-employed photographers have very high earnings. Unlike photojournalists and commercial photographers, very few fine arts photographers are successful enough to support themselves solely through this profession.

Median annual earnings of photographers were $30,867 in 2012. The lowest ten percent earned less than $18,388, and the highest ten percent earned more than $67,202.

Photographers may receive paid vacations, holidays, and sick days; life and health insurance; and retirement benefits. These are usually paid by the employer. Freelance and self-employed photographers must provide their own benefits.

Metropolitan Areas with the Highest Concentration of Jobs in this Occupation

Metropolitan area	Employment	Employment per thousand jobs	Hourly mean wage
New York-White Plains-Wayne, NY-NJ	3,100	0.60	$25.57
Chicago-Joliet-Naperville, IL	2,140	0.59	$24.93
Los Angeles-Long Beach-Glendale, CA	1,680	0.43	$28.68
Orlando-Kissimmee-Sanford, FL	1,500	1.48	$12.92
Atlanta-Sandy Springs-Marietta, GA	1,280	0.57	$14.21
Minneapolis-St. Paul-Bloomington, MN-WI	970	0.55	$23.88
Houston-Sugar Land-Baytown, TX	960	0.36	$15.91
Seattle-Bellevue-Everett, WA	900	0.64	$14.83

(1) Does not include self-employed. Source: Bureau of Labor Statistics, 2012

EMPLOYMENT AND OUTLOOK

There were approximately 56,000 photographers employed nationally in 2012. However, twice that many were self-employed. Some self-employed photographers have contracts with advertising agencies, magazine publishers, or other businesses to do individual projects for a set fee, while others operate portrait studios or provide photographs to stock-photo agencies. Most salaried photographers work in portrait or commercial photography studios; most of the others work for newspapers, magazines, and advertising agencies.

Employment is expected to grow about as fast as the average for all occupations through the year 2020, which means employment is projected to increase about 13 percent. Demand for portrait photography will increase as the population grows. As the number of electronic versions of magazines, journals and newspapers increases on the internet, commercial photographers will be needed to provide digital images.

Photography is a competitive field, and only those with the most skill and the best business ability will be able to find salaried positions or attract enough work to support themselves as self-employed photographers.

Employment Trend, Projected 2010–20

Total, All Occupations: 14%

Arts, Design, Entertainment, Sports, and Media Occupations: 13%

Photographers: 13%

Note: "All Occupations" includes all occupations in the U.S. Economy. Source: U.S. Bureau of Labor Statistics, Employment Projections Program

Related Occupations

- Art Director
- Camera Operator & Videographer
- Cinematographer
- Motion Picture/Radio/TV Art Director
- Photographic Process Worker

Related Military Occupations

- Audiovisual & Broadcast Technician
- Broadcast Journalist & Newswriter
- Photographic Specialist

Conversation With . . .
STEPHEN DONALDSON
Photographer, 18 years

1. What was your individual career path in terms of education, entry-level job, or other significant opportunity?

I got out of the business world after 13 years and am a self-taught, selfinstructed, self-managed photographer. I came from a profit-loss oriented place in sales, so when I got into this, I brought a sensibility and a skill set for selling my work. I always want to be mid-to-high level price-wise, then overdeliver the product. If you build and build, and consistently produce a good product, your photo business will eventually gain momentum that will carry you forward."

2. Are there many job opportunities in your profession? In what specific areas?

There are so many job opportunities in photography that intersect with other professions: sports photography, fashion, corporate, advertising, product, or tabletop photography. One of the things I do is have a lot of pokers in the fire. For instance, I also am a travel stock photographer and travel all over the planet on my own dime and photograph people, places, landmarks, towns, villages - everything that evokes a sense of the place. Directly or through my agent in New York, my photos get picked up and licensed for a cost for products such as educational books, encyclopedias, text books, calendars, even jigsaw puzzles.

3. What do you wish you had known going into this profession?

I had intermediate to advanced course instruction, mostly in high school. I often wish I had had more formal training as a photographer, and had a taken a more conventional path where I worked with another photographer and had more technical training – such as how to create certain lighting – that I wasn't able to do until I figured it out myself.

4. **How do you see your profession changing in the next five years?**

   You've kind of seen early developments of it. Photography, to me, is going in the direction of television: everything is supernatural, hypersaturated, and doesn't look like what it looks like in the real world to the naked eye. Everything looks too perfect. But I do understand that's what people's expectations are gravitating to. That is part of what technology is making possible and driving, this unnatural representation of the natural world. In addition, royalty-free photography options are increasing. When people are in need of something very different, something that is going Photographer 13 to put their product in a different space, or service, that's where they will gravitate away from royalty free imagery.

5. **What role will technology play in those changes, and what skills will be required?**

   Technology is creating and forcing certain changes regarding how to deliver theproduct. For instance, how long are coffee table - my published books – going to be marketable to the public? How much do I migrate from print work – framed – to digital copies of my work buyers can put on their TV screen on the wall, and how do I actually do that? How do I sell that file to them so they don't reproduce it or turn it over to five or six friends? Also, one of the strange conundrums for photographers: advances in technology have not made the equipment you use cheaper. When I started, a Nikon F5 was $1,800 to $2,000. Now, the top Nikon digital is $8,000. The price for professional level equipment has actually been rising as more technology goes into it, as opposed to dropping, like you see with computers and televisions.

6. **Do you have any general advice or additional professional insights to share with someone interested in your profession?**

   You need to learn how to use a camera and become technically proficient. Young people now, their world is very woven into new forms of media, including social media. If they embrace the media and they study the media and how photography and imagery is being used in new media – for editorial, for news, for fashion – they will see how photography is being used in the here and now in the most cutting edge ways to say what they want to say with an image.

7. **Can you suggest a valuable "try this" for students considering a career in your profession?**

   I would go into Facebook and create a photo page and post a picture a day or a week – maybe one out of 100 taken of a particular subject. For example, photograph the high school football team and put your best picture up and see if people like it. See how successful you are in building an audience, see what kind of comments and criticism you get. It's not always your friends – it's people who may be friends of friends and may not know you.

SELECTED SCHOOLS

Many colleges and universities offer bachelor's degree programs in the arts; some have majors or programs in photography. The student may also gain initial training through enrollment at a community college. Below are listed some of the more prominent institutions in this field.

Art Institute of Chicago
36 S. Wabash
Chicago, IL 60603
800.232.7242
www.saic.edu

California College of the Arts
5212 Broadway
Oakland, CA 94618
510.594.3600
www.cca.edu

California Institute of the Arts
24700 McBean Parkway
Valencia, CA 91355
661.255.1050
www.calarts.edu

Columbia College Chicago
600 S. Michigan Avenue
Chicago, IL 60605
312.369.1000
www.colum.edu

New York University
70 Washington Square S
New York, NY 10012
212.998.1212
www.nyu.edu

Rhode Island School of Design
2 College Street
Providence, RI 02903
800.364.7473
www.risd.edu

Rochester Institute of Technology
1 Lomb Memorial Drive
Rochester, NY 14623
585.475.2411
www.rit.edu

University of California, Los Angeles
405 Hilgard Avenue
Los Angeles, CA 90095
310.825.4321
www.ucla.edu

University of New Mexico
1 University Boulevard NE
Albuquerque, NM 87131
505.277.0111
www.unm.edu

Yale University
New Haven, CT 06520
203.432.4771
www.yale.edu

MORE INFORMATION

American Society of Media Photographers
150 North 2nd Street
Philadelphia, PA 19106
215.451.2767
www.asmp.org

American Society of Photographers
3120 N. Argonne Drive
Milwaukee, WI 53222
www.asofp.com

Association of Independent Colleges of Art and Design
236 Hope Street
Providence, RI 02906
401.270.5991
www.aicad.org

National Press Photographers Association, Inc.
3200 Croasdaile Drive, Suite 306
Durham, NC 27705
919.383.7246
www.nppa.org

North American Nature Photography Association
6382 Charleston Road
Alma, IL 62807
618.547.7616
www.nanpa.org

Professional Photographers of America, Inc.
229 Peachtree Street, NE, Suite 2200
Atlanta, GA 30303
800.786.6277
www.ppa.com
PPA Awards:
www.ppa.com/competitions/

Briana Nadeau/Editor

Prepress Technician

Snapshot

Career Cluster: Media & Communications, Technology, Manufacturing
Interests: Print Media, Graphic Design, Technology
Earnings (Yearly Average): $38,457
Employment & Outlook: Decline Expected

OVERVIEW

Sphere of Work

Prepress technicians work to prepare and format print jobs and to maintain operations and equipment related to the print-production process. Prepress technicians are employed in all fields of printing, from books and newspapers to brochures, magazines, and advertising inserts. Prepress technicians also hold important postproduction responsibilities, including monitoring the printing process and examining newly printed items for imperfections. Although their role may overlap with printing machine operators, especially in smaller facilities,

prepress technicians are primarily concerned with ensuring that all of a client's electronic text and image files are in order and have been formatted for print according to specifications. Technicians may also be responsible for daily, weekly, and annual maintenance tasks for print production equipment.

Work Environment

Prepress technicians work in print-operations facilities and similar industrial settings. While some of their tasks may require use of administrative offices, technicians typically spend the majority of their time in and around printers and printing presses, particularly the set-up and control equipment. The work environment for prepress technicians is exclusively indoors, traditionally in a temperature-controlled environment. Given the number of steps involved in the completion of a printing project, prepress technicians may work closely with a multitude of other professionals, including editors, designers, account managers, graphic artists, and production coordinators.

Profile

Working Conditions: Office/Production Studio Some Out Side Work
Physical Strength: Light To Moderate Work
Education Needs: Technical/ Community College Bachelor's Degree
Licensure/Certification: Recommended
Physical Abilities Not Required: No Strenuous Work
Opportunities For Experience: Apprenticeship, Military Service Volunteer Work, Part-Time Work
Holland Interest Score*: RCE

* See Appendix A

Occupation Interest

Prepress technicians are traditionally process-oriented, results-driven professionals who have an appreciation for and dedication to print media and the graphic arts, coupled with a diverse knowledge of technology (including desktop publishing software) and machinery. The profession traditionally attracts creative minds who enjoy team-oriented projects in addition to individuals who are able to simultaneously handle several tasks of varying priority.

A Day in the Life—Duties and Responsibilities

The daily occupational duties and responsibilities of prepress technicians include setting up and prioritizing different print jobs, reviewing test prints, maintaining equipment, and interacting with clients and project managers. Preprint responsibilities include retrieving graphics and text files from computers and transferring this information to printing software. Technicians must then make any necessary adjustments to the graphics or the text in order to ensure the quality of their print reproduction. Depending on the type and scope of a particular project, this process may require extensive collaboration with content creators and other production personnel. Prepress technicians must also be on the lookout for any last-minute changes that could be submitted prior to an actual print run.

Preprint technicians monitor printing jobs while the jobs are in process, examining each page, graphic, and photo for clarity and resolution. In addition to ensuring that the printing apparatus is functioning properly and has enough ink and printing material to complete a project from beginning to end, prepress technicians must also monitor machinery to ensure its proper function throughout a printing project. Additionally, they often discuss the efficiency of print runs upon their completion and strategize with managerial staff to emphasize continued quality and efficiency in future projects.
and anything else that needs to be taken into account. They then develop the requested design, often showing samples to the client at different points in the process. The artist may work independently, or as part of a team overseen by an art director. In a team setting, the art director's job is to assign tasks, give the artists advice and feedback, and approve and present the final product.

Duties and Responsibilities

- **Using computers to prepare text and pictures for printing**
- **Handling special equipment that alters the look of text**
- **Using sophisticated photograph and color separation equipment**
- **Laying out text and photos in aesthetically pleasing ways**
- **Working with other members of the prepress team**

WORK ENVIRONMENT

Physical Environment

Multimedia artists and animators work primarily in video production Prepress technicians typically work in indoor, temperature-controlled environments or print-manufacturing facilities. Typical businesses include newspaper-printing facilities, design shops, art studios, and even clothing mills (for printed apparel).

Relevant Skills and Abilities

Analytical Skills

- Checking work against specifications

Communication Skills

- Speaking effectively
- Writing concisely

Interpersonal/Social Skills

- Being able to work both independently and as part of a team

Organization & Management Skills

- Following instructions
- Managing time
- Meeting goals and deadlines
- Paying attention to and handling details

Technical Skills

- Working with machines, tools or other objects
- Working with your hands and eyes

Human Environment

Prepress technicians often work with other professionals, from designers, artists, and fellow print professionals to salespeople, outside vendors, and repair technicians.

Technological Environment

Prepress technicians are traditionally well versed in a variety of administrative, design, and print software programs. They are equally adept at contemporary printing systems (including color separations and offset printing) and may possess knowledge related to the development and continued evolution of printing technology.

EDUCATION, TRAINING, AND ADVANCEMENT

High School/Secondary

High school students can best prepare for a job as a prepress technician by completing courses in basic mathematics, chemistry, photography, desktop publishing, and computer use. Drafting, industrial arts, and traditional art classes can also be useful for future design work. High school journalism and yearbook production projects can provide students with a basic background in publishing and printing.example, future animators are advised to take cartooning and media classes.

Suggested High School Subjects

- Computers
- Graphic Arts & Desktop Publishing
- Industrial Arts
- Mathematics

Famous First

The first typesetting machine not to employ metal type was the "photographic line composing machine" manufactured by Intertype Corporation of Brooklyn, N.Y. in 1949. It used film negatives in place of the more traditional metal.

Postsecondary

Professionals come to the printing industry from a variety of educational backgrounds. While postsecondary education is not traditionally a requirement for entry-level positions, managerial roles do often require postsecondary or certificate-level study in a related field, such as communications, graphic design, lithography, fashion design, or business.

Printing and document-imaging certification courses are available at many community colleges nationwide. Such instruction provides aspiring printing professionals with a basic understanding of print-and-scan processes, electromechanical components, color theory, and printing-apparatus safety.

Related College Majors

- Desktop & Digital Publishing
- Graphic Arts & Printing

Adult Job Seekers

A job as a prepress technician can be ideal for many adult job seekers, depending on the type of printing and the volume of work a company prints on a weekly basis. Prepress technicians employed by small-scale or specialty print operations or publishing houses often work traditional weekday hours, with holidays and weekends off. Those who work for large publishers, manufacturers, or media companies that create printed items on a daily basis may be required to work sporadic shifts, frequent overtime, and weekends to meet demand.

Professional Certification and Licensure

Certification is not a traditional prerequisite for employment as a prepress technician.

Additional Requirements

A strong commitment to detail and quality are the hallmarks of printing professionals. Many are specialized, creatively fueled professionals who pride themselves on delivering the highest-quality product possible to clients, on budget and in a timely manner.

EARNINGS AND ADVANCEMENT

Earnings depend on the size, geographic location and extent of unionization of the employer, and the specific occupation and years of experience of the employee. Advancement is usually dictated by years of experience, capability, and whether or not the employee has interest in going into management.

Median annual earnings of prepress technicians were $38,457 in 2012. Unionized prepress technicians may receive paid vacations, holidays, and sick days; life and health insurance; and retirement benefits. These are usually paid by the employer. Hourly or salaried prepress technicians in non-union shops may or may not have these benefits.

Metropolitan Areas with the Highest Employment Level in This Occupation

Metropolitan area	Employment[1]	Employment per thousand jobs	Hourly mean wage
Chicago-Joliet-Naperville, IL	1,350	0.37	$22.91
Los Angeles-Long Beach-Glendale, CA	1,320	0.34	$21.44
Minneapolis-St. Paul-Bloomington, MN-WI	1,270	0.73	$23.08
New York-White Plains-Wayne, NY-NJ	1,260	0.24	$22.23
Santa Ana-Anaheim-Irvine, CA	900	0.64	$20.19
Philadelphia, PA	820	0.45	$20.18
Dallas-Plano-Irving, TX	780	0.37	$18.76
Washington-Arlington-Alexandria, DC-VA-MD-WV	680	0.29	$24.61

(1) Does not include self-employed Source: Bureau of Labor Statistics, 2012

EMPLOYMENT AND OUTLOOK

Nationally, in 2012, prepress technicians held about 41,000 jobs. Employment is expected to decline through the year 2020. This country is experiencing an ongoing need for printed material, due to rising personal income, increased school enrollment, and higher levels of educational attainment, but the use of computers in desktop publishing and similar applications will contribute to the elimination of many jobs for prepress technicians.

Employment Trend, Projected 2010–20

Total, All Occupations: 14%

Printing Press Operators: -1%

Print Binding and Finishing Workers: -3%

Printing Workers: -4%

Prepress Technicians and Workers: -16%

Note: "All Occupations" includes all occupations in the U.S. Economy Source: U.S. Bureau of Labor Statistics, Employment Projections Program

Related Occupations

- Desktop & Digital Publishing Specialist
- Photoengraver & Lithographer
- Photographer
- Photographic Process Worker
- Printing Machine Operator

Conversation With . . .

JULIO PEREIRA

Prepress Technician, 29 years

1. What was your individual career path in terms of education, entry-level job, or other significant opportunity?

I came out of a technical high school that provided a two year major in printing/graphic arts. They provided an introduction to hand composition, provided classes in camera work, a little bit of art, and an overview of the actual careers within the printing industry you could go into. Typesetting back then was a career. Printing as a whole provided a lot of flexibility. It was the dawn of the digital age, and I was interested in that.

2. Are there many job opportunities in your profession? In what specific areas?

Unfortunately prepress is an area where jobs are being eliminated more and more as everything becomes more automated. We don't actually do the creative component anymore; we're not putting books and catalogs together. We're taking something that's already formatted and are inspecting, fixing, and cleaning up the file, making sure it's going to print correctly. We provide expert help and consulting to help those files come in correctly. If you want to create a beautiful piece, you still have to learn the basics of design, but it's mostly done by the customer, even if they hire a design studio.

3. What do you wish you had known going into this profession?

Things change so fast. I wouldn't have made a different choice, but anybody starting out needs to realize everything changes. Those who will survive are those who can be flexible and adapt. Sometimes that means going back to school, maybe upgrading your skills at the college level.

4. How do you see your profession changing in the next five years?

I see more automation. In five years' time, fewer and fewer people will be needed in the prepress industry. My own personal opinion is that a prepress operator is almost becoming an expert on workflow systems, to consult on the whole flow of how to manage and perfect the design of a file coming into a company until it goes to press.

5. What role will technology play in those changes?

You may need more than a high school education. Most people we have hired in recent years have a university education. Knowing basic programming is an asset. For example, the ability to write Applescripts will go a long way in automating repetitive tasks. A prepress operator should also be a creative thinker because he or she may also be involved in setting up automated workflows and may be asked to come up with solutions to help with automation processes.

6. Do you have any general advice or additional professional insights to share with someone interested in your profession?

This is not specific to prepress, but don't assume that the job you're doing is the only job you need to be doing. Learn the other jobs in your company; learning these other functions is going to help you do your job better because you'll know what your co-workers need. Learn the entire process, and you'll become more valued and have a better knowledge of the business as a whole.

7. Can you suggest a valuable "try this" for students considering a career in your profession?

Volunteer to do internships for a couple of months in the summer, if you can, for a printing company. See what goes on, and see if it's something you want to do. The other thing to keep in mind is to learn some of the tools in pre-press. Some are used in other areas of media and communications, such as Photoshop or Illustrator in web design.

SELECTED SCHOOLS

Many technical and community colleges offer programs in graphic arts and printing technology, as well as desktop and digital publishing. Below are listed some of the more prominent four-year institutions in this field.

Black Hills State University
1200 University Street
Spearfish, SD 57799
800.255.2478
www.bhsu.edu

California Polytechnic State University
San Louis Obispo, CA 93407
805.756.1111
www.calpoly.edu

California State University, Los Angeles
5151 State University Drive
Los Angeles, CA 90032
323.343.3000
www.calstatela.edu

Ferris State University
1201 S. State Street
Big Rapids, MI 49307
231.591.2000
www.ferris.edu

Idaho State University
921 S. 8th Street
Pocatello, ID 83209
208.282.0211
www.isu.edu

Rochester Institute of Technology
1 Lomb Memorial Drive
Rochester, NY 14623
585.475.2411
www.rit.edu

St. Mary's University of Minnesota
700 Terrace Heights
Winona, MN 55987
507.457.6987
www.smumn.edu

Texas State University, San Marcos
601 University Drive
San Marcos, TX 78666
512.245.2111
www.txstate.edu

University of Houston
4800 Calhoun Road
Houston, TX 77004
713.743.2255
www.uh.edu

Western Illinois University
1 University Circle
Macomb, IL 61455
309.298.1414
www.wiu.edu

MORE INFORMATION

Graphic Arts Education and Research Foundation
1899 Preston White Drive
Reston, VA 20191
703.264.7200
www.gaerf.org

Graphic Communications International Union
International Brotherhood of Teamsters
25 Louisiana Avenue, NW
Washington, DC 20001
202.624.6800
www.teamster.org/content/graphics-communications

National Association for Printing Leadership
1 Meadowlands Plaza, Suite 1511
East Rutherford, NJ 07073
800.642.6275
www.napl.org

Printing Industries of America
200 Deer Run Road
Sewickley, PA 15143
800.910.4283
www.printing.org

John Pritchard/Editor

Production Coordinator

Snapshot

Career Cluster: Manufacturing, Media & Communications, Distribution & Logistics, Arts & Entertainment
Interests: Business Administration, Manufacturing, Industrial Processing, Quality Control
Earnings (Yearly Average): $44,753
Employment & Outlook: Slower Than Average Growth Expected

OVERVIEW

Sphere of Work

Production coordinators oversee the efficiency and productivity of goods at manufacturing and industrial processing facilities. They also work in editorial, graphic design, and other such offices, where they track and handle materials prior to their reaching the manufacturing stage. In addition, they work as stage and television production employees. Production coordinators are sometimes called manufacturing supervisors, production managers, or operations supervisors/ managers, depending on the type of business and the individual's

level of experience. The production coordinator is traditionally a junior management– or management-level position. A (manufacturing) coordinator's primary responsibility is to ensure that production, processing, or manufacturing work orders are met in a cost efficient and timely manner. They also ensure that products are created according to quality specifications, customer expectations, and with respect to worker safety. Similar responsibilities fall to production coordinators in other fields, where the components being monitored are not tangible goods but other materials or processes involved in a production effort.

Work Environment

Production coordinators are employed in all facets of industrial manufacturing and related areas. They work in processing facilities and manufacturing complexes that produce such goods as fabricated metal, textiles, transportation equipment, chemicals, computers, and books and magazines. Production coordinators in the agricultural, livestock, and food processing industries may be required to work outdoors and in inclement conditions, depending on their particular realm of industry. Those in the media industry, on the other hand, work in offices, studios, or printing plants.

Profile

Working Conditions: Office/Production Studio Some Out Side Work
Physical Strength: Light To Moderate Work
Education Needs: Technical/ Community College Bachelor's Degree
Licensure/Certification: Recommended
Physical Abilities Not Required: No Strenuous Work
Opportunities For Experience: Apprenticeship, Military Service Volunteer Work, Part-Time Work
Holland Interest Score*: RCE

* See Appendix A

Occupation Interest

team players who possess the ability to explicate instructions and complex systems in an informed but easily understandable manner. Production coordinators are also often innately sensitive to the potential for problems, both within production systems and in work processes and among workers assigned to a job. They possess a keen ability to handle situations and relationships in a manner that is beneficial to organizational productivity.

A Day in the Life—Duties and Responsibilities

Production coordinators have numerous daily responsibilities that are made more complex by the fact that they are traditionally the sole senior representative of a production branch within a particular company or organization.

Production coordinators must stay in constant contact with both their supervisors, fellow managers, and team of subordinates, keeping them informed of success and failures in the production processes, suggesting arenas for improvement, and ensuring that all necessary equipment maintenance and facility upkeep is completed.
In addition to routinely monitoring the production processes, its materials, procedures, and surroundings, production coordinators are also responsible for making sure each process is undertaken in the most efficient and productive way. It is the responsibility of production managers to suggest improvements to processes. These changes are done through systematic changes, the inclusion of new or updated equipment, or through eliminating steps coordinators deem unnecessary or redundant.

Production coordinators work closely with account management and sales teams to ensure that clients are satisfied with the goods and services they order. Similarly, they are often the key point of contact for outside vendors who sell supplies and ingredients to manufacturing facilities. They also oversee plant safety and quality control and ensure all production systems and related equipment is operating within the specifications of local, state, and federal regulations.

Duties and Responsibilities

- **Distributing work orders to departments**
- **Contacting sellers to verify shipment of goods on promised shipping dates**
- **Revising schedules according to work order specifications, priorities and availability of workers and equipment**
- **Compiling production records**
- **Establishing completion dates for material**
- **Keeping inventory**
- **Communicating with transportation companies to prevent delays in transit**

OCCUPATION SPECIALTIES

Material Coordinators

Material Coordinators coordinate and expedite the flow of material, parts, and assemblies within or between departments in accordance with production and shipping schedules or department priorities

Customer Service Coordinators

Customer Service Coordinators coordinate the production of printed materials, prepress or printing services with customers' requirements, and confer with customers throughout job production to keep them informed of the status of the job. They determine the materials to be used for the job, plan and draw the layout of the job, and route the materials to the proper work areas.

Production Clerks

Production Clerks compile data from customers' orders, production estimates, and perpetual (continuing) inventory to prepare production schedules, records and reports.

WORK ENVIRONMENT

Physical Environment

Production coordinators work primarily in industrial and manufacturing facilities. However, the position is required in any workflow that results in an end product, including publishing, agriculture, food services, and broadcasting.

Human Environment

Strong collaboration and management skills are required of all production coordinator positions. Production coordinators are required to direct and motivate their staff on a daily basis and often act as

Skills and Abilities

Communication Skills
- Checking work against specifications

Interpersonal/Social Skills
- Cooperating with others
- Working as a member of a team

Organization & Management Skills
- Coordinating tasks
- Making decisions
- Managing people/groups

Organization & Management Skills
- Paying attention to and handling details
- Performing duties that may change frequently

Planning & Research Skills
- Analyzing information
- Developing evaluation strategies

Technical Skills
- Working with computers, machines, or other technologies

the point person in production departments to other senior management staff.

Technological Environment

The technological parameters of each production coordinator position vary from industry to industry. However, familiarity with basic technological and mechanical processes is required. Often, some form of inventory management and tracking software is used in carrying out the job, typically in combination with some form of scheduling and cost-control software.

EDUCATION, TRAINING, AND ADVANCEMENT

High School/Secondary

High school students can best prepare for a career as a production coordinator by engaging in coursework such as mathematics, business administration, and computer science. Advanced placement classes in these subjects are especially recommended. Drafting, industrial arts, and engineering classes can also serve as important precursors related to systems design.

Participation in team sports, student government, and other intramural or extra-curricular activities can also lay the groundwork for future leadership positions

Suggested High School Subjects

- Bookkeeping
- Business
- English
- Mathematics

Famous First

The first bar code and scanner were invented in 1949, but it wasn't until 1961 that bar codes came into use in commerce. Their first use there was in tracking railroad cars on the Boston & Maine line. Later, bar codes were used primarily in retail settings. In recent years, they have made their way back to logistics, as managers track the flow of materials and goods from one point to another using scanning technology.

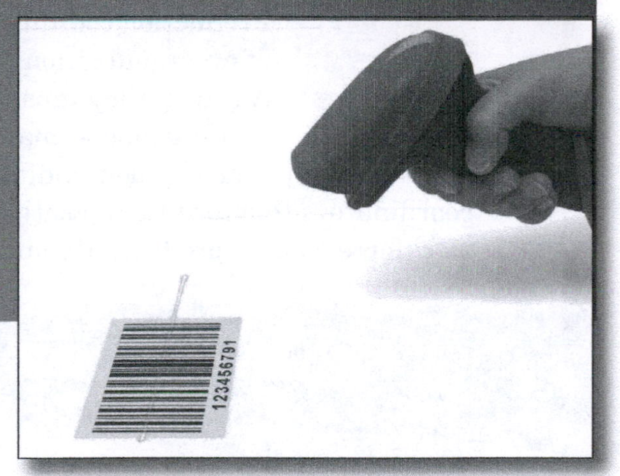

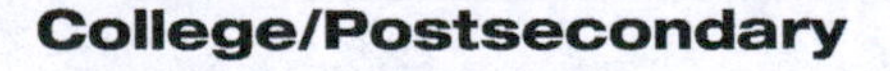

College/Postsecondary

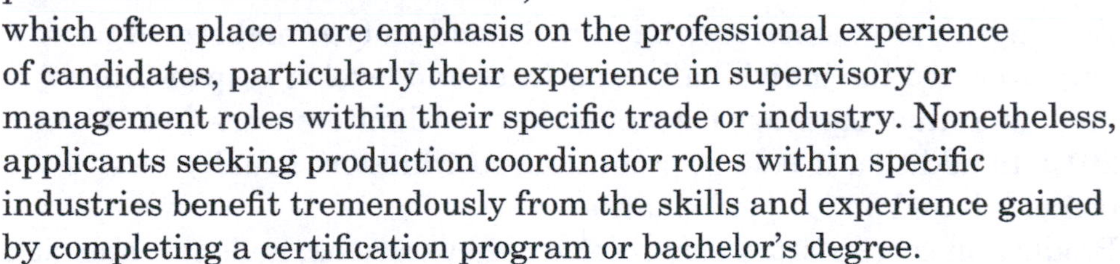

Postsecondary education is not traditionally a requirement for production coordinator vacancies, which often place more emphasis on the professional experience of candidates, particularly their experience in supervisory or management roles within their specific trade or industry. Nonetheless, applicants seeking production coordinator roles within specific industries benefit tremendously from the skills and experience gained by completing a certification program or bachelor's degree.

Related College Majors

- Business Administration
- Industrial Production Management
- Operations Management & Supervision

Adult Job Seekers

Production coordinators are often required to work lengthy hours in addition to late night and weekend shifts. They may be required to be on-call and may be called into work during emergencies or as substitutes for absent employees. Depending on their particular industry, production coordinators often possess experience as production employees.

Professional Certification and Licensure

Certification and licensure for production coordinators is contingent on their particular realm of industry. Facilities supervisors and managers may also be required to possess annually updated certification issued by organizations such as the Occupational Safety and Health Administration.

Additional Requirements

Production coordinators play a major role in the morale of an organization, regardless of its size or output. As such, they must possess the ability to motivate staff members, many of whom have jobs that may be repetitive or physically demanding. It is often the task of production coordinators to maintain a positive morale among the production workforce so that productivity and profits can be maximized.

EARNINGS AND ADVANCEMENT

Earnings of production coordinators depend on type and size of the employer and the individual's experience and level of responsibility. Median annual earnings for production coordinators were $44,753 in 2012. In addition to salary, production coordinators usually receive bonuses based on job performance.

Production coordinators may receive paid vacations, holidays, and sick days; life and health insurance; and retirement benefits. These are usually paid by the employer.

Metropolitan Areas with the Highest Employment Level in This Occupation

Metropolitan area	Employment[1]	Employment per thousand jobs	Hourly mean wage
Los Angeles-Long Beach-Glendale, CA	4,820	1.25	$48.33
Houston-Sugar Land-Baytown, TX	3,930	1.49	$60.71
Chicago-Joliet-Naperville, IL	3,740	1.03	$46.17
Minneapolis-St. Paul-Bloomington, MN-WI	3,520	2.01	$51.25
Detroit-Livonia-Dearborn, MI	2,780	3.99	$54.85
Cleveland-Elyria-Mentor, OH	2,720	2.74	$45.64
Warren-Troy-Farmington Hills, MI	2,680	2.50	$54.76
New York-White Plains-Wayne, NY-NJ	2,470	0.48	$59.36

[1] Does not include self-employed Source: Bureau of Labor Statistics, 2012

EMPLOYMENT AND OUTLOOK

Nationally, there were approximately 161,000 production managers employed in 2012. Employment is expected to grow slower than the average for all occupations through the year 2020, which means employment is projected to increase about 9 percent. As more pressure is put on companies to manufacture and deliver their products more quickly and efficiently, the need for production coordinators will grow. However, the expected employment decline in manufacturing will limit the overall growth of this occupation.

Employment Trend, Projected 2010–20

Total, All Occupations: 14%

Industrial Production Managers: 9%

Management Occupations: 7%

Note: "All Occupations" includes all occupations in the U.S. Economy Source: U.S. Bureau of Labor Statistics, Employment Projections Program

Related Occupations

- Cost Estimator
- Dispatcher
- Operations Research Analyst
- Purchasing Agent
- Transportation Manager

Conversation With . . . Harold Cabrera

Project Manager, 13 years

1. What was your individual career path in terms of education, entry-level job, or other significant opportunity?

I graduated with a Bachelor of Technology degree in Graphic Communications Management from Ryerson University in Toronto, Ontario, CA. This 4-year program catered to the graphic arts industry, including media, print, and business. There is a third year internship requirement, which opens network opportunities between students and industry contacts. I was fortunate enough to have multiple offers for my internship and pursued the commercial print sector for the experience and exposure I'd gain from producing a variety of print products. I also was exposed to many sides of the business - estimating, sales, customer service and operations.

I graduated with the knowledge and background employers were looking for in such a dynamic industry. I continued working in the commercial print sector where new technology at the time was shaping the industry. It was clear that change is critical and businesses must adapt in order to compete. I took an entry level position as a customer service representative and was exposed to every department, from estimating and sales to production. My interests were more into the technical side, working with sales and operations to understand and come up with a plan to support customer needs. This includes testing files and automating workflow – essentially, we are simplifying the technical part of the business and making our approach to clients smooth.

I then had an opportunity to work for Webcom; the company specialized in book manufacturing. Coming from a commercial print background, I had the experience in the print process side. However, this was a different market and a longer manufacturing cycle. I started as a Junior Project Manager and, with experience and training, gradually became a Senior Project Manager and take on very simple to complicated projects.

2. Are there many job opportunities in your profession? In what specific areas?

Yes, in print, media and packaging.

3. What do you wish you had known going into this profession?

How critical Business Information Systems development would be in today's business world.

4. How do you see your profession changing in the next five years?

We will see a greater online presence and improved business systems to support the business and customers.

5. What role will technology play in those changes, and what skills will be required?

It will be significant for digital print technology and business systems. On the printing side, this will mean more new roles to support digital print technology. On the business side, there will be a wider variety of solutions you can provide to customers. You are not just a printer anymore. You have digital technology that provides many solutions, such as variable data and packaging, in different markets.

6. Do you have any general advice or additional professional insights to share with someone interested in your profession?

Technology is always changing. Keep tuned in and up-to-date with companies in your field.

7. Can you suggest a valuable "try this" for students considering a career in your profession?

Research companies and request a tour through their human relations department. This will give you a better understanding of the overall operation. Ask lots of questions regarding technology and positions, so you get a feel of what kinds of jobs are out there after you graduate.

SELECTED SCHOOLS

Many colleges and universities offer bachelor's degrees in business and production management; some have programs in operations management and industrial operations. The student may also gain solid training at a technical or community college. Below are listed some of the more prominent four-year institutions in this field.some of the more prominent four-year institutions in this field.

Carnegie Mellon University
5000 Forbes Avenue
Pittsburgh, PA 15213
412.268.2000
www.cmu.edu

Indiana University, Bloomington
107 S. Indiana Avenue
Bloomington, IN 47405
812.855.4848
www.iub.edu

Massachusetts Institute of Technology
77 Massachusetts Avenue
Cambridge, MA 02139
617.253.1000
www.mit.edu

Ohio State University, Columbus
281 W. Lane Avenue
Columbus, OH 43201
614.292.6446
www.osu.edu

Purdue University, West Lafayette
610 Purdue Mall
West Lafayette, IN 47907
765.494.4600
www.purdue.edu

University of California, Berkeley
101 Sproul Hall
Berkeley, CA 94704
510.642.6000
www.berkeley.edu

University of Michigan, Ann Arbor
1031 Greene Street
Ann Arbor, MI 48109
734.764.1817
www.umich.edu

University of North Carolina, Chapel Hill
220 E. Cameron Avenue
Chapel Hill, NC 27514
919.962.2211
unc.edu

University of Pennsylvania
3451 Walnut Street
Philadelphia, PA 19104
215.898.5000
www.upenn.edu

University of Texas, Austin
110 Inner Campus Drive
Austin, TX 78712
512.471.3434
www.utexas.edu

MORE INFORMATION

APICS–The Association for Operations Management
8430 W. Bryn Mawr Avenue, Suite 1000
Chicago, IL 60631
800.444.2742
www.apics.org

Production and Service Operations Management Society
5521 Research Park Drive, Suite 200
Catonsville, MD 21228
443.757.3500
www.informs.org

John Pritchard/Editor

Public Relations Specialist

Snapshot

Career Cluster: Business Management, Marketing, Sales & Service
Interests: Mass Communications, Media Relations, Public Opinion, Crisis Management
Earnings (Yearly Average): $55,215
Employment & Outlook: Faster Than Average Growth Expected

OVERVIEW

Sphere of Work

Public relations (PR) specialists are communication professionals who handle a wide range of functions to support clients or employers in their efforts to build and maintain a positive public image, seek positive media exposure, and forge strong relationships with the public. Almost any organization or individual can be a client, such as businesses, industries, non-profit organizations, universities, hospitals, government, or celebrities. Companies employ their own PR specialists, as well. PR specialists are responsible for media and community relations,

consumer and industry relations, investor and employee relations, and interest-group representation, as well as political campaigns, fundraising, and conflict mediation.

As part of these functions, public relations specialists focus on maintaining contact with print and broadcast media, arranging media interviews, setting up speaker engagements, hosting events, writing speeches and press releases, and planning and conducting press conferences. Public relations specialists communicate key messages that have been strategically crafted. These messages must be approved by the client or employer, be clear and understandable to the audience or market, and should align with short- and long-term business goals.

Profile

Working Conditions: Work Indoors
Physical Strength: Light Work
Education Needs: Bachelor's Degree
Licensure/Certification: Required
Physical Abilities Not Required: No Heavy Labor
Opportunities For Experience: Internship, Apprenticeship, Military Service, Volunteer Work, Part-Time Work
Holland Interest Score*: EAS

* See Appendix A

Occupation Interest

The public relations field attracts those who enjoy working with people from all industries and environments—who can easily communicate on many levels. Writing is an essential skill for public relations specialists, as is an ability to gauge public opinion, empathize with particular market segments, and assess the public perception of a given message.

Many colleges and universities offer a degree in public relations. Typical coursework includes core classes in English and writing, with specialty coursework in public relations, journalism, news and speech writing, media relations, communications, planning and analysis, crisis management, and public relations ethics.

A Day in the Life—Duties and Responsibilities

Like all communications experts, public relations specialists are consistently on alert for new and creative ways to achieve client/employer goals and to protect, preserve, or enhance a company's image. In a typical day, public relations specialists will write and distribute news releases, prepare copy for annual reports, take and manage calls from journalists, plan press conferences or events, line up media interviews, provide executives with media training and debriefing after interviews, and attend strategy meetings with clients or employers and public relations managers. Within a corporation, "clients" may be divisions or areas inside the company, with the public relations specialist preparing and disseminating various types of information for different departments, all under the banner of one key message.

Public relations specialists often face pressure from eager clients, and work frequently with outside reporters, producers, bloggers, and other social media specialists. In order to avoid the label of a "spin doctor"—a pejorative term often assigned to PR professionals in corporate or government communications—successful PR specialists do well to earn the trust of those in the media by maintaining a professional demeanor and a strict code of ethics. Successful PR specialists communicate a client's message by delivering it to the public in a truthful manner that provides positive exposure for the client and useful information to the customer.

Public relations specialists are employed in nearly every industry in some form or fashion, which makes this a flexible career option. Additionally, because of advances in technology, and through the use of email, videoconferencing, and online social media, public relations specialists can work from almost any location. Self-employment is common among PR specialists; however, most entry-level candidates do not yet have the experience required to branch out on their own.

Duties and Responsibilities

- **Determining the needs of the organization or individual client**
- **reparing and distributing fact sheets, photographs, articles, news releases and/or promotional booklets**
- **Making speeches and conducting background research**
- **Evaluating and maintaining the client's public image**
- **Directing advertising campaigns in all types of media**
- **Coordinating special exhibits, contests or luncheons into the total public relations plan**
- **Helping clients to communicate with the public**

OCCUPATION SPECIALTIES

Lobbyists

Lobbyists contact and confer with members of the legislature and other holders of public office to persuade them to support legislation favorable to their clients' interests.

Fundraising Directors

Fundraising Directors direct and coordinate the solicitation and disbursement of funds for community social-welfare organizations. They establish fund-raising goals according to the financial need of the agency and formulate policies for collecting and safeguarding the contributions.

Media/Communications Specialists

Media specialists, or communications specialists, handle an organization's communication with the public, including consumers, investors, reporters, and other media specialists. In government, public relations specialists may be called press secretaries. They keep the public informed about the activities of government officials and agencies.

Sales-Service Promoters

Sales-Service Promoters generate sales and create good will for a firm's products by preparing displays and touring the country. They call on merchants to advise them of ways to increase sales and demonstrate products.

WORK ENVIRONMENT

Physical Environment

Busy office settings predominate. In an agency environment (i.e., when working for a PR firm), public relations specialists cater to the demands of more than one client and can expect a busy atmosphere with many phone calls and tight deadlines. In-office work includes writing and assistance in strategy sessions with clients and the agency itself. Public relations specialists can also work within a company's larger communication department, often as part of a marketing role. The ability to work as a team, providing a comprehensive communication strategy, is essential.

While most public relations specialists usually work in an office setting, it is not necessarily where they spend all their time. They are often on the road, with clients, meeting with journalists, hosting press conferences or events, and helping executives receive media training. Public relations specialists can be seen at trade shows and conventions, auditoriums, and broadcast or print offices, working with executives from all levels and all industries.

Relevant Skills and Abilities

Analytical Skills
- Assessing social trends

Communication Skills
- Listening attentively
- Speaking and writing effectively
- Persuading others

Interpersonal/Social Skills
- Cooperating with others
- Exhibiting confidence
- Working as a member of a team

Organization & Management Skills
- Coordinating tasks
- Making decisions
- Managing people/groups
- Selling ideas or products

Planning & Research Skills
- Creating ideas
- Developing evaluation strategies
- Solving problems

Human Environment

Public relations specialists must have strong interpersonal skills because they are dealing with a wide variety of environments. They work with fast-paced news reporters and bloggers, broadcast producers, freelance writers, engineers, corporate executives, other business specialists, legal counsel, and the general public. At times, this can produce high stress levels and will require the ability to multitask and delegate. Public relations specialists often work in crisis management, and therefore need to maintain calm while thinking and acting quickly.

Technological Environment

Today, public relations specialists use a wide range of technology to achieve client goals. This technology includes everything from phone and email, to texting, tweeting, blogging, and monitoring online news organizations.

EDUCATION, TRAINING, AND ADVANCEMENT

High School/Secondary

It is best for public relations specialists to have a college degree with some experience, such as an internship. High school students can best prepare to be a public relations specialist through Advanced Placement (AP) English courses that include and encourage non-fiction or news editorial writing, creative writing, reading comprehension, public speaking, critical thinking, and decision making. Extracurricular activities, such as working with the school newspaper, can also help high school students gain admission to the universities they want to attend.

Suggested High School Subjects

- Business
- College Preparatory
- Composition
- English
- Graphic Communications
- Humanities
- Journalism
- Keyboarding
- Literature
- Political Science
- Psychology
- Social Studies
- Sociology
- Speech

Famous First

The first "publicity bureau" is thought to have been founded around 1900 by persons associated with the railroad industry. By the second decade of the 20th century, two prominent pioneers in public relations had emerged: Edward Bernays and Ivy Lee. Both left a lasting imprint on the field, but Bernays outlived Lee by several decades and helped the field to mature.

College/Postsecondary

A bachelor's degree is highly recommended for success as a public relations specialist. Many universities offer communications programs, often specializing in journalism, which can include subspecialties within actual public relations majors.

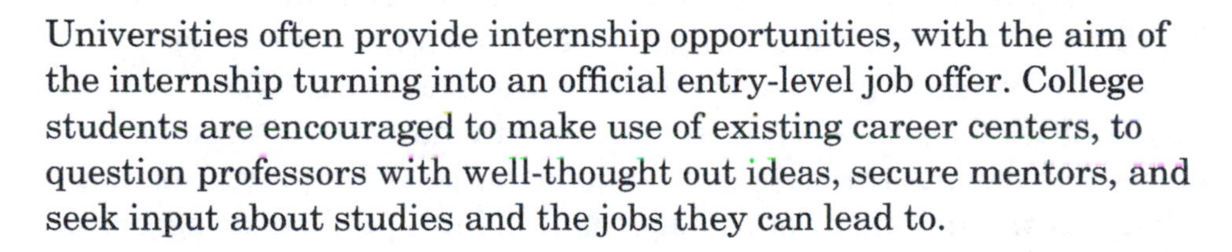

Universities often provide internship opportunities, with the aim of the internship turning into an official entry-level job offer. College students are encouraged to make use of existing career centers, to question professors with well-thought out ideas, secure mentors, and seek input about studies and the jobs they can lead to.

Advanced degrees, such as a master's or PhD, are not necessary for public relations specialists; after earning a bachelor's degree, most of these professionals move through the job ranks through on-the-job experience and a successful portfolio.

Related College Majors

- Business & Personal Services Marketing Operations
- Business Administration & Management, General
- Liberal Arts
- Mass Communications
- public relations ethics

Adult Job Seekers

It is useful to maintain an up-to-date resume with other credentials, such as scholarships, internships, awards, and grants. Being prepared with a portfolio of accomplishments from previous jobs is a good way to demonstrate relevant skills.

Those who do well as public relations specialists are able to articulate the written and spoken word, have confidence, and relate easily to others. They are quick learners and thinkers, calm in the face of pressure, and are persuasive communicators.

Professional associations are often useful sources for those transitioning from another career to public relations, in that they track job openings and provide unique networking opportunities. The Public Relations Society of America (PRSA) and the International Association of Business Communicators (IABC) are two such professional associations.

Professional Certification and Licensure

Accreditations for public relations can be helpful but are not necessary. Employers have varying outlooks on certification. The PRSA has an accreditation program for members who have at least five years of professional experience. The IABC offers opportunities for professionals to be internationally recognized for their achievements through a variety of awards. Work portfolios that include accomplishments such as press clippings, published speeches, or bylined articles are helpful in receiving certification. Professional accreditation can indicate competence in the field which then can help people find jobs in the highly competitive environment of public relations. Consult credible professional associations within your field and follow professional debate as to the relevancy and value of any certification program.

Additional Requirements

Understanding clients' audiences and target markets is essential for aspiring public relations specialists. Public relations specialists must research client background and objectives, understand the business, and "sell" key messages to those people who will benefit from the specific product or service.

EARNINGS AND ADVANCEMENT

Earnings of public relations specialists depend on the type of industry in which the individual is employed and the size and geographic location of the employer. Private consulting firms generally pay more than companies that have their own public relations departments. Median annual earnings of public relations specialists were $55,215 in 2012. The lowest ten percent earned less than $32,394, and the highest ten percent earned more than $100,912.

Public relations specialists may receive paid vacations, holidays, and sick days; life and health insurance; and retirement benefits. These are usually paid by the employer. Some employers may also provide an expense account.

Metropolitan Areas with the Highest Employment Level in This Occupation

Metropolitan area	Employment[1]	Employment per thousand jobs	Hourly mean wage
New York-White Plains-Wayne, NY-NJ	16,210	3.14	$34.28
Washington-Arlington-Alexandria, DC-VA-MD-WV	13,980	5.97	$42.70
Los Angeles-Long Beach-Glendale, CA	7,800	2.02	$36.18
Boston-Cambridge-Quincy, MA	5,750	3.36	$31.28
Philadelphia, PA	4,620	2.54	$33.58
Chicago-Joliet-Naperville, IL	4,570	1.25	$30.24
Dallas-Plano-Irving, TX	3,660	1.74	$32.65
Houston-Sugar Land-Baytown, TX	3,610	1.37	$27.72

(1) Does not include self-employed or PR managers/executives. Source: Bureau of Labor Statistics, 2012

EMPLOYMENT AND OUTLOOK

Nationally, there were approximately 255,000 public relations specialists employed in 2012. Public relations specialists are concentrated in service-providing industries, such as advertising and related services, health care and social assistance, educational services and government. Employment is expected to grow faster than the average for all occupations through the year 2020, which means employment is projected to increase 16 percent to 23 percent. The need for good public relations in a competitive business environment should create demand for public relations specialists in organizations of all types and sizes. With the increasing demand for corporate accountability, more emphasis will be placed on improving the image of the client, as well as building public confidence.

Employment Trend, Projected 2010–20

Public Relations Specialists: 23%

Public Relations Managers and Specialists: 21%

Public Relations and Fundraising Managers: 16%

Total, All Occupations: -14%

Note: "All Occupations" includes all occupations in the U.S. Economy Source: U.S. Bureau of Labor Statistics, Employment Projections Program

Related Occupations

- Advertising Account Executive
- Advertising Agent
- Copywriter
- Electronic Commerce Specialist
- General Manager and Top Executive
- Online Merchant

Related Military Occupations

- Public Information Officer

Conversation With . . .
CHRIS THATCHER

Public Relations Account Supervisor,
6 years in the profession

1. **What was your individual career path in terms of education, entry-level job, or other significant opportunity?**

   I attended SUNY Oswego in upstate New York, one of the few state schools that offered a degree specific to public relations. During college, I was fortunate enough to land a six month internship with one of the top PR agencies in upstate New York, where I worked for 20+ hours a week. I received a B.A in Public Relations, then landed an entry level job the day after graduation in New York City at a boutique public relations agency. (Boutique is an industry firm for smaller agency)

2. **Are there many job opportunities in your profession? In what specific areas?**

   The landscape has changed. I graduated at the peak of the recession and I was the only one of my circle of friends who landed a job. However, over the past few years, businesses have been cutting advertising and switching to public relations because they see a greater value in public relations than advertising – not to mention that PR is significantly cheaper.

   There are many jobs available in the industry, especially at entry level. From consumer products to corporate communications, more and more spots are opening up. My agency has moved twice since I've been with the company because of growth!

3. **What do you wish you had known going into this profession?**

   I majored in PR because someone told me that I would graduate and become a publicist to the stars, essentially working in entertainment. Unfortunately, that is not the case. So many graduates think that PR is the life of glam and fun – planning events, hanging with celebs – but in reality it is hard work, 24/7. The news never stops and if you work with newsmakers, then your life doesn't stop either.

4. How do you see your profession changing in the next five years?

It's hard to say where it is headed. Print media has been slowly disappearing over the past few years and there has been a surge in online influencers (bloggers) and eventually there will be a switch in what is important to publicity: is it going to be a tweet from a newsmaker or a mention in a magazine? What will drive a business further, a social media presence or a traditional platform? Adapting to these changes and being able to express this to clients is going to be a huge factor in the profession.

5. What role will technology play in those changes, and what skills will be required?

Social media has been a huge factor in changing the landscape of public relations. When I first started, I would spend hours researching bloggers and figure out how to reach out to them to cover my clients. Now bloggers want to be paid, sponsored, or otherwise ask for something in return. The journalistic mentality of writing something to let people know about it is disappearing online. It's much harder now to get publicity amid all the "noise."

We're now in a mobile generation, which means having to create the perfect pitch to be viewed on the screen of a mobile phone and not just a computer.

6. Do you have any general advice or additional professional insights to share with someone interested in your profession?

Writing classes. The essential to succeed in this industry is to be able to be a creative writer. Each and every day we are creating content for producers, journalists, and bloggers. Some people become interested in it, some don't. If they don't, then we need to be creative and think of another angle to spark interest from media. It's essential.

Public speaking also helps. A publicist needs to think quickly and be confident in the message they are trying to get across.

7. Can you suggest a valuable "try this" for students considering a career in your profession?

This might sound silly, but students should get a job at their school's telefund. I was a student caller for a year, then got promoted to manager, and this was the smartest thing I did in my college career. Asking people for money is the hardest thing to do, harder than asking media to write about the latest premature ejaculation treatment – and yes, I had to do that. These funds usually provide a general script to follow, but eventually the caller will learn to modify that because he figures out what works, when calling, to secure a donation. This helps build confidence on the phone and enhances creativity. We hear "NO" all the time in the industry. It is something that we learn to accept, then figure out how to get a "YES" next time.

SELECTED SCHOOLS

Most colleges and universities have bachelor's degree programs in the liberal arts, which is a good foundation for work as a public relations specialist. Other institutions have programs devoted to communications and media, another good foundation. The student may also gain initial training at a community college. Below are listed some of the more prominent four-year institutions in this field.

Columbia University
535 W. 116th Street
New York, NY 10027
212.854.1754
www.columbia.edu

Massachusetts Institute of Technology
77 Massachusetts Avenue
Cambridge, MA 02139
617.253.1000
www.mit.edu

New York University
70 Washington Square S
New York, NY 10012
212.998.1212
www.nyu.edu

Stanford University
450 Serra Mall
Stanford, CA 94305
650.723.2300
www.stanford.edu

University of California, Berkeley
101 Sproul Hall
Berkeley, CA 94704
510.642.6000
www.berkeley.edu

University of California, Los Angeles
405 Hilgard Avenue
Los Angeles, CA 90095
310.825.4321
www.ucla.edu

University of Michigan, Ann Arbor
1032 Green Street
Ann Arbor, MI 48109
734.764.1817
www.umich.edu

University of Pennsylvania
3451 Walnut Street
Philadelphia, PA 19104
215.898.5000
www.upenn.edu

University of Texas, Austin
110 Inner Campus Drive
Austin, TX 78712
512.471.3434
www.utexas.edu

Yale University
P.O. Box 208234
New Haven, CT 06520
203.432.4771
www.yale.edu

MORE INFORMATION

American Association of Advertising Agencies
405 Lexington Avenue, 18th Floor
New York, NY 10174-1801
212.682.2500
www.aaaa.org

Association of Fundraising Professionals
4300 Wilson Boulevard
Arlington, VA 22203
703.684.0410
www.afpnet.org

Public Relations Society of America
33 Maiden Lane, 11th Floor
New York, NY 10038-5150
212.460.1400
www.prsa.org

International Association of Business Communicators
601 Montgomery Street, Suite 1900
San Francisco, CA 94111
415.544.4700
www.iabc.com

Susan Williams/Editor

Radio/TV Announcer & Newscaster

Snapshot

Career Cluster: Media & Communications
Interests: Broadcasting, Mass Communication, Journalism, Public Speaking
Earnings (Yearly Average): $42,925
Employment & Outlook: Slower Than Average Growth Expected

OVERVIEW

Sphere of Work

Announcers and newscasters deliver news and commentary on radio and television. Radio announcers and television newscasters are both also traditionally known as broadcasters. In addition to delivering news information to listeners and viewers, broadcasters conduct interviews, moderate discussions, and provide commentary for live Sports Photography competitions, musical selections, and developing news events. Several broadcasters also veer

into journalism, researching and writing about topics for discussion on their particular programs. As such, broadcasting has broadened into a multidisciplinary profession encompassing mass communication, journalism, and reportage.

Work Environment

Broadcasters operate primarily out of radio and television studios, where they work in concert with technical and production staff to prepare radio and television programs. It is not uncommon for broadcasters to travel to areas where important news events are unfolding, presenting their programs from a diverse array of locales from show to show. Broadcasters are also often called upon to visit interview subjects and develop stories from a variety of locations in and around their region, the country, or even the globe. In the past, most broadcasters worked nontraditional hours, including early mornings, late nights, weekends, and holidays, but newer technology has enabled more broadcasts to be prerecorded.

Occupation Interest

While radio announcers and television newscasters traditionally came from media communications backgrounds, the field is now populated by individuals who come from numerous academic and professional backgrounds, including journalism, politics, science, literature, music, and the arts.

Colleges and universities nationwide offer specific academic programs dedicated to both audio and visual broadcasting, which students often reinforce with course work dedicated to their other academic interests, notably English, politics, or sports management. Excellent time management, judgment, and organization are just as imperative as personality and conversational skills.

Profile

Working Conditions: Work Indoors
Physical Strength: Light Work
Education Needs: Bachelor's Degree
Licensure/Certification: Recommended
Physical Abilities Not Required: No Heavy Labor
Opportunities For Experience: Internship, Apprenticeship, Military Service, Volunteer Work, Part-Time Work
Holland Interest Score*: SEC

* See Appendix A

A Day in the Life—Duties and Responsibilities

Radio and television broadcasters spend their days planning future shows, filming or recording new broadcasts, and editing new recordings for public broadcast. On air, broadcasters generally introduce and close programs, present information, and lead discussions. Many of the specific occupational duties and responsibilities of radio and television broadcasters depend on the nature and frequency of the program for which they work.

Developing programs that air live on a daily basis predominantly involves preproduction tasks such as fact gathering, organizing specific questions, and preparing for guest interviews. Live television and radio production is often completed in a fast-paced environment under strict deadlines. As a result, radio and television broadcasters who work in live programming often must effectively adapt to evolving situations and on-air conversations.

Documentary-style radio and television programs conduct a large amount of investigative research and information gathering. Documentary programs tend to air on a less frequent basis, usually weekly or monthly; thus, much of the focus for developing such programs is placed on gathering video and audio copy, narrative construction, fact checking, and follow-up interviews with subjects. The protracted nature of documentary radio and television broadcasting necessitates a lot of editing work prior to presentation.

Duties and Responsibilities

- **Introducing various types of radio or television programs**
- **Announcing news, commercial breaks, and public service messages**
- **Interviewing guests**
- **Describing sports and public events**
- **Writing scripts and news copy**
- **Selling commercial time**
- **Keeping records of programs and preparing program logs**
- **Reviewing and selecting recordings for air play**

OCCUPATION SPECIALTIES

Anchors/Hosts

News Anchors and Program Hosts work in television or radio and specialize in a certain area of interest, such as politics, personal finance, sports, or health. They contribute to the preparation of the program's content, interview guests, and discuss issues with viewers, listeners, or the studio or radio audience.

Commentators

Commentators analyze and write commentaries, based upon personal knowledge and experience with the subject matter, for broadcast. They interpret information on a topic and record their commentary or present it live during the broadcast.

Critics

Critics write and deliver critical reviews of literary, musical, or artistic works and performances for broadcast.

Disc Jockeys (DJs)

Disc Jockeys, or DJs, announce radio programs of musical selections, and choose the selections to be made based upon knowledge of audience preference or requests. They also comment upon the music and other matters of interest to the audience, such as the weather, time, and traffic conditions.

Newsreaders

Newsreaders read prepared news copy over the air. They may or may not be involved in the writing and editing of that copy.

Public Address Announcers

Public Address Announcers provide information to the audience at sporting, performing arts, and other events.

WORK ENVIRONMENT

Physical Environment

Television and radio broadcasting studios are the broadcaster's primary work environment. These spaces are generally bright, soundproof, and temperature controlled. A considerable amount of fieldwork may also be required. Broadcasters may work in a variety of locations, including government buildings, sports arenas, and hospitals. They may also serve as station representatives at public events.

Relevant Skills and Abilities

Communication Skills

- Speaking and writing clearly and effectively
- Being able to pronounce difficult words and phrases with ease
- Being able to speak consistently and at length
- Being able to listen while speaking

Interpersonal/Social Skills

- Being objective
- Being persistent
- Cooperating with others
- Working as a member of a team

Organization & Management Skills

- Paying attention to and handling details
- Performing duties that change frequently

Planning & Research Skills

- Creating ideas
- Laying out a plan
- Researching a topic

Human Environment

Radio and television broadcasters are often the public face of a larger team of technical and production staff with whom they are required to work closely with on a daily basis.

Technological Environment

Radio and television broadcasters use a wide range of communication and broadcasting technology, from microphones and teleprompters to sophisticated editing equipment.

EDUCATION, TRAINING, AND ADVANCEMENT

High School/Secondary

High school students can best prepare for a career in broadcasting with courses in public speaking, composition, the dramatic arts, and computer science. Many high schools have scholastic television and radio stations that instruct students on broadcasting basics. Exposure to local radio and television broadcasting stations through internships or volunteer work may also be highly beneficial. Writing and reporting on local events for a school or community newspaper will provide high school students with reportage and interviewing experience that can benefit a future career in broadcasting.

Suggested High School Subjects

- Applied Communication
- College Preparatory
- Composition
- English
- Foreign Languages
- Journalism
- Literature
- Speech
- Theatre & Drama

Famous First

The first radio station to feature a 24-hour "all-news" format was WINS, 1010 on the AM dial (New York City), beginning in 1965. Other AM stations around the nation quickly followed suit, leading to a spike in the hiring of announcers.

College/Postsecondary

Hundreds of colleges and universities in the United States offer undergraduate- and graduate-level programs in broadcasting. The majority of entry-level radio and television broadcasting positions require a bachelor's degree in communication, broadcasting, or journalism.

Undergraduate programs in journalism outline the techniques and strategies that apply to television and radio reporters while honing students' reporting and storytelling skills. Journalism majors also learn the basic ethical standards that dictate news production across all types and levels of media. Undergraduate work in broadcasting exposes students to the vast array of media technologies and software used in the field and helps them learn the acoustics of speech, vocal delivery, and camera presence.

Graduate-level programs in broadcasting are usually completed in conjunction with an internship at a radio or television news studio. In addition to studying advanced topics such as media law, news production, and directing, graduate students also conduct research for a master's thesis dedicated to an area of their particular interest. Individuals with master's degrees often go on to professional careers as radio and television broadcasters, media researchers, or college-level academic instructors.

Related College Majors

- Acting & Directing
- Broadcast Journalism
- Creative Writing
- Drama/Theater Arts, General
- Film/Cinema Studies
- Journalism
- Music History & Literature
- Music, General
- Radio & Television Broadcasting

Adult Job Seekers

The educational and professional experience requirements of broadcasting can make it a difficult field for adult job seekers to enter.

Due to the highly competitive job market and low turnover rate of established broadcasters, landing a professional role as a broadcaster can require several years of lower-level experience, during which one is expected to master the production, reporting, and editing aspects of the role. Advancement to higher-level, higher-paying positions often depends on proven ratings, contributions to the station's marketing efforts, and the station's size. Relocation is common.

Professional Certification and Licensure

Professional certification and licensure is not required of broadcast professionals, although membership and affiliation with national organizations and associations can boost credentials and improve networking opportunities.

Additional Requirements

Radio announcers and television newscasters are also often entertainers. Therefore, those interested in the field should be comfortable speaking and engaging with interviewees and audiences, have a sense of humor, work well under pressure, and adapt quickly to changing situations and circumstances.

Fun Fact

Almost three out of four U.S. adults (71%) view network newscasts over the course of a month, making television the dominant source of news for Americans at home, according to an October 2013 survey.

Source: Pew Research Center analysis of Nielson data.

EARNINGS AND ADVANCEMENT

Earnings of radio and television announcers and newscasters depend on the employer, the size of the community, the nature of the announcer's or newscaster's work and the announcer's or newscaster's reputation. Salaries are higher in television than in radio, higher in larger markets than in small ones, and higher in commercial than in public broadcasting.

Median annual earnings of announcers were $28,461 in 2012. The lowest ten percent earned less than $17,585, and the highest ten percent earned more than $76,850.

Median annual earnings of newscasters were $57,388 in 2012. The lowest ten percent earned less than $29,214, and the highest ten percent earned more than $155,004.

Radio and television announcers and newscasters may receive paid vacations, holidays, and sick days; life and health insurance; and retirement benefits. These are usually paid by the employer.

Metropolitan Areas with the Highest Employment Level in This Occupation

Metropolitan area	Employment(1)	Employment per thousand jobs	Hourly mean wage
New York-White Plains-Wayne, NY-NJ	1,140	0.22	$28.08
Los Angeles-Long Beach-Glendale, CA	910	0.24	$34.96
Chicago-Joliet-Naperville, IL	480	0.13	$25.39
Boston-Cambridge-Quincy, MA	410	0.24	$42.29
Washington-Arlington-Alexandria, DC-VA-MD-WV	400	0.17	$22.40
Atlanta-Sandy Springs-Marietta, GA	390	0.17	$28.50
Minneapolis-St. Paul-Bloomington, MN-WI	370	0.21	$28.68
Dallas-Plano-Irving, TX	370	0.18	(8)

(1) Does not include self-employed or PR managers/executives. Source: Bureau of Labor Statistics, 2012

EMPLOYMENT AND OUTLOOK

Nationally, there were approximately 31,000 radio and television announcers and newscasters employed in 2012. (An additional 8,000 worked as public address announcers and in similar occupations.) Employment is expected to grow slower than the average for all occupations through the year 2020, which means employment is projected to increase about 7 percent. The slow growth is due to the consolidation of radio and television stations and improving technology.

Employment Trend, Projected 2010–20

Total, All Occupations: 14%

Announcers: 7%

Radio and Television Announcers: 7%

Public Address System and Other Announcers: -5%

Note: "All Occupations" includes all occupations in the U.S. Economy Source: U.S. Bureau of Labor Statistics, Employment Projections Program

Related Occupations

- Actor
- Copywriter
- Journalist
- Writer & Editor

Related Military Occupations

- Broadcast Journalism & Newswriter

Conversation With . . .
NEFERTITI JÁQUEZ

Broadcast Journalist, 9 years

1. What was your individual career path in terms of education, entry-level job, or other significant opportunity?

I actually didn't study journalism. I studied law and politics. However, I interned at NBC in Providence, RI, as an Emma L. Bowen Foundation intern and fell in love with journalism, broadcasting, and storytelling. I interned for five years and in that time I came to the realization this is what I truly wanted to do. I was hired by CBS in Miami after I graduated from Brown University. Since then, I have also worked for FOX News, and I am currently working for NBC.

2. Are there many job opportunities in your profession? In what specific areas?

I think you have to create you own opportunities. This is a very competitive industry. You have to work diligently to brand yourself and make yourself and your work marketable. There are no set steps that you call follow, 1-2-3. It's not that easy. When I did my five-year internship, I made a point to know everyone, from the general manager all the way down to the janitor. Branding always includes networking. I carry a stack of business cards and hand them out to everyone–mailmen, tow truck drivers. It's really being open to the idea that everyone has a story. I think as long as you're willing to work hard and never lose sight of your goals, anything is achievable.

3. What do you wish you had known going into this profession?

It will be an emotional roller coaster. There will be stories you're not prepared for and people you will be surprised to meet. You will see some horrific things. I think people don't always realize how hard it is for us as journalists to cover some of the things we do, like the DC shootings or the bombings in Boston. But sometimes you have to turn off your emotions and tell the story, because we have the responsibility to do that. You will see some amazing things. You will witness history in the making. Simply put: the good and the bad, but it will be well worth it in the end.

4. **How do you see your profession changing in the next five years?**

As journalists, we have more responsibilities now: we have Faceboook, we have tweets, we have the Vine. It's really no different than in the '50s, with Walter Cronkite and the transition from radio to TV. It's one of those moments in time. We have to be open to the idea that there are things in the industry that we have to deal with. The ways that people are getting their news or expecting their news are very different. Who am I to say exactly where it's going? But as journalists with a job to do, as things change, we have to change with it.

5. **What role will technology play in those changes, and what skills will be required?**

Technology plays a huge role in how we tell news now. Social media is changing our audience, and the challenges of developing real-time news. It's very fast-paced and it's very easy to judge someone on their one mistake. Everybody should dot their Is and cross their Ts. In a matter of seconds, you can text or Tweet, but it's always better to be right than to be first. Television is our bread and butter, but there are so many other platforms now.

6. **Do you have any general advice or additional professional insights to share with someone interested in your profession?**

I have two Facebook pages, one for work and one that's private. But even on my private Facebook page, I'm pretty careful about what I post. You really have to be very conscientious and aware of what you upload to the Internet, because once it's there, it's there. You don't ever want to become the news.

I was nominated for an Emmy for a feature piece. It was about a group of professional photographers across the nation who take pictures of stillborn children for families who want to have memories of their children. It was a difficult story. Some people thought it was morbid. There's no class you take in college that prepares you for the emotional ramifications. I never took a journalism class a day in my life. Having a law/political background, I look at stories in a different way. I do a lot of crime reporting.

The best listeners are the best storytellers. Read "Make it Memorable," by Bob Dotson and "Aim for the Heart," by Al Tompkins.

7. **Can you suggest a valuable "try this" for students considering a career in your profession?**

Take an anchor's script and re-write it in your own words. Use a mirror or record yourself practicing the script.

SELECTED SCHOOLS

Many colleges and universities have bachelor's degree programs in journalism; some have programs in broadcast journalism, specifically. The student may also gain initial training at a community college. Below are listed some of the more prominent four-year institutions in this field.

Boston University
1 Silber Way
Boston, MA 02215
617.353.2000
www.bu.edu

Emerson College
120 Boylston Street
Boston, MA 02116
617.824.8500
www.emerson.edu

Columbia University
535 W. 116th Street
New York, NY 10027
212.854.1754
www.columbia.edu

Northwestern University
633 Clark Street
Evanston, IL 60208
847.491.3741
www.northwestern.edu

St. Bonaventure University
3261 West State Road
St. Bonaventure, NY 14778
716.375.2000
www.sbu.edu

Syracuse University
900 S. Crouse Avenue
Syracuse, NY 13210
315.443.1870
syr.edu

University of Georgia
100 Green Street
Athens, GA 30602
706.542.3000
www.uga.edu

University of Missouri, Columbia
230 Jesse Hall
Columbia, MI 65211
573.882.7786
www.missouri.edu

University of North Carolina, Chapel Hill
Jackson Hall
Chapel Hill, NC 27599
919.966.3621
www.unc.edu

University of Southern California
850 W. 37th Street
Los Angeles, CA 90089
323.442.1130
www.usc.edu

MORE INFORMATION

American Women in Radio and Television
1760 Old Meadow Road, Suite 500
McLean, VA 22102
703.506.3290
www.awrt.org

Association for Women in Communications
3337 Duke Street
Alexandria, VA 22314
703.370.7436
www.womcom.org

Broadcast Education Association
1771 N Street, NW
Washington, DC 20036-2891
888.380.7222
www.beaweb.org

National Association of Broadcasters
1771 N Street, NW
Washington, DC 20036
202.429.5300
www.nab.org

National Association of Digital Broadcasters
244 Fifth Avenue, Suite 2757
New York, NY 10001-7945
www.thenadb.org

National Cable Television Association
Careers in Cable
1724 Massachusetts Avenue, NW
Washington, DC 20036
202.222.2300
www.ncta.com

John Pritchard/Editor

Software Developer

Snapshot

Career Cluster: Arts, A/V Technology & Communications, Information Technology
Interests: Computer Software Technology, Math, Science, Information Technology
Earnings (Yearly Average): $96,444
Employment & Outlook: Faster Than Average Growth Expected

OVERVIEW

Sphere of Work

Software developers design and write computer programs or computer applications for use in a variety of media, including computer games. They also modify existing programs to improve functionality or to meet client needs. On large-scale projects, software developers typically work with a team of professionals that includes software engineers, software architects, and computer programmers. In these cases, they might be primarily responsible for developing the functional or "front-end" user interface of the program to ensure that it is compatible

with an existing system and that it works reliably and securely. On smaller jobs, software designers might also handle the programming, engineering, and architecture of the program. In any case, they serve as the creative link between an abstract idea for a program or application and its realization as a functioning piece of software.

Work Environment

Many software developers are self-employed and work at home or in small businesses. Others work for the military, government agencies, or industries such as telecommunications, health care, aerospace, e-commerce, video games, and education. Software developers working for corporations typically work forty-hour weeks, while those who are self-employed may set their own hours. In either case, strict deadlines or unexpected problems may require software developers to work additional hours as needed. A typical workstation includes top-quality computer hardware and systems for designing and writing software.

Profile

Working Conditions: Work Indoors
Physical Strength: Light Work
Education Needs: Bachelor's Degree
Licensure/Certification: Recommended
Physical Abilities Not Required: No Heavy Labor
Opportunities For Experience: Internship, Apprenticeship, Military Service, Volunteer Work, Part-Time Work
Holland Interest Score*: AES, IRE

* See Appendix A

Occupation Interest

People who are attracted to software development careers are analytical and mathematically inclined, with strong problem-solving skills and an aptitude for learning programming languages. They are detail oriented, yet also able to envision the overall design and application of products. Software developers need good communication skills to interact with team members and convey their ideas. Leadership and organizational skills are also important, as is the desire to be knowledgeable about new developments in the industry.

A Day in the Life—Duties and Responsibilities

Most computer programs are born out of a need. Software developers first evaluate that need, usually in consultation with a client, and then conceive of a program to solve the problem. They design computer games, applications for mobile phones, and other highly visible types of software. They also design behind-the-scenes programs known as utilities, which may help users download content from the Internet seamlessly, convert files to different formats, protect computers from malware, or free up computer disk space when needed. Some software developers design programs used in business, education, graphic arts, multimedia, web development, and many other fields, as well as programs intended just for other programmers.

Software developers are often responsible for planning a project within budget and time constraints. They must consider compatibility issues, determining the type of platform on which the software will operate and the oldest version on which it will work reliably. They also consider issues such as the maintainability of the software (how often it will need to be updated).

Software developers then devise a schematic of the program that shows its structure, often displayed as a hierarchy consisting of modules. They develop algorithms, which are sets of instructions or steps needed to solve the problems identified by each module. Developers program the code line by line, or supervise other programmers. They test the modules, locate and correct any errors, and then test the program repeatedly until it is secure, user-friendly, and reliable. They might also add graphics and multimedia components or hand that job over to a graphic designer.

Duties and Responsibilities

- **Identifying the purpose and scope of new software**
- **Outlining new software components and functionality**
- **Providing detailed instructions for programmers**
- **Documenting each step necessary to create new software**
- **Testing to make sure steps are correct and will produce the desired results**
- **Rewriting programs if desired results are not produced**
- **Creating graphics, animation, and sound effects for software**
- **Monitoring maintenance needs and providing upgrades as necessary**
- **Staying abreast of trends in the industry**

OCCUPATION SPECIALTIES

Application Software Developers

Application Software Developers design computer applications, such as word processors and games, for consumers. They may create custom software for a specific customer or commercial software to be sold to the general public. Some applications software developers create complex databases for organizations. They also create programs that people use over the Internet and within a company's intranet.

Systems Software Developers

Systems Software Developers create the systems that keep computers functioning properly. These could be operating systems that are part of computers the general public buys or systems built specifically for an organization. Often, systems software developers also build the system's interface, which is what allows users to interact with the computer. Systems software developers create the operating systems that control most of the consumer electronics in use today, including those in phones or cars.

WORK ENVIRONMENT

Physical Environment

Software developers usually work in comfortable offices or from their homes, although some may also travel to meet with clients. Spaces are usually environmentally controlled. Given the nature of the work, developers may be at risk for developing carpel tunnel syndrome, back problems, and eyestrain owing to prolonged use of computers.

Human Environment

Software developers typically report to a project manager and are usually members of a development team, along with programmers, systems architects, quality assurance specialists, and others. The developer might also manage the team or oversee the work done by programmers. A high level of communication and cooperation is usually necessary for success. Many developers, however, work alone and are responsible only to their clients.

Relevant Skills and Abilities

Analytical Skills
- Identifying technical problems
- Using logical reasoning

Communication Skills
- Speaking and writing effectively
- Using diagrams and flowcharts

Interpersonal/Social Skills
- Being able to work independently and as a member of a team

Organization & Management Skills
- Organizing information or materials
- Paying attention to and handling details
- Performing routine work
- Supervising others as necessary

Planning & Research Skills
- Creating ideas
- Laying out a strategy

Technological Environment

Software developers use a variety of stationary and portable computers and computer devices, video game consoles, and related hardware. They use and interface with various operating systems and database management programs. While software developers do not necessarily do programming, they should be familiar with various computer and markup languages, including C++, Java, ColdFusion, and HTML, as well as related compilers and interpreters.

EDUCATION, TRAINING, AND ADVANCEMENT

High School/Secondary

Students should take a strong college-preparatory program that includes English, chemistry, physics, and four years of mathematics, including trigonometry, calculus, and statistics. Computer science or technology, engineering, and electronics courses are also important. Students interested primarily in designing video games or visual-heavy programs should take computer graphics and drawing courses. Other potentially beneficial subjects include psychology, sociology, and business. Participation in technology clubs, science fairs, mathematics competitions, and other related extracurricular activities is encouraged, as is independent study and creation of programs.

Suggested High School Subjects

- Accounting
- Algebra
- Applied Communication
- Applied Math
- Bookkeeping
- Business & Computer Technology
- Business Data Processing
- Calculus
- College Preparatory
- Computer Programming
- Computer Science
- English
- Geometry
- Graphic Communications
- Keyboarding
- Mathematics
- Statistics
- Trigonometry

Famous First

The first software program to receive a patent was a program called Swift-Answer, designed in 1981 by Satya Pal Asija of St. Paul, Minn. The program searched a database in response to a query posed by a user. Since that time, applications for software patents have become so numerous that the U.S. Patent Office can barely keep up—and patent litigation (one person or firm suing another over allegations of patent infringement) has become a multibillion-dollar industry.

College/Postsecondary

Although some employers consider job applicants with an associate's degree, most prefer to hire workers with a bachelor's degree or higher in computer science, computer engineering, or a related technical field. Prospective software developers must be familiar with different types of computers and operating systems, systems organization and architecture, data structures and algorithms, computation theory, and other related topics. Internships and independent projects are recommended.

Related College Majors

- Computer Engineering
- Computer Engineering Technology
- Computer Maintenance Technology
- Computer Programming
- Computer Science
- Design & Visual Communications
- Educational/Instructional Media Design
- Graphic Design, Commercial Art & Illustration
- Information Sciences & Systems
- Management Information Systems & Business Data Processing

Adult Job Seekers

Adults with a computer science or programming background who are returning to the field can update their skills and knowledge by taking continuing education courses offered by software vendors or colleges. Some courses are available online. Those with family obligations might want to consider self-employment, although regular full-time employment may offer more financial stability. Professional associations may provide networking opportunities, as well as job openings and connections to potential clients.

Advancement is partially dependent on the size of the company and the scale of projects. In large companies, software developers with leadership skills typically move into project management and higher-ranked positions as experience and education warrant. Experienced developers may also establish their own businesses, while developers with advanced degrees may move into college teaching.

Professional Certification and Licensure

There are no mandatory licenses or certifications needed for these positions, although voluntary certification from the Institute of Electrical and Electronics Engineers (IEEE), the Institute for Certification of Computing Professionals (ICCP), and other professional organizations can be especially advantageous for job hunting and networking. Software developers can be certified as Software Development Associates (CSDA) or Software Development Professionals (CSDP) through IEEE or as Computing Professionals (CCP) and Associate Computing Professionals (ACP) through ICCP. Software developers are encouraged to consult prospective employers and credible professional associations within the field as to the relevancy and value of any voluntary certification program.

Additional Requirements

Software developers must have excellent conceptual skills in addition to nuts-and-bolts programming skills. Although some developers may serve as the "creative genius" behind an important project, the first requirement is a combination of conceptual and logical skills.

Fun Fact

Portio Research estimates that 1.2 billion people worldwide were using mobile apps at the end of 2012, a figure estimated to grow at a 29.8 percent rate each year and reach 4.4 billion users by the end of 2017.

Source: socialmediatoday.com

EARNINGS AND ADVANCEMENT

Earnings for software developers vary depending on the size and location of the employer and the education, experience and certification of the employee. Median annual earnings of software developers were $96,444 in 2012. The lowest ten percent earned less than $61,162, and the highest ten percent earned more than $146,514.

Software developers may receive paid vacations, holidays, and sick days; life and health insurance; and retirement benefits. These are usually paid by the employer.

Metropolitan Areas with the Highest Employment Level in This Occupation (Applications Developer)

Metropolitan area	Employment[1]	Employment per thousand jobs	Hourly mean wage
Seattle-Bellevue-Everett, WA	35,650	25.29	$48.99
New York-White Plains-Wayne, NY-NJ	33,360	6.47	$50.86
Washington-Arlington-Alexandria, DC-VA-MD-WV	28,360	12.10	$50.56
San Jose-Sunnyvale-Santa Clara, CA	24,160	26.89	$56.06
Boston-Cambridge-Quincy, MA	19,950	11.66	$50.35

(1) Does not include self-employed. Source: Bureau of Labor Statistics, 2012

Metropolitan Areas with the Highest Employment Level in This Occupation (Systems Developer)

Metropolitan area	Employment[1]	Employment per thousand jobs	Hourly mean wage
Washington-Arlington-Alexandria, DC-VA-MD-WV	28,600	12.20	$54.88
San Jose-Sunnyvale-Santa Clara, CA	24,790	27.58	$61.13
Boston-Cambridge-Quincy, MA	19,430	11.35	$53.93
Seattle-Bellevue-Everett, WA	13,670	9.70	$51.01
Los Angeles-Long Beach-Glendale, CA	13,280	3.43	$54.80

(1) Does not include self-employed. Source: Bureau of Labor Statistics, 2012

EMPLOYMENT AND OUTLOOK

Software developers held about 978,000 jobs nationally in 2012. (586,000 were applications developers, and 392,000 were systems developers.) Employment of software developers is expected to grow much faster than the average for all occupations through the year 2020, which means employment is projected to increase 29 percent or more. The increasing uses of the Internet, and mobile technology such as wireless Internet, have created a demand for a wide variety of new products. In addition, information security concerns have created new software needs. Concerns over cyber security should result in businesses and government continuing to rely on security software that protects their networks from attack. The growth of this technology in the next ten years will lead to an increased need for these workers to design this type of software.

Employment Trend, Projected 2010–20

Software Developers, Systems Software: 32%

Software Developers: 30%

Software Developers, Applications: 28%

Total, All Occupations: 14%

Note: "All Occupations" includes all occupations in the U.S. Economy Source: U.S. Bureau of Labor Statistics, Employment Projections Program

Related Occupations

- Computer & Information Systems Manager
- Computer Engineer
- Computer Operator
- Computer Programmer
- Computer Security Specialist
- Computer Support Specialist

- Computer Systems Analyst
- Computer-Control Tool Programmer
- Information Technology Project Manager
- Multimedia Artist & Animator
- Network & Computer Systems Administrator
- Network Systems & Data Communications Analyst
- Web Administrator
- Website Designer

Related Military Occupations

- Computer Programmer
- Computer Systems Specialist
- Graphic Designer & Illustrator

Conversation With . . .
CRAIG KAHN

Software Developer, 34 years

1. What was your individual career path in terms of education, entry-level job, or other significant opportunity?

Although I have a bachelor's of arts degree, my education did not include any courses in computer science. I wish it had and I certainly recommend taking as many courses in computer science as possible if one's desired profession is to write software code. My education in software programming was strictly "on the job" at first, although I did take classes eventually. My first foray into programming came out of necessity. I was at a company that ran ski trips, via bus, to ski resorts in New England. We were dealing with multiple groups on multiple buses going to multiple resorts utilizing multiple rooms and types of lodging. In addition, some individuals needed rentals and/or lessons. This was 1979 and we were keeping track of all of this information by hand. The PC hadn't been invented yet (MS-DOS, the first popular operating system, had yet to be developed) but the desktop computer existed. It was actually the size of a desktop. Our company bought a dual 8" floppy disk drive computer running the CPM operating system. I learned how to program using a database program called dBase II.

2. Are there many job opportunities in your profession? In what specific areas?

I get the sense that there is a significant demand for programmers who can do more than merely write code. People are looking for programmers who can develop, or help develop, a complete application, including designing the user interface and developing the logic necessary for the program to work. The pure "coding" work seems to be going overseas.

3. What do you wish you had known going into this profession?

I wish I had taken classes and was more informed – there would have been less trial and error and I would have been up to speed much more quickly.

4. **How do you see your profession changing in the next five years?**

This is a tough one to call. My niche is developing small- to medium-scale applications for clients that want to move from keeping track of things on paper to being able to enter, retrieve and report on that information via computer. I think this will pretty much stay the same.

5. **What role will technology play in those changes, and what skills will be required?**

It's difficult to predict how the computer programming profession will change in the next five years. A lot will depend on the economy and the political environment, especially in regards to outsourcing. The good news is that certain types of programming cannot be shipped overseas because they require a lot of face-to-face meetings to go over and revise specifications. Basically, any development that would be considered "Agile Software Development," where requirements and solutions evolve over time as a result of working with others, would most likely need to be local.

As technology evolves, different skill sets will be needed. For example, 10 years ago a programmer didn't need to know much about web programming. These days it is essential to know how to develop for the desktop and for the web. I suspect that as smart phones become more powerful, and as tablets become more common, a requirement may be for an application to work among all platforms.

6. **Do you have any general advice or additional professional insights to share with someone interested in your profession?**

The most important requirement for a software developer is to be aware of what is going on in the world of technology and embrace the advances and changes. Even if you don't deem it necessary to learn how to use the newest technology, you should at least know it's out there and be ready to absorb and learn at a moment's notice.

Also, one of the things clients look for is someone with good communication skills – including being a good listener. If the choice is between two equally good coders, the one who the client feels can "get it" – and can explain what he or she is doing – will get the job.

7. **Can you suggest a valuable "try this" for students considering a career in your profession?**

I would suggest coming up with an idea for a program and spending time developing it in one's language of choice. Make mistakes and learn on your own time instead of on the client's time. If a potential client wants to know what you've developed in the past, you'll have something to show them.

SELECTED SCHOOLS

Many colleges and universities have bachelor's degree programs in computer science; some have programs in software developments, specifically. The student may also gain initial training in programming at a community college. Below are listed some of the more prominent four-year institutions in this field.

California Institute of Technology
1200 E. California Boulevard
Pasadena, CA 91125
626.395.6811
www.caltech.edu

Carnegie Mellon University
5000 Forbes Avenue
Pittsburgh, PA 15213
412.268.2000
www.cmu.edu

Cornell University
401 Thurston Avenue
Ithaca, NY 14850
607.255.5241
www.cornell.edu

Georgia Institute of Technology
225 North Avenue NW
Atlanta, GA 30332
404.894.2000
www.gatech.edu

Massachusetts Institute of Technology
77 Massachusetts Avenue
Cambridge, MA 02139
617.253.1000
www.mit.edu

Stanford University
450 Serra Mall
Stanford, CA 94305
650.723.2300
www.stanford.edu

University of California, Berkeley
101 Sproul Hall
Berkeley, CA 94704
510.642.6000
www.berkeley.edu

University of Illinois, Urbana-Champaign
601 E. John Street
Champaign, IL 61820
217.333-1000
illinois.edu

University of Michigan, Ann Arbor
1031 Greene Street
Ann Arbor, MI 48109
734.764.1817
www.umich.edu

University of Texas, Austin
110 Inner Campus Drive
Austin, TX 78712
512.471.3434
www.utexas.edu

MORE INFORMATION

Association for Computing Machinery
2 Penn Plaza, Suite 701
New York, NY 10121-0701
800.342.6626
www.acm.org

Computing Research Association
1828 L Street NW, Suite 800
Washington, DC 20036
202.234.2111
www.cra.org

Institute for the Certification of Computer Professionals
2400 East Devon Avenue, Suite 281
Des Plaines, IL 60018-4610
800.843.8227
www.iccp.org

Institute of Electrical and Electronics Engineers (IEEE) Computer Society
2001 L Street, NW, Suite 700
Washington, DC 20036-4928
202.371.0101
www.computer.org

National Center for Women and Information Technology
University of Colorado
Campus Box 322 UCB
Boulder, CO 80308
303.735.6671
www.ncwit.org

Software & Information Industry Association
1090 Vermont Avenue NW, Sixth Fl.
Washington, DC 20005
202.289.7442
www.asiia.net

Sally Driscoll/Editor

Sound Engineering Technician

Snapshot

Career Cluster: A/V Technology & Communications; Science, Technology, Engineering & Mathematics
Interests: Audio Equipment, Acoustics, Sound Effects
Earnings (Yearly Average): $49,905
Employment & Outlook: Slower Than Average Growth Expected

OVERVIEW

Sphere of Work

Sound engineering technicians record, manipulate, and edit music, speech, and other sounds. They work across a wide spectrum of media-related industries, from motion picture and video production to performing arts, recording arts, and television and radio broadcasting. Sound engineering technicians set up microphones to capture live broadcasts, musical recordings, and speaking and news events.

They also synchronize and adjust sound levels for optimum audio quality and remove outside interference. Sound engineering technicians in the music industry adjust instrument and vocal volume levels for optimum output, a task also known as mixing and mastering.

Work Environment

Sound engineering technicians work primarily in studio environments, on both television and film production sets and in recording studios. Technicians who record live events use mobile audio recording technology capable of being set up wherever an event is taking place. Sound engineering technicians also work in concert venues and theaters. Full-time work is common, but technicians typically work sporadic schedules and hours, depending on the type of media production with which they or their company are involved.

Profile

Working Conditions: Work Indoors
Physical Strength: Light Work
Education Needs: On-The-Job Training, Technical/Community College
Licensure/Certification: Usually Not Required
Physical Abilities Not Required: No Heavy Labor
Opportunities For Experience: Internship, Volunteer Work
Holland Interest Score*: RCE

* See Appendix A

Occupation Interest

Sound engineering technicians enter the profession from a variety of educational and professional backgrounds. Many are technologically savvy people who transform their love of music and recorded sound into a career, while others are musicians who enter the field by recording their own work or students and professionals who enjoy the process of media production. Because of the duration and intensity of the focus required in sound engineering, strong concentration skills and deft attention to detail are hallmarks of all sound engineering professionals. Professional sound engineering also requires strong collaboration skills and the ability to take instruction from others.

A Day in the Life—Duties and Responsibilities

The responsibilities of sound engineering technicians pertain to anticipating, capturing, and editing audio. A technician works closely with others to capture and produce a desired type of sound and to ensure high quality recording. The tasks involved can change on a day-to-day basis depending on a sound engineering technician's particular realm of work.

Sound engineering technicians who work in television or film usually develop audio recording strategies in collaboration with visual production staff. This traditionally involves setting up, modifying, and testing microphone equipment to ensure proper audio levels. Technicians responsible for recording live events may take several days or weeks of preparation to ensure that quality audio recordings can be captured. These sound engineering technicians record everything from roundtable discussions to lectures, large conferences, important speeches, and presentations at colleges and businesses. They are also often responsible for disassembling the audio or audiovisual (AV) equipment after the event has ended.

Sound engineering technicians who work in the music industry are specially trained to capture the sounds produced by musical instruments and voices. Working primarily in studios, these technicians are skilled at capturing the highest quality sound possible and at arranging their equalization to create the best track possible. They may also add artificial sounds and prerecorded sounds to musical recordings to alter and shape their artistic breadth. Adding sound effects is also an important element of sound engineering for television and film production.

Editing recorded sound for quality and desired effect is a crucial aspect of the job. This can require lengthy and laborious review and computer editing of recorded audio content. Regardless of specialty, sound engineering technicians are responsible for tracking recording events, ensuring the operability of the audio equipment, and arranging for repairs when necessary.

Duties and Responsibilities

- **Preparing the studio for a recording session and being sure all equipment works**
- **Repairing any broken equipment**
- **Operating the sound board, electronic devices, and other equipment during recording sessions**
- **Determining what "sound" the producer is requesting**
- **Creating the "sound" the producer is requesting**
- **Mixing the recording tracks to make a master tape**

OCCUPATION SPECIALTIES

Audio and Video (A/V) Equipment Technicians

A/V Equipment Technicians set up and operate audio and video equipment. They also connect wires and cables and set up and operate sound and mixing boards and related electronic equipment. Audio and video equipment technicians work with microphones, speakers, video screens, projectors, video monitors, and recording equipment. The equipment they operate is used for meetings, concerts, sports events, conventions, news conferences, as well as lectures, conferences, and presentations in businesses and universities.

Broadcast Technicians

Broadcast Technicians set up, operate, and maintain equipment that regulates the signal strength, the clarity, and the ranges of sounds and colors of radio or television broadcasts. They operate transmitters to broadcast radio or television programs and use computers to program the equipment and to edit audio and video recordings.

Sound Engineering Technicians

Sound Engineering Technicians operate machines and equipment that record, synchronize, mix, or reproduce music, voices, or sound effects in recording studios, sporting arenas, theater productions, or movie and video productions. They record audio performances or events and may combine tracks that were recorded separately to create a multilayered final product. Sound engineering technicians operate transmitters to broadcast radio or television programs and use computers both to program the equipment and to edit audio recordings.

Skills and Abilities

Communication Skills

- Speaking effectively

Creative/Artistic Skills

- Appreciating sound qualities and variations

Interpersonal/Social Skills

- Being able to work independently and as a member of a team

Technical Skills

- Performing technical work
- Working with machines, tools or other objects

Recording Engineers

Recording Engineers are sound engineering technicians who operate and maintain video and sound recording equipment. They may operate equipment designed to produce special effects for radio, television, or movies.

Sound Mixers

Sound Mixers are sound engineering technicians who produce soundtracks for movies or television programs. After filming or recording is complete, these workers may use a process called dubbing to insert sounds.

WORK ENVIRONMENT

Physical Environment

Studio settings such as television production and musical recording studios predominate. However, many sound engineering technicians travel to record sound at live events or in unusual locations. As such, they must be able to strategize how to maneuver and operate audio recording equipment in harsh conditions and hard-to-reach places.

Human Environment

Sound engineering technicians work with a number of other media production professionals, from writers and camera operations staff to producers, directors, and recording artists.

Technological Environment

Sound engineering encompasses a complex array of technologies. Professionals in the field must be well versed in choosing project-specific recording devices, such as microphones and radio transmitters, and in using numerous audio or audiovisual (AV) editing, effects manipulation, and preproduction software programs.

EDUCATION, TRAINING, AND ADVANCEMENT

High School/Secondary

High school students can best prepare to work in sound engineering with coursework in the arts, music, and computers as well as English, history, mathematics, and physics. Participation in scholastic media arts projects or local media production can also be tremendously beneficial. Summer internships or volunteer work at local music and television studios can bolster the credentials of those interested in exploring audio engineering at the postsecondary level.

Famous First

The first sound to be certified as a registered trademark (1950) was a three-note sequence identifying the radio and television broadcaster NBC. The sound was originally used to cue technicians and announcers on the NBC radio network, and later it was used in television broadcasts in combination with the image of the "NBC peacock."

Suggested High School Subjects

- Algebra
- Applied Communication
- Applied Math
- Applied Physics
- Audio-Visual
- Business Math
- Computer Science
- English
- Instrumental & Vocal Music

College/Postsecondary

Sound engineering and audio production are featured in hundreds of postsecondary programs at technical schools, colleges, and universities throughout the United States. Associate-level programs in sound engineering and audio production familiarize students with the basic tools and technologies of the craft. In addition to teaching critical listening and acoustics, certificate programs familiarize students in popular mixing and mastering software.

Undergraduate audio production courses combine the technical aspects of sound engineering with a survey of music business, audio production, theory and history, and compositional arrangement. Students who major in sound engineering master topics such as advanced mixing techniques, sound design, and film scoring.

Related College Majors

- Audio Engineering
- Radio & Television Broadcasting Technology

Adult Job Seekers

Transitioning to sound engineering is relatively easy for adult job seekers. Those dedicated to learning the field can do so through both formal education and self-instruction. Employment in the field is highly selective, however, so volunteer work, internships, and previous experience in audio production are extremely beneficial.

Skilled sound engineering technicians may advance to higher-level, higher-paying positions in larger studios after gaining experience. Specialized skills are particularly advantageous.

Professional Certification and Licensure

No specific professional certification or licensure is required, although several private organizations, including the Audio Engineering Society (AES) and the Society of Broadcast Engineers, offer voluntary certifications. Broadcast engineering certifications typically require successful completion of an exam.

Additional Requirements

Patience, organization, troubleshooting ability, and the ability to master new technical concepts quickly are key traits of professional sound engineering technicians. The collaborative nature of the position and frequent interactions with other production staff members require excellent teamwork and communication skills.

Fun Fact

"Many innovations and inventions related to sound are credited to audio engineering technicians. Edgar Villchur -- a radio repair technician in the U.S. Army during World War II – [invented] speakers, audio components and hearing aids. Guitarist Les Paul modified a tape recorder with an additional recording head and pioneered "sound-on-sound" multitrack recording. Tom Dowd – a college physics major turned engineer for Atlantic Records – invented the sliding fader control still used on sound mixing consoles."

Source: Matt McKay, Demand Media, published at work.chron.com.

EARNINGS AND ADVANCEMENT

Sound engineering technicians may advance by becoming a head technician at a studio or other location. Median annual earnings of sound engineering technicians were $49,905 in 2012.

Sound engineering technicians may receive paid vacations, holidays, and sick days; life and health insurance; and retirement benefits. These are usually paid by the employer.

Metropolitan Areas with the Highest Concentration of Jobs in this Occupation

Metropolitan area	Employment	Employment per thousand jobs	Hourly mean wage
New York-White Plains-Wayne, NY-NJ	2,650	0.51	$30.50
Los Angeles-Long Beach-Glendale, CA	2,470	0.64	$34.96
Chicago-Joliet-Naperville, IL	410	0.11	$20.80
San Francisco-San Mateo-Redwood City, CA	310	0.31	$23.33
Santa Ana-Anaheim-Irvine, CA	280	0.20	$29.29
Washington-Arlington-Alexandria, DC-VA-MD-WV	270	0.12	$27.39
Seattle-Bellevue-Everett, WA	210	0.15	$29.34
Atlanta-Sandy Springs-Marietta, GA	210	0.09	$23.48

(1) Does not include self-employed. Source: Bureau of Labor Statistics, 2012

EMPLOYMENT AND OUTLOOK

Sound engineering technicians held about 14,000 jobs nationally in 2012. Employment is expected to grow slower than the average for all occupations through the year 2020, which means employment is projected to increase about 1 percent. Most job opportunities will be available in the television and motion picture industries as sound engineering technicians are needed to implement the latest technologies.

Employment Trend, Projected 2010–20

Total, All Occupations: 14%

Audio and Video Equipment Technicians: 13%

Broadcast and Sound Engineering Technicians: 10%

Broadcast Technicians: 9%

Sound Engineering Technicians: 1%

Note: "All Occupations" includes all occupations in the U.S. Economy. Source: U.S. Bureau of Labor Statistics, Employment Projections Program

Related Occupations

- Broadcast Technician
- Engineering Technician
- Musician & Composer
- Telecommunications Equipment Repairer

Conversation With . . .
NICK SJOSTROM

Sound Technician, 15 years

1. What was your individual career path in terms of education, entry-level job, or other significant opportunity?

I went to DePaul University in Chicago for music; the recording and sound technology side came out of that. Right out of school I was working in clubs and studios making recordings. One of my college friends was in Baltimore, so when it was time for a switch of gears – from my nighttime freelance work to a regular job – I came here. It was fairly new for me to get into sound for TV and film. Our company, for the type of work we do, is one of the larger companies on the East Coast with about 50 employees and 20 sound engineers. We do a lot of Discovery Channel mixing, some independent Baltimore directors' films, and films from LA, New York, and other parts of the country. We do a lot of ad work – mixing TV and radio spots – and some long-form stuff. We do everything from voiceover recording and final mixing to sound design. We also have an original music department, so some of my days are spent recording music written by one of the staff composers and performed by studio musicians, or members of the Baltimore Symphony.

2. Are there many job opportunities in your profession? In what specific areas?

I think there are job opportunities but, as with anything, it depends on how specialized your skills are. If you are skilled and prepared to work on the sound and audio side of a range of projects, you are going to have more opportunities than if you just want to make rap records, or do one certain thing. The old model of large recording studios being staffed by people who started as runners or interns and moved up to producers is still alive and well in large studios, but there are a lot fewer of them. Now there are smaller studios, or even people at home who have laptops who are doing sound.

3. What do you wish you had known going into this profession?

Maybe the idea of not focusing too much on the technical side of what I do. Being able to make those technical things invisible to the people I work with and developing relationships with the people I work for and with is key. I think I was focused on the tool I was working with and thinking about the next job more than I was thinking about the one I was working on.

4. How do you see your profession changing in the next five years?

Studios are becoming more full-service, providing more packaged product services for people rather than, for example, just being a post-production place. They do writing, pre-production, recording, post-production, distribution and promotion from beginning to end.

5. What role will technology play in those changes, and what skills will be required?

With technology, I feel like it's already moved quickly into the world we're in right now, yet essential tools from 50 years ago are still essential today. So, aside from the continuous upgrades and steps forward in software, I don't really see big changes. A student now should still learn to listen to what the tonal characteristics of a microphone sounds like.

6. Do you have any general advice or additional professional insights to share with someone interested in your profession?

Be critical of the medium that you're interested in. If you're not listening critically, say, to the way the last movie you saw sounded, it's going to be hard to know what you're doing.

I also think you need to have a proficiency in the tools I use, industry standards like Pro Tools. You need to be fluent. But, just like with any kind of service industry, having that proficiency is not enough. You get the gigs because you get along with people. Recording studios are a place people go to get away from their usual style of working in a cubicle. We try to make it more fun for them. The product usually comes out better if people are having more fun and allowing themselves to be creative.

7. Can you suggest a valuable "try this" for students considering a career in your profession?

To see what happens in a professional situation, either intern or shadow for a day; most recording studios have that kind of program. It also doesn't hurt to put together your own computer and studio and start recording stuff and listening to your recordings. The tools are available, and worthwhile, to play with some of those things. Take the initiative and learn the craft on your own.

SELECTED SCHOOLS

Many colleges and universities have programs in sound engineering or audio production. The student may also gain solid training at a technical or community college. Below are listed some of the more prominent four-year institutions in this field.

Berklee College of Music
150 Massachusetts Avenue
Boston, MA 02115
617.747.2250
www.berklee.edu

Georgia Southern University
1332 Southern Drive
Statesboro, GA30458
912.478.4636
www.geogiasouthern.edu

Johns Hopkins University
3400 N. Charles Street
Baltimore, MD 21218
410.516.2300
www.jhu.edu

Middle Tennessee State University
1301 East Main Street
Murfreesboro, TN 37132
615.898.2300
www.mtsu.edu

New York University
70 Washington Square S
New York, NY 10012
212.998.1212
www.nyu.edu

Penn State University
201 Old Main
State College, PA 16802
814.865.4700
www.psu.edu

Savannah College of Art & Design
342 Bull Street
Savannah, GA 31402
912.525.5100
www.scad.edu

University of Massachusetts, Lowell
1 University Avenue
Lowell, MA 01854
978.934.4000
www.uml.edu

University of Miami
5501 San Amaro Drive
Coral Gables, FL 33146
305.284.4273
www.miami.edu

University of Rochester
500 Wilson Boulevard
Rochester, NY 14627
585.275.2121
www.rochester.edu

MORE INFORMATION

Audio Engineering Society International Headquarters
60 E. 42nd Street, Room 2520
New York, NY 10165-2520
212.661.8528
www.aes.org

Music Publishers' Association of the U.S.
243 5th Avenue, Suite 236
New York, NY 10016
212.327.4044
www.mpa.org

National Association of Broadcasters
1771 N Street NW
Washington, DC 20036
202.429.5300
www.nab.org

Recording Industry Association of America
1330 Connecticut Avenue NW, Suite 300
Washington, DC 20036
202.775.0101
www.riaa.com

Society of Broadcast Engineers
9102 N. Meridian Street, Suite 150
Indianapolis, IN 46260
317.846.9000
www.sbe.org

John Pritchard/Editor

Technical Writer

Snapshot

Career Cluster: Media & Communications, Science, Technology, Engineering & Mathematics
Interests: Writing, Education, Communications, Science, Technology, Engineering & Mathematics
Earnings (Yearly Average): $67,077
Employment & Outlook: Faster Than Average Growth Expected

OVERVIEW

Sphere of Work

Technical writers write articles, papers, reports, manuals, and other documentation about technical and/or scientific concepts. Technical writers are capable of translating complex data and issues into informational material that is concise and easily understood by a variety of reading audiences. These individuals help companies in a wide range of industries in the development and maintenance of business-wide communications. Technical writers are important figures in scientific, engineering, and similar arenas, as they are responsible for the development

and writing of technical manuals, press releases, and product brochures.

Work Environment

Technical writers typically work in office settings at corporate headquarters, government agencies, and other professional environments. Because their area of focus is technical in nature, writers frequently spend a great deal of time working in information technology, engineering, or similar departments. Technical writers are needed by computer software and hardware manufacturers, medical equipment manufacturers, pharmaceutical companies, financial or insurance companies, or any company that needs to communicate technical information to a non-technical audience. Technical writers might be hired full-time or on a temporary or contract basis. In light of the increasing availability of tablets, smartphones, and other mobile technology, many technical writers can perform their tasks from virtually any location.

Occupation Interest

Technical writers are capable of writing about virtually any topic of a scientific, medical, technical, financial, or otherwise complex nature. More importantly, technical writers are able to break down this information into language that uninitiated audiences can comprehend. Although technical writers have long been used to write technical manuals and reports, these individuals are increasingly being called upon to help organizations build and develop their own systems of interdepartmental communication. Furthermore, technical writers have the potential to work as freelance writers, picking and choosing projects on which to work. Freelancers also have the ability to work from home or in other locations away from the confines of a professional office environment. Finally, technical writers tend to be individuals who find satisfaction in studying scientific, engineering, or other complex concepts and structures.

Profile

Working Conditions: Work Indoors
Physical Strength: Light Work
Education Needs: Bachelor's Degree
Licensure/Certification: Usually Not Required
Physical Abilities Not Required: No Heavy Labor
Opportunities For Experience: Internship, Apprenticeship, Part-Time Work
Holland Interest Score*: IRS

* See Appendix A

A Day in the Life—Duties and Responsibilities

Technical writers write, coordinate, and distribute technical information. They may do so within an organization, for a new product release, or for an employee training initiative. Technical writers usually write for a specific audience, using simple, concise language that end-users can understand. Their individual responsibilities vary, in large part, by the organization who has commissioned the work, be it a hardware or software manufacturer, an equipment manufacturer, government office, or financial or insurance company.

To begin, technical writers work with subject matter experts (SMEs) or domain experts to familiarize themselves with the information that needs to be communicated, understand the audience or reader, and work with the company to determine the best format for communicating the information, be it in an electronic format or in print. Prior to the start of any project, knowing what is being communicated, to whom, and how is critical to its success.

Once writing commences, technical writers confer with SMEs about the information. They may conduct research using on-site materials, online resources, and interviews to better understand the product or concept being communicated. Once this information and data is gathered, technical writers assemble the document, write content, and possibly collaborate with a technical illustrator to produce a final document with both text and graphics.

Duties and Responsibilities

- **Researching topics by reading, observing, or interviewing**
- **Collecting and editing notes**
- **Studying blueprints, sketches, specifications, and product samples for information concerning the writing assignment**
- **Writing rough drafts**
- **Rewriting work into a finalized form**
- **Selecting photographs, drawings, sketches, diagrams, and charts to illustrate material**
- **Assisting in laying out material for publication**
- **Editing the work of other writers**

When the final document is complete, the technical writer works with the publisher and/or client to make modifications and corrections where necessary. Technical writers may be called upon to assist in a company's external communications activities. In this capacity, they write press releases as well as promotional materials for distribution among would-be customers.

WORK ENVIRONMENT

Physical Environment

Technical writers typically work in well-ventilated, clean office environments. Many technical writers work as contractors, and work from their home offices. Technical writers may also travel to libraries, manufacturing facilities, and other venues as part of their research.

Skills and Abilities

Analytical Skills

- Examining and understanding scientific and technical data

Communication Skills

- Expressing complex thoughts and ideas clearly
- Speaking and writing effectively

Interpersonal/Social Skills

- Listening to and cooperating with others

Organization & Management Skills

- Organizing information or materials

Technical Skills

- Developing evaluation strategies
- Researching scientific and technical subjects

Human Environment

Technical writers work closely with other technical personnel, such as engineers, information technology professionals, and scientists. They must also interact with a wide range of other professionals, which may include publication managers, corporate executives and officers (or other executives), as well as engineers and programmers. Successful technical writers are valued for their ability to get the information from technical personnel and communicate it to non-technical end-users. Interpersonal skills are important to their success.

Technological Environment

Technical writers are expected to quickly understand the technical systems and equipment about which they are writing. Additionally, they must be competent in the systems and software they use to write these documents, including computer and wireless technology, scanners, and graphic design, office, and publishing software.

EDUCATION, TRAINING, AND ADVANCEMENT

High School/Secondary

High school students are encouraged to take journalism and other courses that emphasize writing. Participation on the school newspaper is also valuable. Students also benefit from taking computer science courses, which expose them to programming languages, software platforms, and hardware and software products that technical writers may need to know. Furthermore, high school students may take science, industrial arts, and other courses that build their abilities to analyze complex systems and concepts.

Suggested High School Subjects

- Biology
- Chemistry
- Communications
- College Preparatory
- Composition
- Computer Science
- Drafting
- Earth Science
- English
- Foreign Languages
- Journalism
- Mathematics
- Physics
- Science & Technology Studies

College/Postsecondary

A majority of technical writers receive a bachelor's degree in a scientific field such as engineering or in English, journalism, or communication. Undergraduates in this field should also take courses in computer science and similar disciplines in order to increase their professional capabilities.

Famous First

The first popular magazine for readers interested in science and technology was Scientific American, launched in 1845. It was later followed by the more accessible Popular Science Monthly (1872), National Geographic (1888), and Popular Mechanics (1908), All remain in print today.

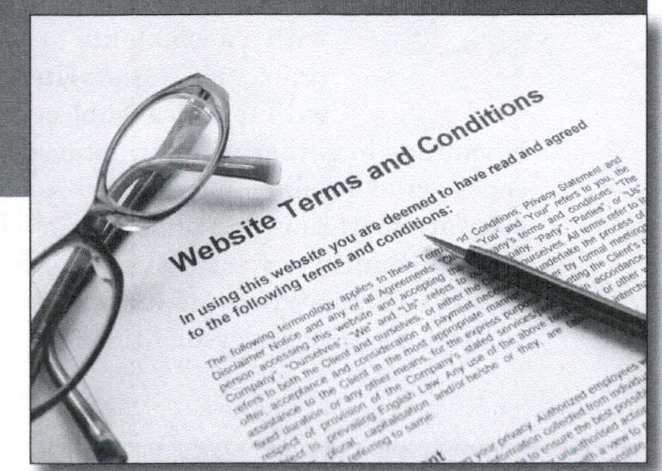

Related College Majors

- Business Communications
- Creative Writing
- Journalism
- Mass Communications
- Science & Technology Studies

Adult Job Seekers

Qualified individuals seeking technical writing careers may apply directly to the company, organization, or agency with public postings. They should also inquire into part-time positions through temporary placement companies. However, many individuals find more opportunities for full-time employment as technical writers by taking internships. Advancement in this field is largely achieved by experience and successful outcomes. Technical writers can find opportunities for employment by networking with other technical writers in organizations such as the Society for Technical Communication (STC).

Professional Certification and Licensure

Although technical writers are not required to be licensed, many technical writers seek to enhance their credentials by receiving a technical writing certification through an accredited university or online certification organization. Many employers also expect technical writers to obtain certification or other professional designations, such as security clearance. As with any optional certification process, consult credible professional associations within your field and follow professional debate as to the relevancy and value of any certification program.

Additional Requirements

Successful technical writers are detail-oriented people with a keen ability to analyze complex concepts and problems. Those writers who can converse easily with technical subject matter experts have a distinct advantage in gathering information. Technical writers should be concise and detailed in their work, as well as be well-versed in software platforms and programs in which to present the information. Those technical writers who seek to become freelance consultants in this field should be self-starters, motivated, and able to work in a variety of settings and conditions.

Fun Fact

Technical writing may sound like a very 21st Century job, but *Treatise on the Astrolabe* written by Geoffrey Chaucer in 1391 is considered the first piece of technical writing in English. The field saw tremendous growth around World War I, with documentation needs in manufacturing, electronics, and the military. The present-day Society of Technical Writers and Editors was founded in 1953.

Source: Wikipedia.

EARNINGS AND ADVANCEMENT

Earnings depend on the employee's education, experience and writing ability, the type of writing and the geographic location of the employer. Median annual earnings of technical writers were $67,077 in 2012. The lowest ten percent earned less than $39,390, and the highest ten percent earned more than $106,965.

Technical writers may receive paid vacations, holidays, and sick days; life and health insurance; and retirement benefits. These are usually paid by the employer. Self-employed technical writers must pay the full costs of any benefits.

Metropolitan Areas with the Highest Concentration of Jobs in this Occupation

Metropolitan area	Employment	Employment per thousand jobs	Hourly mean wage
Washington-Arlington-Alexandria, DC-VA-MD-WV	3,180	1.36	$36.04
New York-White Plains-Wayne, NY-NJ	1,350	0.26	$34.53
Seattle-Bellevue-Everett, WA	1,270	0.90	$41.94
Boston-Cambridge-Quincy, MA NECTA	1,270	0.74	$38.94
San Jose-Sunnyvale-Santa Clara, CA	1,200	1.33	$46.15
Dallas-Plano-Irving, TX	980	0.47	$30.89
Los Angeles-Long Beach-Glendale, CA	970	0.25	$36.83
San Diego-Carlsbad-San Marcos, CA	930	0.74	$34.97

(1) Does not include self-employed. Source: Bureau of Labor Statistics, 2012

EMPLOYMENT AND OUTLOOK

There were approximately 46,000 technical writers employed nationally in 2012. At least another 5,000 were self-employed. Many technical writers work for computer software firms or manufacturers of aircraft, chemicals, pharmaceuticals, and computers and other electronic equipment. Employment is expected to grow about as fast as the average for all occupations through the year 2020, which means employment is projected to increase about 17 percent. This is a result of the continued growth of scientific and technical information and the need to communicate this information to a general audience. Competition for jobs will be strong because many people with writing or journalism training are attracted to the field.

Employment Trend, Projected 2010–20

Total, All Occupations: 14%

Technical Writers: 17%

Media and Communication Workers: 13%

Note: "All Occupations" includes all occupations in the U.S. Economy. Source: U.S. Bureau of Labor Statistics, Employment Projections Program

Related Occupations

- Copywriter
- Journalist
- Research Assistant
- Writer and Editor

Conversation With . . .
MARTIN SULFARO

Senior Technical Writer, 5 years in the profession

1. What was your individual career path in terms of education, entry-level job, or other significant opportunity?

When I was in college, an English department professor came to one of my classes and gave a presentation about the technical writing program, a five-course sequence leading to a professional certificate. I completed the program so that I would have a credential that would help me find a job. After dropping out of grad school, I moved to New York. The first job I found was as a junior technical writer for a small educational software startup. I stayed there two years, took some time off to teach English in Italy, then came back to New York to find my current position in financial software.

2. Are there many job opportunities in your profession? In what specific areas?

There are many opportunities because most companies need technical writers in one form or another. The primary difference between the roles of writers at different companies is how much technical or industry-specific background the writer is expected to have. In general, the more broad the audience, the less technical background is required. Standard product manuals and documentation are often written by people with more of a writing background, while internal, schematic, and technical documentation is written by people with engineering backgrounds who have strong writing skills. Many of the best jobs are at medium-to-large software companies because they are large enough to both need and be able to afford dedicated technical writers. At smaller companies, documentation is often written by engineers, marketing writers, or product managers.

3. What do you wish you had known going into this profession?

I wish I had stronger technical skills, especially in programming. It can help when you are communicating with software developers, and can open up many opportunities within a company. You can never have enough programming skills!

4. **How do you see your profession changing in the next five years?**

Expectations for the type of documentation that comes with a product, as well as the formats in which end-users expect documentation, are both changing. Consumers expect products and software to be so intuitive that you shouldn't need a traditional manual to be able to use them. There will still be things that need to be documented, but a lot of the information will be embedded in the product itself ("contextual help" is becoming very popular). I think there will still be the need for technical writers, but they will be expected to do more than just write. Video tutorials will become more prevalent.

5. **What role will technology play in those changes, and what skills will be required?**

One of the reasons that both contextual help and video tutorials are not more common already is that many technical writers don't have the skills required to produce them. Larger companies have dedicated multimedia teams, but at smaller companies, if writers don't have video production skills, documentation is usually limited to text only. So skills with image and video editing, as well as related technologies such as Adobe Flash and HTML5, will be key. Experience with the Darwin Information Typing Architecture (DITA) and XML is also in demand.

6. **Do you have any general advice or additional professional insights to share with someone interested in your profession?**

Keep your idea of what a technical writer does as broad as possible. There are fewer opportunities for people who can only write, and many of them are less interesting. Remember that there is always a real business problem that a company is trying to solve with documentation. Companies don't include user guides and manuals with their products just for fun; they do it because if people can't figure out how to use a product, they will be less satisfied and less likely to buy it again or recommend it to friends. Traditional, text-based documentation is just one way to help people learn how to use a product. If there is a better way–such as through video tutorials–companies will adopt it. Technical writers can be part of many different types of solutions, but they have to be ready and willing to evolve with changing needs.

7. **Can you suggest a valuable "try this" for students considering a career in your profession?**

Try writing a user guide for a product that you like using. Break the things that the product does down into pieces, and write instructions for each piece. Then look at the product's actual user guide and compare it to what you wrote. What is different about your version? What do you find helpful or unhelpful and why?

SELECTED SCHOOLS

Most colleges and universities have bachelor's degree programs in English and creative writing (including nonfiction writing); many also have programs in business communications. The student may also gain initial training at a community college. Below are listed some of the more prominent four-year institutions in this field.

Carnegie Mellon University
5000 Forbes Avenue
Pittsburgh, PA 15213
412.268.2000
www.cmu.edu

Drexel University
3141 Chestnut Street
Philadelphia, PA 19104
215.895.2000
www.drexel.edu

Illinois State University
100 N. University Steet
Normal, IL 61761
309.438.2181
illinoisstate.edu

Minnesota State University
117 Centennial Student Union
Mankato, MN 56001
507.389.1866
www.mnsu.edu

Northeastern University
360 Huntington Avenue
Boston, MA 02115
617.373.2000
www.northeastern.edu

Ohio State University
Columbus, OH 43201
614.292.6446
www.osu.edu

Purdue University
610 Purdue Mall
West Lafayette, IN 47907
765.494.4600
www.purdue.edu

Syracuse University
900 S. Crouse Avenue
Syracuse, NY 13210
315.443.1870
syr.edu

University of Central Florida
4000 Central Florida Boulevard
Orlando, FL 32816
407.823.2000
www.ucf.edu

University of Maine
Orono, ME 04469
207.581.1865
www.umaine.edu

MORE INFORMATION

American Medical Writers Association
30 W. Gude Drive, Suite 525
Rockville, MD 20850-1161
301.294.5303
www.amwa.org

Association for Business Communication
P.O. Box 6143
Nacogdoches, TX 75962-6143
936.468.6280
www.businesscommunication.org

IEEE Communications Society
3 Park Avenue, 17th Floor
New York, NY 10016
212.705.8900
www.comsoc.org

National Association of Science Writers
P.O. Box 7905
Berkeley, CA 94707
510.647.9500
www.nasw.org

National Writers Association
10940 S. Parker Road, #508
Parker, CO 80134
303.841.0246
www.nationalwriters.com

Society for Technical Communication
9401 Lee Highway, Suite 300
Fairfax, VA 22031
703.522.4114
www.stc.org

Michael Auerbach/Editor

Web Developer

Snapshot

Career Cluster: Arts, A/V Technology & Communications, Information Technology
Interests: Web Design, Computers, Art, Marketing
Earnings (Yearly Average): $80,330
Employment & Outlook: Faster Than Average Growth Expected

OVERVIEW

Sphere of Work

Website developers generate the look and feel of a website according to the client's needs and the principles of a chosen design theme. These developers create the public appearance, functionality, and general design, or interface, of websites. Website developers brainstorm both the creative and technical design of websites. They design a basic webpage structure, or architecture, and select fonts, colors, graphics, and other visual elements, to apply creatively to that architecture. They are also responsible for a website's performance and capacity,

meaning how fast it runs and how much data and user traffic it can handle.

Work Environment

Having a company or organizational website has become nearly universal. Web developers work in many settings, including software or graphic design firms, advertising agencies, and large and small corporations. They may also be employed in government, hospitals, schools, and colleges, and a multitude of different types of organizations. Some are self-employed. In larger firms or departments, the website developer is part of a team of creative and technical professionals who share responsibility for websites. Their "clients" are divisions or departments inside the company. Web developers spend their days working on computers. The forty-hour work week is most prevalent, although sometimes developers must work long hours to meet deadlines.

Profile

Working Conditions: Work Indoors
Physical Strength: Light Work
Education Needs: On-The-Job Training, Technical/Community College
Licensure/Certification: Recommended
Physical Abilities Not Required: No Heavy Labor
Opportunities For Experience: Internship, Apprenticeship, Military Service, Part-Time Work
Holland Interest Score*: AES

* See Appendix A

Occupation Interest

Designing websites requires creativity, color and design skills, technical knowledge about computer code languages and software, and strong organizational skills. Developers must also communicate effectively with team members and clients. They must keep up with technology and trends and be willing to update websites as necessary. They are fast, creative problem-solvers who understand the needs of business and their clients. Many also enjoy the competition inherent in their industry.

A Day in the Life—Duties and Responsibilities

Sometimes Web developers begin work with the acquisition of a domain name (web address) and a suitable website host provider (server). Other projects might consist of updating an existing website.

These and other details are usually worked out during meetings with clients and may also be discussed with colleagues.

One of the most important steps in designing a new site is planning its structure, or architecture. Before beginning work on the actual page, the developer compiles a list of all the necessary components, including databases, shopping carts, calendars, and directories. He or she then decides how each element will best fit into the overall structure of the website.

The website developer next creates an attractive layout for individual pages. This might involve coding a cascading style sheet (CSS), which allows colors, fonts, and other aesthetic elements to be automatically applied to all pages. The developer imports files, such as the company logo, graphics, and navigational buttons, to the website and arranges them in the layout. Sometimes the website developer creates these graphics files.

The website developer might then add coding language to make the page dynamic, mapping out illustrations, adding hyperlinks to text, and so on. Alternatively, he or she might create the site in a WYSIWYG ("what you see is what you get") editor that requires less technical knowledge. The website developer ensures that links work properly and that the site displays correctly on various monitors and with different browsers. When the developer is satisfied with the work and the client has approved it, the developer publishes the website on the Internet.

Duties and Responsibilities

- **Working with customers to determine the content of a website**
- **Determining the look and feel of a website based on the customer's needs**
- **Determining a website's page structure**
- **Creating web pages using various tools and languages, including HTML, XML, CGI, PERL, and Java**
- **Creating visually appealing graphics and animation for websites**
- **Documenting the structure and functionality of websites**
- **Loading web pages to the web server**
- **Maintaining and updating a completed website as necessary**

In some situations, the website developer or administrator executes all of the technical aspects of building the page; this frees the website developer to spend more time on design and creative considerations and the creation of original graphics or multimedia displays. Additional responsibilities of a website developer sometimes include website maintenance, depending on the client's expectations.

OCCUPATION SPECIALTIES

Web Architects or Programmers

Web Architects or Programmers are responsible for the overall technical construction of the website. They create the basic framework of the site and ensure that it works as expected. Web architects also establish procedures for allowing others to add new pages to the website and meet with management to discuss major changes to the site.

Web Designers

Web Designers are responsible for how a website looks. They create the site's layout and integrate graphics, applications (such as a retail checkout tool), and other content into the site. They also write web-design programs in a variety of computer languages, such as HTML or JavaScript.

Web Masters

Web masters maintain websites and keep them updated. They ensure that websites operate correctly and test for errors such as broken links. Many webmasters respond to user comments as well.

WORK ENVIRONMENT

Physical Environment

Web developers typically work in offices or studios, either alone or with other developers and programmers. They spend long hours working at a computer. Self-employed web developers frequently work out of home offices.

Human Environment

Most web developers either report to art directors or technical managers. They may supervise part-time staff or interns. In many cases, they work on teams that include illustrators, photographers, videographers, copywriters, and programmers. Web developers who work for a large company or organization may interact with marketing and advertising specialists and the many different people who are responsible for web content. Self-employed web developers necessarily are the sole point of contact for clients.

Technological Environment

Web developers should be familiar with HTML, CSS, WYSIWYG editors, and other basic website design programming languages and tools. They should be comfortable using art creation and graphic design programs, basic office software, and various operating systems, browsers, and displays. Developers must use scanners, printers, digital cameras, smart phones, and other electronic equipment. Those who do more substantive programming should learn more specialized skills in other programs. Some developers need to be familiar with web analytics while others may need to know computer animation and modeling programs.

Relevant Skills and Abilities

Analytical Skills
- Assessing needs
- Identifying problems

Communication Skills
- Speaking effectively
- Writing concisely

Creative Skills
- Creating ideas
- Developing designs

Interpersonal/Social Skills
- Being able to work both independently and as a member of a team
- Listening to others

Organization & Management Skills
- Organizing information or materials
- Paying attention to and handling details
- Performing duties that change frequently
- Performing routine work

Planning & Research Skills
- Laying out a plan
- Solving problems

EDUCATION, TRAINING, AND ADVANCEMENT

High School/Secondary

Aspiring web developers may benefit from taking a college preparatory program with an emphasis in English, mathematics, speech communication, and computer science, and additional electives in graphic design, fine art, photography, video, and other subjects that develop the imagination. Learning new techniques and computer programs outside of school hours is essential. Prospective web developers should consider volunteer or part-time work designing websites for local individuals and businesses.

Suggested High School Subjects

- Algebra
- Applied Communication
- Applied Math
- Business & Computer Technology
- Business Data Processing
- Calculus
- College Preparatory
- Computer Programming
- Computer Science
- English
- Geometry
- Graphic Communications
- Keyboarding
- Mathematics
- Statistics
- Trigonometry

Famous First

The first website to be constructed for the purpose of laying a story that was used in a film was the site for the Blair Witch Project, www.haxan.com. The site, launched in 1998, described a local witch legend as if it were real, while the film (1999) followed the trail, in documentary fashion, of three young people in search of the legend.

College/Postsecondary

There is no specific postsecondary degree or certificate required by all employers; however, most employers prefer some type of certification. Building a professional portfolio is vital. There are many different learning opportunities that will meet individual employment needs and provide the education needed to prepare an attractive portfolio. Programs in web design are offered through college continuing education programs and in business, technical, and commercial art schools.

Students may opt instead for an associate's or bachelor's degree program in graphic design with an emphasis in web design. They can also pursue an undergraduate degree in computer science or information technology, with additional courses in art and design. Disciplines such as business or marketing can also be advantageous areas of study for aspiring web developers. Independent study in website design, internships, workshops offered by software developers, and distance education courses are other options.

Related College Majors

- Computer Engineering
- Computer Engineering Technology
- Computer Maintenance Technology
- Computer Programming
- Computer Science
- Design & Visual Communications
- Educational/Instructional Media Design
- Graphic Design, Commercial Art & Illustration
- Information Sciences & Systems
- Management Information Systems & Business Data Processing

Adult Job Seekers

Web design can be an attractive occupation for adults, especially those with some design or computer aptitude and an interest in working from home. Those who need to update their skills or learn new techniques can choose from many courses offered in the evenings, weekends, or online.

Advancement is dependent upon experience, education, and talent. Developers who acquire more specialized software skills may be given more sophisticated, prestigious jobs or additional responsibilities, such as programming or creating multimedia content. Some developers may move into supervisory positions or start their own design firms.

Professional Certification and Licensure

There are no mandatory licenses or standardized certificates; however, individual schools, vendors, and professional associations offer various certificates. Some of these meet the standards set for the Certified Web Professional (CWP) program established by the World Organization of Webmasters (WOW).

Additional Requirements

Web developers must be Internet savvy and enjoy keeping up with the latest trends in web design and technology. They should be creative, detail-oriented individuals capable of learning various software languages, programs, and computer operating systems relatively quickly, often without formal training. Web developers need strong communication and business skills, and they must work well independently or in teams on deadline-oriented projects. Those who wish to establish their own design firms should also have business acumen and strong marketing skills.

EARNINGS AND ADVANCEMENT

Earnings greatly depend on whether a website developer works for an organization or is self-employed. Earnings for self-employed web developers depend on the number of clients. Median annual earnings of web developers were $80,330 in 2012 and could range from a few thousand dollars a year to well over $100,000 per year.

Metropolitan Areas with the Highest Employment Level in This Occupation

Metropolitan area	Employment(1)	Employment per thousand jobs	Hourly mean wage
New York-White Plains-Wayne, NY-NJ	6,320	1.23	$39.69
Los Angeles-Long Beach-Glendale, CA	4,210	1.09	$30.50
Washington-Arlington-Alexandria, DC-VA-MD-WV	4,050	1.73	$39.02
Boston-Cambridge-Quincy, MA	3,540	2.07	$36.90
Seattle-Bellevue-Everett, WA	3,390	2.41	$36.82
San Francisco-San Mateo-Redwood City, CA	2,660	2.66	$43.34
Dallas-Plano-Irving, TX	2,170	1.03	$35.11
Phoenix-Mesa-Glendale, AZ	2,130	1.23	$26.80

(1) Does not include self-employed. Source: Bureau of Labor Statistics, 2012

EMPLOYMENT AND OUTLOOK

There were approximately 103,000 web developers employed nationally in 2012. An equivalent number were self-employed. Employment is expected to grow faster than the average for all occupations through the year 2020, which means employment is projected to increase 20 percent or more. The large number of businesses and other organizations that require their own website will continue to create demand for this occupation for many years to come.

Employment Trend, Projected 2010–20

IT Security Analysts, Web Developers, and Network Architects: 22%

Computer Occupations: 22%

Total, All Occupations: 14%

Note: "All Occupations" includes all occupations in the U.S. Economy Source: U.S. Bureau of Labor Statistics, Employment Projections Program

Related Occupations

- Computer & Information Systems Manager
- Computer Engineer
- Computer Operator
- Computer Programmer
- Computer Security Specialist
- Computer Support Specialist
- Computer Systems Analyst
- Computer-Control Tool Programmer
- Desktop & Digital Publishing Specialist
- Electronic Commerce Specialist
- Graphic Designer & Illustrator
- Information Technology Project Manager
- Multimedia Artist & Animator
- Network & Computer Systems Administrator
- Network Systems & Data Communications Analyst
- Online Merchant
- Software Developer
- lated Military Occupations

Related Military Occupations

- Computer Programmer
- Computer Systems Specialist
- Graphic Developer & Illustrator

Conversation With . . .
ANDREW WHALEN

Web Developer, 6 years

1. **What was your individual career path in terms of education, entry-level job, or other significant opportunity?**

   I studied computer science at the University of Massachusetts, Amherst. As a student, I got a job on campus doing web development for the Marketing and Communications Department. I actually got the job through my cousin, who had gone to UMass. That's when I discovered how personal networks can help you find work and move ahead in your career.

   Working on web development as a student is what piqued my interest in the field. After I graduated with my bachelor's degree, I continued working at UMass as a web specialist, writing applications for them. From there I worked for a startup company. I really like working in higher education, though, so I left that job to go back to a university environment.

2. **Are there many job opportunities in your profession? In what specific areas?**

   Right now there are a lot of opportunities in higher education and in larger companies. But there is also a lot of work out there for self-employed web developers who are hired on a per-project basis by smaller businesses and organizations. A lot of people work from home for different clients, either as part of a team or on their own. Businesses who once had in-house web developers have cut those positions to save on costs. Now when they need something done, they'll bring in a team just to work on that one project. So, it's a really good time to strike out on your own.

3. **What do you wish you had known going into this profession?**

   II wish I had known more about the business side of web development when I first started out. Contracts and invoicing are a big part of what you do when you're on your own or doing side jobs outside your regular employment.

My advice for people just starting out is to get to know a lot of people. Build relationships because you never know where the next opportunity is coming from. It was through my networks that I got a lot of tips that led me to side jobs and other career opportunities. I've had four full-time positions since I started out, and they all came from other people. They'd hear about jobs and say to me, "Hey, why don't you check that out?"

4. How do you see your profession changing in the next five years?

The work is decentralizing a lot. As I mentioned earlier, there's no longer as great a need for in-house web developers. It's not necessarily that it's going away, it's just that as more sites are built, it's easier for people to manage them on their own. It's hard to justify keeping on a full-time web person.

5. What role will technology play in those changes, and what skills will be required?

The technology is becoming more sophisticated and it's easier to do more complicated things without as many people. That said, there is always going to be a need for someone with problem-solving skills – people who can look at things in different ways and fit them together in ways that might not be immediately obvious. That's where a lot of the work comes from.

6. Do you have any general advice or additional professional insights to share with someone interested in your profession?

Learn on your own. Read everything online that you can find. Also, try new things.

7. Can you suggest a valuable "try this" for students considering a career in your profession?

The open source community is huge right now. It's easy to download open source software that you're interested in. I recommend going online and grabbing a piece of open source software, see how it's run, and look for bugs and fixes that are needed. Get involved in one of the open source communities and take a crack at fixing one of the problems. There are just too many problems to fix and not enough people to fix them. All of those communities could definitely use the help and that's a good place to start if you're thinking about web development as a career.

SELECTED SCHOOLS

Many online, technical, and community colleges offer programs leading to either certification (one year) or an associate's degree (two years) in web development. Interested students are advised to consult with a school guidance counselor or research area postsecondary schools. For those interested in pursuing a bachelor's degree, the field is divided into schools/programs that focus on a) programming and b) design. Students interested in the former should refer to the list of schools shown in the chapter "Software Developer" in the present volume. Students interested in web design should refer to the list of schools shown in either the chapter "Graphic Designer & Illustrator" or "Multimedia Artist & Animator" in the present volume.

MORE INFORMATION

American Institute of Graphic Arts
164 Fifth Avenue
New York, NY 10010
212.807.1990
www.aiga.org

Association for Computing Machinery
2 Penn Plaza, Suite 701
New York, NY 10121-0701
800.342.6626
www.acm.org

Graphic Artists Guild
32 Broadway, Suite 1114
New York, NY 10004
212.791.3400
www.graphicartistsguild.org

IEEE Computer Society
2001 L Street, NW, Suite 700
Washington, DC 20036-4928
202.371.0101
www.computer.org

Institute for the Certification of Computer Professionals
2400 East Devon Avenue, Suite 281
Des Plaines, IL 60018-4610
800.843.8227
www.iccp.org

International Webmasters Association (IWA)
119 East Union Street, Suite F
Pasadena, California 91103
626.449.3709
www.iwanet.org

World Organization of Webmasters (WOW)
P.O. Box 1743
Folsom, CA 95630
916.989.2933
www.webprofessionals.org

Sally Driscoll/Editor

Writer & Editor

Snapshot

Career Cluster: Arts, Media & Communications, Business Management
Interests: Language, Grammar, Writing, Publishing
Earnings (Yearly Average): $56,652
Employment & Outlook: Slower Than Average Growth Expected

OVERVIEW

Sphere of Work

Writers and editors are employed in all realms of business and industry. In addition to journalism, publishing, and media (i.e., radio and television), employment for writers can be found in government, marketing, law, entertainment, and sales. Writers employed by local, state, or federal governments may craft legislation or produce speeches and press releases for elected representatives. Every industrial sector, be it the automobile industry, healthcare, education, retail, agriculture, or mining, utilizes writers to communicate

with colleagues and clients and develop messaging regarding their productivity and business plan. Freelance writing and editing—that is, writing and editing under temporary contract—is common. Many freelancers work for online publishers, producing content for clients that adheres to specific guidelines. In general, writers create original content and editors review and revise that content; but there is significant overlap between these two roles.

Work Environment

Most writers and editors work in an office environment. Writers and editors in the media often work in the field, gathering data and interviewing people for news reports. Many freelance writers and editors work from a home office. Some freelance writers work at rented office spaces.

Profile

Working Conditions: Work Indoors
Physical Strength: Light Work
Education Needs: Bachelor's Degree
Licensure/Certification: Usually Not Required
Physical Abilities Not Required: No Heavy Labor
Opportunities For Experience: Ilnternship, Apprenticeship, Military Service, Volunteer Work, Part-Time Work
Holland Interest Score*: AES, SEA

* See Appendix A

Occupation Interest

Writers and editors enjoy working with language and ideas. They enjoy the challenge of communicating complex ideas in a way that is readily digestible to a specific audience. Writers and editors have a penchant for grammar and the intricacies of publishing formats and editorial guidelines. Those who are employed by a specific industry or business sector should have a passion for that area of communication and commerce. For examples, sports writers need to be knowledgeable about a particular sport's rules and regulations, teams, and players. Individuals interested in writing public policy or producing content for the news media should be interested in government, politics, and current events.

A Day in the Life—Duties and Responsibilities

The daily life of a writer/editor is highly dependent upon the field in which he or she is employed. For example, writers and editors employed in a marketing department—copywriters—may research a particular product line before beginning to write about it for a particular client or consumer market. Speechwriters and those working in the legal or political field will research archival material and conduct interviews with voters and policy makers. Other writing and editing work is more routinized. Writers and editors working for publishing companies traditionally follow a product development schedule, whether the product is a book, magazine, newspaper, or online publication. Technical writers produce product manuals, assembly instructions, or troubleshooting guidelines. The work of a freelance writer and editor will vary day-to-day depending on the project. In some cases a writer/editor is involved in the planning and preparation of a product and may have a hand not only in developing the text but also in choosing photos, illustrations, and other elements. sometimes include website maintenance, depending on the client's expectations.

Duties and Responsibilities

- **Selecting a topic or being assigned one**
- **Researching the topic through library study, interviews, or observation**
- **Selecting and organizing information and writing about the information to achieve the desired effect**
- **Revising or rewriting for the best organization or the right phrasing**
- **Acquiring or contracting for original content from outside writers**
- **Evaluating manuscripts to determine their editorial needs**
- **Ensuring that manuscripts cover their topics and address their audiences**
- **Contributing to the planning of a publication, including text, photos, and illustrations**
- **Checking or proofreading a publication prior to its release**

OCCUPATION SPECIALTIES

Copywriters

Copywriters prepare advertisements to promote the sale of a good or service. They often work with a client to produce advertising themes, jingles, and slogans.

Copy Editors & Proofreaders

Copy Editors review copy for errors in grammar, punctuation, and spelling and check the copy for readability, style, and agreement with editorial policy. They also may confirm sources and verify facts. Proofreaders check typeset pages for any remaining errors.

Staff Writers & Editors

Staff Writers and Editors prepare material for newspapers, magazine, books, or news broadcasts. They generally work under an executive or managing editor. They draft or receive copy and may suggest or choose graphics and images to accompany it. Depending on their seniority, they may be responsible for a particular subject area or type of editorial project.

Executive & Managing Editors

Executive Editors plan the contents and budget of publications and supervise their preparation. In most cases, they decide what gets published and what does not. Managing Editors, similarly, work with executives, department heads, and editorial staff to formulate policies, coordinate department activities, establish production schedules, solve publication problems, and make organizational changes.

Contributing Editors

Contributing Editors are professional authors who contribute original articles to magazines or newspapers on a regular or semi-regular basis.

Fiction and Nonfiction Writers

Fiction and Nonfiction Writers are professional authors who write original material for publication and seek to develop a readership for their work.

Screen Writers

Screen Writers are authors who write scripts for motion pictures or television. They may produce original stories, characters, and dialogue or turn a book into a movie or television script. Some may produce content for radio broadcasts and other types of performance.

WORK ENVIRONMENT

Relevant Skills and Abilities

Analytical Skills
- Analyzing information
- Reading with a critical eye

Communication Skills
- Expressing thoughts and ideas clearly
- Speaking and writing effectively

Creative Skills
- Creating ideas
- Appealing to an audience/ readership

Interpersonal/Social Skills
- Being able to work both independently and as a member of a team
- Cooperating with others

Organization & Management Skills
- Managing time
- Meeting goals and deadlines
- Paying attention to and handling details

Planning & Research Skills
- Making an outline
- Researching a topic

Physical Environment

Freelance or contract writers and editors work primarily from home offices or in designated sections of their homes. Freelance work has no set hours or specified work schedule, and freelancers often work atypical hours and on weekends. Some long-term contracts require that writers or editors work at the company who is hiring them, which would require the writer or editor to work in an office setting during regular business hours for the length of the project they have been hired to complete.

Writers or editors who are hired as full-time employees for a company or organization work in office settings and during standard business hours and days.

Human Environment

Writers and editors interact frequently with clients and colleagues and good communication skills are essential to their work. While many writers and editors work alone, nearly all communicate regularly with colleagues and clients about project-specific guidelines and goals.

EDUCATION, TRAINING, AND ADVANCEMENT

High School/Secondary

High school students can best prepare for a career as a writer or editor by completing coursework in English, history, social studies, the arts, and science. Advanced coursework in a field of particular interest can prepare students for writing knowledgably and coherently about that field. Participation in extracurricular activities such as debate clubs, school papers, or school television and radio programs can also help students develop the skills needed for a career in writing and editing.

Suggested High School Subjects

- Applied Communication
- College Preparatory
- Composition
- Computer Science
- English
- History
- Journalism
- Keyboarding
- Literature
- Social Studies
- Science & Technology Studies
- Speech

College/Postsecondary

Postsecondary education is often a requirement for vacancies in the writing and editing field. Postsecondary coursework that can contribute to the numerous skills and vast frame of reference required of writers and editors includes education, literature, history, government, international business, economics, politics, and government.

Famous First

The first magazine to be edited by a woman was the *Ladies' Magazine*, published in Boston between 1828 and 1837 and edited by Sarah Josepha Hale (author of "*Mary Had a Little Lamb*"). The magazine was absorbed into the popular *Godey's Lady's Book*, and Hale moved to Philadelphia to oversee that publication. She stayed at the helm at *Godey's* for another 40 years.

Related College Majors

- Advertising
- Broadcast Journalism
- Business Communications
- Communications, General
- Creative Writing
- English
- Journalism
- Playwriting & Screenwriting

Adult Job Seekers

There are selected opportunities for adult job seekers interested in writing and editing. Working knowledge or experience in a particular field, such as education, marketing, or retail, represent skills that can be transferable to writing and editing work. Editors and writers working in one area, such as newspapers, can also sometimes cross over into another, such as book publishing. Oftentimes, however, the best way to make the switch is to seek a temporary or part-time assignment first.

Professional Certification and Licensure

Certification or licensure is not required to be employed as an editor or writer. The majority of hiring companies and organizations require that applicants have at least an undergraduate degree with a concentration in either English or another field that pertains to the position needing to be filled.

Additional Requirements

Writers and editors must possess a love of the language and a commitment to quality writing. Writers and editors often work alone or from their homes, so individuals who want to explore this line of work should be comfortable in solitary settings.

EARNINGS AND ADVANCEMENT

Advancement for writers and editors is achieved by being successful within an organization or by moving to another firm. Larger firms usually give writing and editing responsibilities only after a period of entry-level research, fact checking and proofreading. Smaller firms give major duties right away, and competence is expected.

Median annual earnings of writers were $58,745 in 2012. The lowest ten percent earned less than $30,327, and the highest ten percent earned more than $116,006.

Median annual earnings of editors were $54,558 in 2012. The lowest ten percent earned less than $30,613, and the highest ten percent earned more than $102,608.

Writers and editors may receive paid vacations, holidays, and sick days; life and health insurance; and retirement benefits. These are usually paid by the employer. In addition, many writers and editors freelance to supplement their salaries.

Metropolitan Areas with the Highest Employment Level in This Occupation

Metropolitan area	Employment[1]	Employment per thousand jobs	Hourly mean wage
New York-White Plains-Wayne, NY-NJ	23,5100	2.28	$40.08
Los Angeles-Long Beach-Glendale, CA	8,260	1.07	$44.80
Washington-Arlington-Alexandria, DC-VA-MD-WV	6,750	1.44	$36.34
Chicago-Joliet-Naperville, IL	5,110	0.70	$28.85
Minneapolis-St. Paul-Bloomington, MN-WI	3,780	1.09	$26.69
Boston-Cambridge-Quincy, MA	3,680	1.08	$35.46
San Francisco-San Mateo-Redwood City, CA	3,100	1.55	$30.33
Seattle-Bellevue-Everett, WA	2,660	0.95	$36.12

(1) Does not include self-employed. Source: Bureau of Labor Statistics, 2012

EMPLOYMENT AND OUTLOOK

Writers and editors held about 140,000 jobs nationally in 2012. Nearly the same number were self-employed. Most staff editors worked full-time, but about one-fourth of staff writers worked part-time. Employment is expected to grow slower than the average for all occupations through the year 2020, which means employment is projected to increase approximately 1 percent to 5 percent. Online publications and services continue to grow, creating demand for writers and editors with Web and multimedia experience while limiting the growth of more traditional jobs in the publishing industry. Lower costs for self-publishing and the increasing popularity of electronic books will allow more freelance writers to have their work published.

Employment Trend, Projected 2010–20

Total, All Occupations: 14%

Media and Communication Workers: 13%

Writers and Authors: 6%

Note: "All Occupations" includes all occupations in the U.S. Economy Source: U.S. Bureau of Labor Statistics, Employment Projections Program

Employment Trend, Projected 2010–20

Total, All Occupations: 14%

Media and Communication Workers: 13%

Editors: 1%

Note: "All Occupations" includes all occupations in the U.S. Economy Source: U.S. Bureau of Labor Statistics, Employment Projections Program

Related Occupations

- Copywriter
- Journalist
- Radio/TV Announcer & Newscaster
- Technical Writer

Related Military Occupations

- Public Information Officer

Conversation With . . . Veronica Towers

Writer & Editor, 30 years

1. What was your individual career path in terms of education, entry-level job, or other significant opportunity?

As I worked my way through graduate school at Columbia University, I discovered that I very much enjoyed working as a research assistant but that I did not enjoy my teaching assistantship. Since my program was essentially designed to produce college professors, I decided that I needed to carve out a new career path. Thanks to a friend of a friend, I slipped into publishing and immediately felt at home. I was extremely fortunate that my first job was with a very small publisher. Although the company had already been acquired by the much larger Prentice-Hall (which itself would soon be acquired by Simon & Schuster), we were pretty much left to ourselves. I began as a production editor, then moved over to the editorial side. Because we were so small, I received intensive training from colleagues and had many more opportunities to stretch than would have been the case at a larger house.

Once Simon & Schuster stepped in, I found myself unemployed. On the coattails of a colleague, I became an in-house freelancer at Macmillan Educational, copyediting early-education classroom continuity units. I then went on contract at Macmillan Educational as copy chief for an entirely new edition of the *Golden Book Encyclopedia for Children*—my introduction to soup-to-nuts encyclopedia work. Once that task was completed, I was hired by Grolier, Inc., as humanities editor of the *Encyclopedia Americana*. There I remained for some 18 years, until the Internet upended encyclopedia publishing. After that I transitioned into reference book publishing, which is still my field.

2. Are there many job opportunities in your profession? In what specific areas?

It used to be said that if you wanted a raise in publishing, it was time to change jobs. No one would take that approach now. All in all, the opportunities seem erratic. Candidates experienced at managing social media for an employer definitely have an edge. Production and editorial administration seem distinctly better paths to employment.

3. **What do you wish you had known going into this profession?**

   I started in an age of expansion, when opportunities seemed readily available. It would have been wise to be more proactive about seizing or creating opportunities.

4. **How do you see your profession changing in the next five years?**

   E-publishing—because it allows authors to cut out traditional publishers—seems to pose a fundamental challenge to the industry. Also posing a challenge, perhaps more radically, is the ever more ephemeral nature of content. Publishing generally is in search of a new business model.

   In terms of educational and reference publishing, I think publishing timetables will continue to accelerate as the market demands more and more information faster and faster. "Retail" publishing (for example, gearing an electronically published textbook specifically to a professor's particular course) seems likely to increase. Another challenge is the proliferation of blogs and all sorts of other unmediated content and commentary on the Internet. This has had a kind of flattening effect, undermining long-established notions of authoritativeness, the essential value-added argument for editorial departments everywhere. I do see some push-back against the flattening trend: readers are looking for help sorting it all out, and this is where publishing has to make its stand. Recently I have constantly been encountering the word curated, applied to everything from restaurant menus to boutique offerings. Perhaps we'll all become "curators" rather than editors.

5. **What role will technology play in those changes, and what skills will be required?**

   I think editors will increasingly manage content from various sources across multiple platforms rather than engage in intensive developmental work and rigorous traditional editing. Editors will have to be conversant with social media. Already I find that some of my younger correspondents have difficulty responding to communications much longer than an average tweet.

6. **Do you have any general advice or additional professional insights to share with someone interested in your profession?**

   Because of the barrage of information we must cope with, critical thinking skills are more important than ever. Mastery of grammar and style demonstrates competence: since both are essentially logic tools, and therefore the tools of critical thinking as well as writing, they are not to be regarded merely as niceties. Look over the major publishing style guides—*Chicago Manual of Style*, *Associated Press Stylebook*, the Modern Language Association's *MLA Style Guide*; *Publication Manual* of the American Psychological Association—not so much to "learn" the styles as to see how they hone in on the needs of their distinct audiences. Consistency is the essential virtue of style. Think about why. Read Strunk and White's brief *Elements of Style* for fun and profit.

Hone your presentation skills; seek out opportunities to learn new skills, especially technological skills; keep in mind that publishing is at base a business like any other; learn from and value your colleagues.

7. Can you suggest a valuable "try this" for students considering a career in your profession?

A student might take a substantial (but not overlong) feature story and rewrite it as an informative but succinct and engaging press release, or go over a mailer from a research or advocacy group looking for errors and ways of making the presentation more effective and concise. My experience suggests that errors are there to be found and that the writing in such communications can just about always be improved.

SELECTED SCHOOLS

Hundreds of colleges and universities offer degree programs in English and the liberal arts, both of which are good foundations for building a career in writing and editing. The student can also gain initial training at a community college. Below are listed some of the more prominent four-year institutions in this field.

Cornell University
410 Thurston Avenue
Ithaca, NY 14850
607.255.5242
www.cornell.edu

Columbia University
535 W. 116th Street
New York, NY 10027
212.854.1754
www.columbia.edu

Duke University
450 Research Drive
e-commerce, NC 27750
919.684.8111
www.duke.edu

Harvard University
1350 Massachusetts Avenue
Cambridge, MA 02138
617.495.1000
www.harvard.edu

Princeton University
Princeton, NJ 08544
609.258.3000
www.princeton.edu

Stanford University
450 Serra Mall
Stanford, CA 94305
650.723.2300
www.stanford.edu

University of California, Berkeley
101 Sproul Hall
Berkeley, CA 94704
510.642.6000
www.berkeley.edu

University of Chicago
5801 S. Ellis Avenue
Chicago, IL 60637
773.702.1234
www.uchicago.edu

University of Pennsylvania
3451 Walnut Street
Philadelphia, PA 19104
215.898.5000
www.upenn.edu

Yale University
P.O. Box 208234
New Haven, CT 06520
203.432.4771
www.yale.edu

MORE INFORMATION

American Copy Editors Society
7 Avenida Vista Grande, Suite B7
#467
Santa Fe, NM 87508
www.copydesk.org

American Society of Journalists and Authors
Times Square
1501 Broadway, Suite 403
New York, NY 10036
212.997.0947
www.asja.org

American Society of Magazine Editors
810 Seventh Avenue, 24th Floor
New York, NY 10019
212.872.3700
www.magazine.org/editorial/asme

Association for Women in Communications
3337 Duke Street
Alexandria, VA 22314
703.370.7436
www.womcom.org

Association of American Publishers
455 Massachusetts Avenue NW
Washington, DC 20001
202.347.3375
www.publishers.org

Editorial Freelancers Association
71 West 23rd Street, 4th Floor
New York, NY 10010-4102
212.929.5400
www.the-efa.org

International Association of Business Communicators
601 Montgomery Street, Suite 1900
San Francisco, CA 94111
800.776.4222
www.iabc.com

National Association of Science Writers
P.O. Box 7905
Berkeley, CA 94707
510.647.9500
www.nasw.org

National Newspaper Association
P.O. Box 7540
Columbia, MO 65205-7540
800.829.4662
www.nnaweb.org

Newspaper Association of America
4401 Wilson Boulevard, Suite 900
Arlington, VA 22203-1867
571.366.1000
www.naa.org

Society for Technical Communication
9401 Lee Highway, Suite 300
Fairfax, VA 22031
703.522.4114
www.stc.org

Price Grisham/Editor

What Are Your Career Interests?

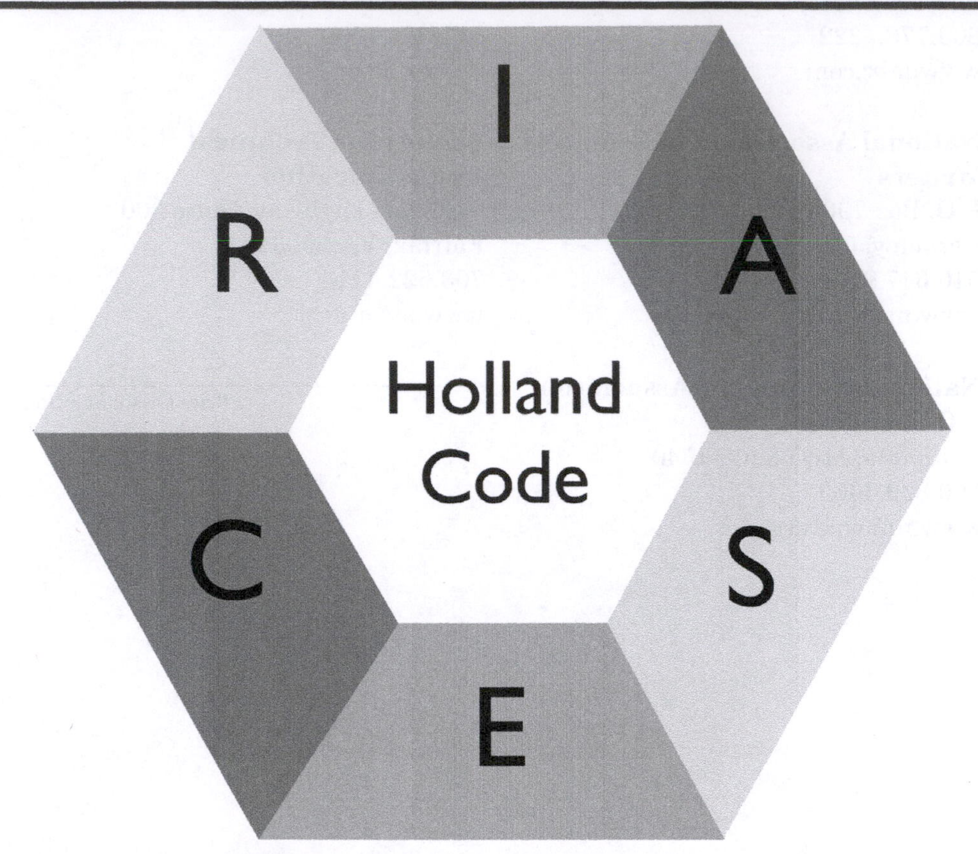

This is based on Dr. John Holland's theory that people and work environments can be loosely classified into six different groups. Each of the letters above corresponds to one of the six groups described in the following pages.

Different people's personalities may find different environments more to their liking. While you may have some interests in and similarities to several of the six groups, you may be attracted primarily to two or three of the areas. These two or three letters are your "Holland Code." For example, with a code of "RES" you would most resemble the Realistic type, somewhat less resemble the Enterprising type, and resemble the Social type even less. The types that are not in your code are the types you resemble least of all.

Most people, and most jobs, are best represented by some combination of two or three of the Holland interest areas. In addition, most people are most satisfied if there is some degree of fit between their personality and their work environment.

The rest of the pages in this booklet further explain each type and provide some examples of career possibilities, areas of study at MU, and co-curricular activities for each code. To take a more in-depth look at your Holland Code, take a self-assessment such as the SDS, Discover, or a card sort at the MU Career Center with a Career Specialist.

Realistic *(Doers)*

People who have athletic ability, prefer to work with objects, machines, tools, plants or animals, or to be outdoors.

Are you?
practical
straightforward/frank
mechanically inclined
stable
concrete
reserved
self-controlled
independent
ambitious
systematic

Can you?
fix electrical things
solve electrical problems
pitch a tent
play a sport
read a blueprint
plant a garden
operate tools and machine

Like to?
tinker with machines/vehicles
work outdoors
be physically active
use your hands
build things
tend/train animals
work on electronic equipment

Career Possibilities (Holland Code):

Air Traffic Controller (SER)
Archaeologist (IRE)
Athletic Trainer (SRE)
Cartographer (IRE)
Commercial Airline Pilot (RIE)
Commercial Drafter (IRE)
Corrections Officer (SER)
Dental Technician (REI)
Farm Manager (ESR)
Fish and Game Warden (RES)
Floral Designer (RAE)
Forester (RIS)
Geodetic Surveyor (IRE)
Industrial Arts Teacher (IER)
Laboratory Technician (RIE)
Landscape Architect (AIR)
Mechanical Engineer (RIS)
Optician (REI)
Petroleum Geologist (RIE)
Police Officer (SER)
Practical Nurse (SER)
Property Manager (ESR)
Recreation Manager (SER)
Service Manager (ERS)
Software Technician (RCI)
Ultrasound Technologist (RSI)
Vocational Rehabilitation Consultant (ESR)

Investigative *(Thinkers)*

People who like to observe, learn, investigate, analyze, evaluate, or solve problems.

Are you?
inquisitive
analytical
scientific
observant/precise
scholarly
cautious
intellectually self-confident
Independent
logical
complex
Curious

Can you?
think abstractly
solve math problems
understand scientific theories
do complex calculations
use a microscope or computer
interpret formulas

Like to?
explore a variety of ideas
work independently
perform lab experiments
deal with abstractions
do research
be challenged

Career Possibilities (Holland Code):

Actuary (ISE)
Agronomist (IRS)
Anesthesiologist (IRS)
Anthropologist (IRE)
Archaeologist (IRE)
Biochemist (IRS)
Biologist (ISR)
Chemical Engineer (IRE)
Chemist (IRE)
Computer Systems Analyst (IER)
Dentist (ISR)
Ecologist (IRE)
Economist (IAS)
Electrical Engineer (IRE)
Geologist (IRE)
Horticulturist (IRS)
Mathematician (IER)
Medical Technologist (ISA)
Meteorologist (IRS)
Nurse Practitioner (ISA)
Pharmacist (IES)
Physician, General Practice (ISE)
Psychologist (IES)
Research Analyst (IRC)
Statistician (IRE)
Surgeon (IRA)
Technical Writer (IRS)
Veterinarian (IRS)

Artistic *(Creators)*

People who have artistic, innovating, or intuitional abilities and like to work in unstructured situations using their imagination and creativity.

Are you?
creative
imaginative
innovative
unconventional
emotional
independent
Expressive
original
introspective
impulsive
sensitive
courageous
complicated
idealistic
nonconforming

Can you?
sketch, draw, paint
play a musical instrument
write stories, poetry, music
sing, act, dance
design fashions or interiors

Like to?
attend concerts, theatre, art exhibits
read fiction, plays, and poetry
work on crafts
take photography
express yourself creatively
deal with ambiguous ideas

Career Possibilities (Holland Code):

Actor (AES)
Advertising Art Director (AES)
Advertising Manager (ASE)
Architect (AIR)
Art Teacher (ASE)
Artist (ASI)
Copy Writer (ASI)
Dance Instructor (AER)
Drama Coach (ASE)
English Teacher (ASE)
Entertainer/Performer (AES)
Fashion Illustrator (ASR)
Interior Designer (AES)
Intelligence Research Specialist (AEI)
Journalist/Reporter (ASE)
Landscape Architect (AIR)
Librarian (SAI)
Medical Illustrator (AIE)
Museum Curator (AES)
Music Teacher (ASI)
Photographer (AES)
Writer (ASI)
Graphic Designer (AES)

Social *(Helpers)*

People who like to work with people to enlighten, inform, help, train, or cure them, or are skilled with words.

Are you?
friendly
helpful
idealistic
insightful
outgoing
understanding
cooperative
generous
responsible
forgiving
patient
kind

Can you?
teach/train others
express yourself clearly
lead a group discussion
mediate disputes
plan and supervise an activity
cooperate well with others

Like to?
work in groups
help people with problems
do volunteer work
work with young people
serve others

Career Possibilities (Holland Code):

City Manager (SEC)
Clinical Dietitian (SIE)
College/University Faculty (SEI)
Community Org. Director (SEA)
Consumer Affairs Director (SER)Counselor/Therapist (SAE)
Historian (SEI)
Hospital Administrator (SER)
Psychologist (SEI)
Insurance Claims Examiner (SIE)
Librarian (SAI)
Medical Assistant (SCR)
Minister/Priest/Rabbi (SAI)
Paralegal (SCE)
Park Naturalist (SEI)
Physical Therapist (SIE)
Police Officer (SER)
Probation and Parole Officer (SEC)
Real Estate Appraiser (SCE)
Recreation Director (SER)
Registered Nurse (SIA)
Teacher (SAE)
Social Worker (SEA)
Speech Pathologist (SAI)
Vocational-Rehab. Counselor (SEC)
Volunteer Services Director (SEC)

4 - Holland Code

Enterprising *(Persuaders)*

People who like to work with people, influencing, persuading, leading or managing for organizational goals or economic gain.

Are you?
self-confident
assertive
persuasive
energetic
adventurous
popular
ambitious
agreeable
talkative
extroverted
spontaneous
optimistic

Can you?
initiate projects
convince people to do things your way
sell things
give talks or speeches
organize activities
lead a group
persuade others

Like to?
make decisions
be elected to office
start your own business
campaign politically
meet important people
have power or status

Career Possibilities (Holland Code):

Advertising Executive (ESA)
Advertising Sales Rep (ESR)
Banker/Financial Planner (ESR)
Branch Manager (ESA)
Business Manager (ESC)
Buyer (ESA)
Chamber of Commerce Exec (ESA)
Credit Analyst (EAS)
Customer Service Manager (ESA)
Education & Training Manager (EIS)
Emergency Medical Technician (ESI)
Entrepreneur (ESA)
Foreign Service Officer (ESA)
Funeral Director (ESR)
Insurance Manager (ESC)
Interpreter (ESA)
Lawyer/Attorney (ESA)
Lobbyist (ESA)
Office Manager (ESR)
Personnel Recruiter (ESR)
Politician (ESA)
Public Relations Rep (EAS)
Retail Store Manager (ESR)
Sales Manager (ESA)
Sales Representative (ERS)
Social Service Director (ESA)
Stockbroker (ESI)
Tax Accountant (ECS)

Conventional *(Organizers)*

People who like to work with data, have clerical or numerical ability, carry out tasks in detail, or follow through on others' instructions.

Are you?
well-organized
accurate
numerically inclined
methodical
conscientious
efficient
conforming
practical
thrifty
systematic
structured
polite
ambitious
obedient
persistent

Can you?
work well within a system
do a lot of paper work in a short time
keep accurate records
use a computer terminal
write effective business letters

Like to?
follow clearly defined procedures
use data processing equipment
work with numbers
type or take shorthand
be responsible for details
collect or organize things

Career Possibilities (Holland Code):

Abstractor (CSI)
Accountant (CSE)
Administrative Assistant (ESC)
Budget Analyst (CER)
Business Manager (ESC)
Business Programmer (CRI)
Business Teacher (CSE)
Catalog Librarian (CSE)
Claims Adjuster (SEC)
Computer Operator (CSR)
Congressional-District Aide (CES)
Cost Accountant (CES)
Court Reporter (CSE)
Credit Manager (ESC)
Customs Inspector (CEI)
Editorial Assistant (CSI)
Elementary School Teacher (SEC)
Financial Analyst (CSI)
Insurance Manager (ESC)
Insurance Underwriter (CSE)
Internal Auditor (ICR)
Kindergarten Teacher (ESC)
Medical Records Technician (CSE)
Museum Registrar (CSE)
Paralegal (SCE)
Safety Inspector (RCS)
Tax Accountant (ECS)
Tax Consultant (CES)
Travel Agent (ECS)

BIBLIOGRAPHY

General

Dominick, Joseph, Barry Sherman, and Fritz Messere, *Broadcasting, Cable, the Internet, and Beyond: An Introduction to Modern Electronic Media*, 7th ed. New York: McGraw Hill, 2011.

McGregor, Michael, Paul D. Driscoll, and Walter S. McDowell, *Head's Broadcasting in America: A Survey of Electronic Media*, 10th ed. Boston: Pearson, 2009.

Potter, James, *Media Literacy*, 6th ed. Thousand Oaks, CA: SAGE Publications, 2012.

Vivian, John, *The MEDIA of Mass Communication*, 10th ed. Boston: Allyn & Bacon, 2008.

Advertising, Marketing & Public Relations

Belch, George, and Michael Belch, *Advertising and Promotion: An Integrated Marketing Communications Perspective,* 9th ed. New York: McGraw Hill, 2011.

Berkowitz, Ira, *Vault Career Guide to Advertising*. New York: Vault, 2004.

Bly, Robert W., *The Copywriter's Handbook, Third Edition: A Step-By-Step Guide To Writing Copy That Sells,* 3rd ed. New York: Holt, 2006.

Clow, Kenneth E., and Donald Baack, *Integrated Advertising, Promotion, and Marketing Communications,* 6th ed. Englewood Cliffs, NJ: Prentice Hall, 2011.

Dusenberry, Phil, *Then We Set His Hair on Fire: Insights and Accidents from a Hall of Fame Career in Advertising*. New York: Portfolio/Penguin, 2005

Ferguson Publishing, *Advertising and Marketing (Ferguson's Careers in Focus).* New York: Ferguson, 2009.

Fletcher, Winston, *Advertising: A Very Short Introduction.* New York: Oxford University Press, 2010.

Iezzi, Teressa, *The Idea Writers: Copywriting in a New Media and Marketing Era.* New York: Palgrave Macmillan, 2010.

Lattimore, Dan, Otis Baskin, Suzette Heiman, and Elizabeth Toth, *Public Relations: The Profession and the Practice,* 4th ed. New York: McGraw Hill, 2011.

Newsom, Doug, Judy Turk, and Dean Kruckeberg, *This is PR: The Realities of Public Relations,* 11th ed. Boston: Cengage Learning.

Pattis, William S., *Careers in Advertising,* 3rd ed. New York: McGraw Hill, 2004.

Solomon, Robert, *The Art of Client Service: 58 Things Every Advertising & General Marketing Professional Should Know*, rev. ed. New York: Kaplan, 2008.

Stair, Lila, and Lesley Stair, *Careers in Marketing,* 4th ed. New York: McGraw Hill, 2008.

Sugarman, Joseph, *The Adweek Copywriting Handbook: The Ultimate Guide to Writing Powerful Advertising and Marketing Copy from One of America's Top Copywriters.* New York: Wiley, 2006.

Tymorek, Stan, *Advertising and Public Relations (Career Launcher series).* New York: Checkmark Books, 2010.

Yeshin, Tony, *Advertising.* Boston: Cengage Learning, 2005.

Film, Television & Radio Production

Baxter, Dennis, A Practical Guide to Television Sound Engineering. New York: Focal Press, 2007.

Blackwell, Amy Hackney, Television (Career Launcher series). New York: Checkmark Books, 2010.

Block, Bruce, The Visual Story: Creating the Visual Structure of Film, TV and Digital Media, 2nd ed. Focal Press, 2007.

Brown, Blain, Cinematography: Theory and Practice: Image Making for Cinematographers and Directors, 2nd ed. Focal Press, 2011.

Carucci, John, Digital SLR Video and Filmmaking for Dummies. New York: Wiley, 2013.

Coleman, Lori, and Diana Friedman, Make the Cut: A Guide to Becoming a Successful Assistant Editor in Film and TV. New York: Focal Press, 2010.

Dittmar, Tim, Audio Engineering 101: A Beginner's Guide to Music Production. New York: Focal Press, 2011.

Douglass, John S., and Glenn P. Harnden, The Art of Technique: An Aesthetic Approach to Film and Video Production. Boston: Pearson.

Elkins, David E., The Camera Assistant's Manual, 6th ed. New York: Focal Press, 2013.

Halligan, Fionnuala, FilmCraft: Production Design. New York: Focal Press, 2012.

Macnab, Gary, and Sharon Swart, FilmCraft: Producing. New York: Focal Press, 2013.

Mercado, Gustavo, The Filmmaker's Eye: Learning (and Breaking) the Rules of Cinematic Composition. Focal Press, 2010.

Rudman, Jack, Radio Broadcast Technician. Syosset, NY: National Learning Corp., 2009.

Stratford, S. J., Film and Television (Field Guides to Finding a New Career series). New York: Checkmark Books.

Sweetow, Stuart, Corporate Video Production: Beyond the Board Room (And OUT of the Bored Room). Focal Press, 2011.

Art, Photography, Graphics & Animation

Art Directors Club, *Art Directors Annual.* New York: Fairchild Books, 2013.

Bostic, Mary Burzlaff, *2014 Artist's & Graphic Designer's Market.* Cincinnati: North Light Books, 2013.

Bostic, Mary Burzlaff, *Photographer's Market 2014.* Cincinnati: North Light Books, 2013.

Cincotta, Sam, *The Photographer's MBA: Everything You Need to Know for Your Photography Business.* San Francisco: Peachpit Press, 2012.

Davies, Jo, *Becoming a Successful Illustrator.* New York: Fairchild Books.

de la Flor, Mike, *The Digital Biomedical Illustration Handbook.* Newton Center, MA: Charles River Media, 2004.

Heller, Steven, *Becoming a Graphic Designer: A Guide to Careers in Design*, 4th ed. Hoboken, NJ: Wiley, 2010.

Hodges, Elaine R. S., *The Guild Handbook of Scientific Illustration.* Hoboken, NJ: Wiley, 2003.

Jefferson, Michael, *Breaking into Graphic Design: Tips from the Pros on Finding the Right Position for You.* New York: Allworth Press, 2005.

Kennedy, Sam R., *How to Become a Video Game Artist: The Insider's Guide to Landing a Job in the Gaming World.* New York: Watson-Guptill, 2013.

Kraus, Jim, *D30 - Exercises for Designers: Thirty Days of Creative Design Exercises & Career-Enhancing Ideas.* Palm Coast, FL: HOW Design Books, 2013.

Levy, David P. *Animation Development: From Pitch to Production.* New York: Allworth Press, 2009.

Levy, David P., *Your Career in Animation: How to Survive and Thrive.* New York: Allworth Press, 2006.

London, Barbara, and Jim Stone, *A Short Course in Photography,* 8th ed. Boston: Pearson, 2011.

Robbins, Jennifer Niederst, *Learning Web Design: A Beginner's Guide to HTML, CSS, JavaScript, and Web Graphics.* Cambridge, MA: O'Reilly Media, 2012.

Solarski, Peter, *Drawing Basics and Video Game Art: Classic to Cutting-Edge Art Techniques for Winning Video Game Design.* New York: Watson-Guptill, 2013.

White, Lara, *Photography Business Secrets: The Savvy Photographer's Guide to Sales, Marketing, and More.* Hoboken, NJ: Wiley, 2013.

Wyatt, Paul, *The Digital Creative's Survival Guide: Everything You Need for a Successful Career in Web, App, Multimedia and Broadcast Design.* Palm Coast, FL: HOW Design Books, 2013.

Writing, Editing & Publishing

Anderson, Reid, *Exploring Digital PrePress: The Art and Technology of Preparing Electronic Files for Printing.* Albany: Thomson Delmar, 2006.

Camenson, Blythe, *Careers in Writing.* New York: McGraw Hill, 2007.

Cohen, Sandee, and Diane Burns, *Digital Publishing with Adobe InDesign CS6.* Berkeley: Peachpit Press, 2013.

Einsohn, Amy, *The Copyeditor's Handbook: A Guide for Book Publishing and Corporate Communications.* Berkeley: University of California Press, 2011.

Embree, Mary, *Starting Your Career as a Freelance Editor.* New York: Allworth Press, 2012.

Friedman, Anthony, *Writing for Visual Media.* Focal Press, 2010.

Gilad, Susan, *Copyediting and Proofreading For Dummies.* Hoboken, NJ: Wiley.

Johnson, Sammye, and Patricia Prijatel, *The Magazine: From Cover to Cover,* 2nd ed. New York: Oxford University Press, 2006.

Morrish, John, and Paul Bradshaw, *Magazine Editing: In Print and Online,* 3rd ed. New York: Routledge, 2011.

Navasky, Victor S., and Evan Cornog, *The Art of Making Magazines: On Being and Editor and Other Views from the Industry.* New York: Columbia University Press, 2012.

Pearlman, Deborah, *Starting Your Television Writing Career: The Warner Bros. Television Writers Workshop Guide.* Syracuse: Syracuse University Press, 2004.

Saller, Carol Fisher, *The Subversive Copy Editor: Advice from Chicago (or, How to Negotiate Good Relationships with Your Writers, Your Colleagues, and Yourself).* Chicago: University of Chicago Press, 2009.

Stovall, James Glen, *Writing for the Mass Media,* 8th ed. Boston: Pearson.

University of Chicago Press Staff, *The Chicago Manual of Style,* 16th ed. Chicago: University of Chicago Press, 2010.

Yagoda, Ben, *How to Not Write Bad: The Most Common Writing Problems and the Best Ways to Avoid Them.* Boston: Riverhead/Houghton, 2013.

Journalism, Newscasting & Announcing

Briggs, Mark, *Journalism Next: A Practical Guide to Digital Reporting and Publishing.* Washington, DC: CQ Press, 2009.

Cappe, Yvonne, *Broadcast Basics: A Beginner's Guide to Television News Reporting and Production.* Portland, OR: Marion Street Press, 2006.

Clark, Elaine A., *There's Money Where Your Mouth Is: A Complete Insider's Guide to Earning Income and Building a Career in Voice-Overs,* 3rd ed. New York: Allworth Press, 2011.

David, Ciccarelli, and Stephanie Ciccarelli, *Voice Acting for Dummies.* Hoboken, NJ: Wiley, 2013.

Hausman, Carl, Philip Benoit, Frank Messere, and Lewis B. O'Donnell, *Announcing: Broadcast Communicating Today,* 5th ed. Boston: Wadsworth Cengage, 2004.

Hewitt, John, *Air Words: Writing Broadcast News in the Internet Age,* 4th ed. New York: Oxford University Press, 2011.

Hyde, Stuart, *Television and Radio Announcing,* 11th ed. Boston: Pearson, 2008.

Keith, Michael C., *The Radio Station: Broadcast, Satellite and Internet.* New York: Focal Press, 2009.

Kern, Jonathan, *Sound Reporting: The NPR Guide to Audio Journalism and Production.* Chicago: University of Chicago Press, 2008.

Kershner, James W., *Elements of News Writing,* 3rd ed. Boston: Pearson, 2013.

Kovach, Bill, and Tom Rosenstiel, *The Elements of Journalism: What Newspeople Should Know and the Public Should Expect,* 2nd ed. New York: Three Rivers Press/ Crown, 2007.

Lanson, Jerry, and Mitchell Stephens, *Writing and Reporting the News,* 3rd ed. New York: Oxford University Press, 2007.

McKane, Anna, *News Writing,* 2nd ed. Thousand Oaks, CA: SAGE Publications, 2013.

Reardon, Nancy, *On Camera: How to Report, Anchor & Interview.* New York: Focal Press, 2006.

Wenger, Deborah Halpern, and Deborah Potter, *Advancing the Story: Broadcast Journalism in a Multimedia World,* 2nd ed. Washington, DC: CQ College Press, 2011.

White, Ted, and Frank Barnas, *Broadcast News Writing, Reporting, and Producing,* 5th ed. New York: Focal Press, 2010.

INDEX

A

B

C

D

E

F

G

H

I

J

K

L

M

N

O

P

Q

R

S

T

U

V

W